Creating a New Consensus on Population

The International Conference on Population and Development

Jyoti Shankar Singh

Earthscan Publications Ltd, London

First published in the UK in 1998 by
Earthscan Publications Ltd

A catalogue record for this book is available from the British Library

ISBN: 1 85383 565 X (paperback)
ISBN: 1 85383 566 8 (hardback)

Typesetting and page design by JS Typesetting, Wellingborough, Northants.
Printed and bound by Clays Ltd, St Ives plc
Cover design by John Gosling
Cover photo © Panos Pictures

For a full list of publications please contact:

Earthscan Publications Ltd
120 Pentonville Road
London, N1 9JN, UK
Tel: +44 (0)171 278 0433
Fax: +44 (0)171 278 1142
email: earthinfo@earthscan.co.uk
http://www.earthscan.co.uk

Earthscan is an editorially independent subsidiary of Kogan Page Limited
and publishes in association with WWF-UK and the International Institute for
Environment and Development.

Creating a New Consensus on Population

TABLE OF CONTENTS

Contents

LIST OF TABLES

LIST OF ACRONYMS AND ABBREVIATIONS

ACC	Administrative Committee on Coordination
AIDS	acquired immune deficiency syndrome
ASEAN	Association of South-East Asian Nations
CBR	crude birth rate
CEDPA	Center for Development and Population Activities
CELADE	Latin American Demographic Centre
CEPIA	Citizenship, Studies, Information, Action
CIDA	Canadian International Development Agency
CONGO	Conference of Non-Governmental Organizations in Consultative Status with ECOSOC
CPR	contraceptive prevalence rate
DAC	Development Assistance Committee
DESIPA	Department for Economic and Social Information and Policy Analysis
DIESA	Department for International Economic and Social Affairs
ECA	Economic Commission for Africa
ECE	Economic Commission for Europe
ECLAC	Economic Commission for Latin America and the Caribbean
ECOSOC	Economic and Social Council
ESCAP	Economic and Social Commission for Asia and the Pacific
ESCWA	Economic and Social Commission for Western Asia
EU	European Union
FAO	Food and Agriculture Organization
FP	family planning
G77	Group of 77
GA	General Assembly
GNP	gross national product
HIV/AIDS	human immunodeficiency virus/acquired immune deficiency syndrome

HRP	Special Programme of Research, Development and Research Training in Human Reproduction, World Health Organization
ICPD	International Conference on Population and Development
IEC	information, education and communication
ILO	International Labour Organization
IOM	International Organization for Migration
IPPF	International Planned Parenthood Federation
IPU	Inter-Parliamentary Union
IUSSP	International Union for the Scientific Study of Population
IWHC	International Women's Health Coalition
MCH	maternal and child health
MMR	maternal mortality rate
NGO	non-governmental organization
NIEO	new international economic order
NRDC	Natural Resources Defense Council
OAU	Organization for African Unity
ODA	official development assistance
OECD	Organization for Economic Cooperation and Development
OMB	US Office of Management and Budget
PAI	Population Action International
PrepCom	Preparatory Committee Session
SAARC	South Asian Association for Regional Cooperation
SIDA	Swedish International Development Authority
STD	sexually transmitted diseases
TED	Technical and Evaluation Division
TFR	total fertility rate
UKODA	United Kingdom Overseas Development Administration
UNAIDS	Joint United Nations Programme on HIV/AIDS
UNCED	United Nations Conference on Environment and Development
UNDP	United Nations Development Programme
UNESCO	United Nations Educational, Scientific and Cultural Organization
UNFPA	United Nations Population Fund
UNHCR	United Nations High Commissioner for Refugees
UNICEF	United Nations Children's Fund
UNIFEM	United Nations Development Fund for Women
USAID	United States Agency for International Development
WAY	World Assembly of Youth
WEDO	Women's Environment and Development Organization
WHO	World Health Organization
WPC	World Population Conference

WPPA   World Population Plan of Action
WPY   World Population Year
YWCA   Young Women's Christian Association

ACKNOWLEDGEMENTS

This book would not have been possible without the constructive and helpful advice and assistance provided by numerous colleagues and friends. It is impossible to mention all of them here. But I would like to record my profound gratitude to several of them.

Dr Nafis Sadik, Executive Director of UNFPA and Secretary General of the 1994 International Conference on Population, has patiently and carefully read several drafts of this book and offered incisive comments and suggestions. Other colleagues in the ICPD Secretariat and UNFPA whose advice and comments on several or all of the chapters have helped shape this book are German Bravo-Casas, Joseph Chamie, David Payton, Stafford Mousky and Arthur Erken of the ICPD Secretariat; and SLN Rao, Catherine Pierce, Mari Simonen, and Stan Bernstein of UNFPA. I also received extremely useful and valuable comments from Steven Sinding, Director, Population Sciences, Rockefeller Foundation.

During the course of writing the book, I was able to interview several key participants in the ICPD process on their impressions and recollections. These are Timothy E Wirth, former US Under Secretary of State, and now President of the UN Foundation; Nicolaas Biegman, former Permanent Representative and Ambassador of the Netherlands at the UN; Haryono Suyono, Minister of Population, Indonesia; Elizabeth Maguire, Director, and Barbara Crane, Adviser, Office of Population, US Agency for International Development (USAID); Hernando Clavijo, former Adviser to the Permanent Mission of Colombia at the UN; Avabai Wadia, President, Family Planning Association of India; Bella Abzug, President, Women's Environment and Development Organization (WEDO); Joan Dunlop, President, and Adrienne Germain, Vice President, International Women's Health Coalition (IWHC); and Werner Fornos, President, Population Institute.

Those who provided personal insights into several key events at the Bucharest and Mexico conferences are Philander Claxton, a former senior official of the US Department of State; Halvor Gille, former Deputy Executive Director, UNFPA; Carl Wahren, former Director of the Health and Population Division, SIDA; and Anwarul Karim Chowdhury, Deputy Permanent Representative of Bangladesh at the UN in the early 1980s and currently Permanent Representative and Ambassador of Bangladesh at the UN.

UNFPA representatives in the field who were extremely helpful, during my visits in 1995–1997, in providing updated information on ICPD follow-up include Ugur Tuncer in Indonesia, KC Bal Gopal in Thailand, Alain Mouchiroud in Bangladesh, Wasim Zaman in India, Claude Paulet in Tunisia, and Reiner Rosenbaum in Mexico. During visits to Geneva and London, several senior officials of the World Health Organization (WHO), including Dr Tomris Turmen, Executive Director of the Family and Reproductive Health Programme, and Dr Giuseppe Benegiano, then Director of WHO Special Programme of Research, Development and Research Training in Human Reproduction (HRP), and of the International Planned Parenthood Federation (IPPF), including Ingar Brueggemann, Secretary General, and Mark Laskin, Assistant Secretary General, were kind enough to provide me with extensive updates on their programmes and plans on the implementation of the ICPD Programme of Action.

I would especially like to acknowledge the research assistance provided to me by Yunae Yi, Technical Adviser, UNFPA, and the secretarial and clerical support provided by Alicia Long, Secretary. I would also like to thank my wife Mariluz Molares for helping me extensively with proof-reading and other editorial tasks.

UNFPA has provided me with every possible assistance, both at the headquarters and in the field, in undertaking the research required for this book. I would also like to record my gratitude to the Rockefeller Foundation for providing partial support for a research project associated with the writing of this book.

Many of the tables used in the book have been reproduced from UN documents prepared by the UN Population Division. Though these documents were issued in 1997, the tables provide data and estimates which are generally similar to those available during the ICPD process (1991–1994). Among the other tables, Table 7.1 comes from a UNFPA document, and Table 2.1 from a paper by Mr Sinding.

INTRODUCTION

Soon after the International Conference on Population and Development (ICPD), several of my colleagues and friends suggested that I write a comprehensive commentary on the Conference, from the vantage point of an insider, for readers interested in population and development issues. This book, which has been written in response to that suggestion, examines, first, how during the ICPD process various issues in the politics of population were dealt with by government officials, representatives of non-governmental organizations (NGOs), academics, experts, religious leaders, politicians and the media; second, what kind of strategic role the Conference Secretariat, led by the Secretary General of the Conference Dr Nafis Sadik, played in initiating, promoting and coordinating in-depth consideration of these issues; and, finally, how the conceptual framework and substantive content of the ICPD Programme of Action emerged at the Conference, through a protracted and complex process of negotiations and consensus-building.

The issues that came up during the ICPD process were examined in a variety of settings – three preparatory meetings for the ICPD (involving the entire membership of the United Nations), five regional conferences (Asia and the Pacific, Africa, Europe and North America, Arab states, and Latin America and the Caribbean), six expert group meetings and seven round tables. As Executive Coordinator of the ICPD, I was actively involved in the preparation for these events and attended all of them. Additionally, there were numerous sub-regional and national consultations as well as meetings organized by NGOs. I had the opportunity to participate in many of these meetings as well. The book reviews the evolution of the debates on various issues at these events and related activities, also outlining how specific national and regional perceptions and positions evolved during 1991–1994 and what contributions they made to the emergence of a new global consensus on population.

Five of the seven chapters of the book are devoted to the major issues, which I have grouped under the following clusters: family planning, reproductive health and reproductive rights; population and development; empowerment of women; partnership with the non-governmental sector; and mobilization of resources for population programmes. The other two are in the nature of a prologue and an epilogue.

Since the ICPD was the third in a series of global, intergovernmental conferences on population, the first chapter provides a historical perspective through an overview of the World Population Conference (WPC) (1974) and the International Conference on Population (1984), in particular their legislative history, organizational and preparatory activities, the structure of the secretariat, finances, host country arrangements, highlights of the political debates and the main achievements. On the ICPD (1994), the information provided here covers the legislative, organizational and preparatory aspects, leaving the technical, policy and political issues to be elaborated and analysed in the subsequent five chapters.

The second chapter deals with the cluster of issues that generated the most discussion: family planning, reproductive health and reproductive rights. It provides an overview of how discussion on these themes evolved, with a brief account of various issues and controversies, particularly on abortion, which arose during the process, and an analysis of the political processes through which these controversies were finally resolved, leading to a broad consensus at the Conference on a comprehensive definition of reproductive health, including family planning and sexual health.

The third chapter deals with policy developments from Bucharest to Cairo under four broad themes: integration of population and development strategies; population growth and structure; reduction of mortality and morbidity; and population distribution and migration, particularly international migration.

The fourth chapter examines why, given increasing support at the global level for the concept of equality between men and women, there was a wide divergence of opinion on such issues as gender equity *vs* gender equality, age at marriage, family structure and composition and inheritance rights. It also deals with such emerging issues as female genital mutilation and violence against women. The fifth chapter traces the highly significant role NGOs, in particular women's groups, played in the ICPD process and what impact this had on the outcome of Cairo.

The sixth chapter documents the efforts undertaken since Bucharest to mobilize resources for population programmes and provides a step-by-step account of how resource estimates for the ICPD were developed and negotiated between the Group of 77 (G77) representing developing countries and the donors' group constituted by most of the industrialized countries.

The final chapter of the book reports on the substantive as well as practical steps taken by the international community (including the UN Population Fund (UNFPA), the UN and its agencies and organizations and the World Bank) on ICPD follow-up and outlines briefly the action being taken by national governments and NGOs, under the five theme clusters, to follow up on the Programme of Action adopted by the ICPD.

In the process of preparing this book, I have had the opportunity to visit several countries in Asia, Africa, Latin America and Europe and to talk to government officials and NGO representatives as well as representatives of international organizations. I have also benefited from conversations with many of the key participants in the ICPD process and members of the ICPD Secretariat, and in a separate section I have acknowledged their contributions. However, the views and opinions expressed in the book are, in the final analysis, my own, as are all the shortcomings.

1   BUCHAREST, MEXICO AND CAIRO

The International Conference on Population and Development (ICPD), which was held in Cairo, Egypt, from 5 to 13 September 1994, has earned a place in history as one of the most significant global conferences ever. It radically transformed the views and perceptions of thousands of policy makers and programme managers on how population policies and programmes should be formulated and implemented in future – moving away from top–down approaches and pre-planned demographic goals to those that would seek to respond to the needs of 'couples and individuals'. At the same time, the unparalleled exposure it received through newspapers, radio, television and the internet helped to bring issues relating to reproductive health, reproductive rights and women's empowerment to the attention of millions of women and men around the world, and may indeed have enhanced their understanding and appreciation of these issues in a positive manner.

Cairo also set clear benchmarks to measure progress over a period of two decades (1995–2015) towards goals relating to the reduction of infant, child and maternal mortality; ensuring the availability of reproductive health services to all those who need them; education, particularly of young girls and women; and the empowerment of women. Finally, it brought to the fore the critical role of the non-governmental sector in population activities, and firmly established the concept of 'partnership' between governments and non-governmental organizations (NGOs).

Cairo broke new ground in so many ways that it must be regarded as a unique event. But it was also part of a series of United Nations (UN) conferences on population, which included the World Population Conference (WPC) held in Bucharest, Romania, in 1974 and the International Conference on Population held in Mexico City, Mexico, in 1984.

The Bucharest, Mexico and Cairo conferences shared one common characteristic: all three were global intergovernmental conferences organized by the UN. But to complete the record, I should mention two other world conferences on population, sponsored by the Population Division of the UN in cooperation with the International Union for the Scientific Study of Population (IUSSP) – Rome (31 August–10 September 1954) and Belgrade (30 August–10 September 1965). These two conferences were designed as scientific meetings of individual experts (drawn mostly from among the community of demographers) and did not, therefore, formulate any substantive resolutions or recommendations on population and development issues.

Various sessions of the Rome and Belgrade conferences focused on themes and issues of professional concern to individual experts, but taken together they also reflected emerging issues and concerns in the population field. This was particularly noticeable at the Belgrade Conference where, for the first time, a significant number of participants from developing countries were in attendance. On the basis of the latest available information, many of the papers submitted to the Belgrade Conference sought to examine the interrelationship between population growth and economic and social development, especially for developing countries, and as the report of the Conference points out, it provided a forum 'where experts could examine together the present and prospective trends in population growth, composition and distribution, the problems arising from these trends, and the techniques required to improve the knowledge of such trends in many parts of the world' (UN, 1966: 2). Proposing or recommending action on questions of policy was not within the remit of the Conference.

In its organization, format and procedures, the Bucharest Conference marked a complete departure from the Rome and Belgrade conferences. In contrast to these two conferences, which were attended by participants in their individual capacity, Bucharest was an intergovernmental conference. It was attended by 138 governmental delegations from the member states of the UN and its specialized agencies, and its recommendations and decisions were negotiated and formulated on the basis of the UN rules and practices governing intergovernmental meetings. The Mexico Conference, organized ten years after Bucharest, attracted the participation of 146 governments and the Cairo Conference, which came ten years after Mexico City, was attended by 179 governments as full participants and by the Palestinian Authority, and six governments that are associate members of the UN regional commissions, as observers. The European Union (EU), following the practice established at the UN Conference on Environment and Development (UNCED) (Rio de Janeiro, 1992), was also given full participant status at Cairo.[1]

As in the case of all major UN conferences, the intergovernmental character of the Bucharest, Mexico and Cairo conferences implied the fulfilment of several organizational and political requirements by the UN in preparing for and holding such global events. First of these is always the need to ensure internal coordination. In addition to the unit or units with overall responsibility, many other units of the UN (Finance, Conference Services, Public Information, the Secretariat of the Economic and Social Council (ECOSOC) and Security) have specific functional responsibilities regarding preparations for and organization of UN conferences; and regular and effective collaboration among them is indispensable for the success of such conferences.

The financial arrangements for the conferences follow specially defined procedures and can prove to be quite complicated. A government that offers to host a UN conference is required to cover the difference in costs between holding the Conference at a UN site (eg New York, Geneva or Vienna) and the site proposed by the host. Though working out the cost difference ought to be a straightforward matter, it never is, and lengthy and protracted negotiations are needed to finalize the financial arrangements with the host government. The regular UN budget should in principle cover all the other costs relating to staff, documentation, preparatory meetings and so on. But extra-budgetary contributions are almost always needed to pay for additional costs and these require a good deal of initiative and imagination in fund-raising efforts. This was certainly the case with all three intergovernmental population conferences.

Each major UN conference is expected to be preceded by regional conferences, national preparatory activities, technical workshops and meetings, and meetings of its international preparatory committee. Participating in the planning, organization or coordination of these events and activities worldwide is a major exercise in logistics, patience and diplomacy for the conference secretariat. Most importantly, the preparatory process needs to be designed in such a way as to mobilize the support of national delegations for the emergence of an international consensus on major themes and issues. The practice of consensus-building as it has evolved within the UN can sometimes mean that a single delegation can block an agreement among all the other delegations. More often, consensus is arrived at through negotiations among a bewildering variety of regional, political, economic and other interested groups; and the countries which still do not support the consensus text, or parts thereof, may choose to state their reservations for the record.

When the Bucharest Conference took place, the UN practice still allowed voting, and it was used extensively at Bucharest. In the case of Mexico, it was used once in the Main Committee and twice in the Plenary Session. Voting was not used at all during the Cairo process, and on one occasion when Fred Sai, Chairman of the Preparatory Committee, thought aloud of the possibility of holding a straw vote to determine the preference of members of the Preparatory Committee, his rumination caused considerable consternation among all the major groups – the Group of 77 (G77) and the EU included. Over the last decade, consensus-building has indeed become the accepted norm at the UN.

In order to obtain an overview of the linkages among the three global population conferences, it is useful first to look at what happened at the WPC and the International Population Conference, in particular their legislative history, organizational and preparatory activities, the structure of the secretariat, finances, host country arrangements, highlights of the political debate and the main achievements. On the ICPD this chapter covers the legislative, organizational and preparatory aspects, leaving the technical, policy and political issues to be elaborated and analysed in the subsequent chapters.

BUCHAREST CONFERENCE

The WPC (Bucharest, 19–30 August 1974) was organized under the auspices of ECOSOC, which approved a resolution on 3 April 1970 authorizing the convening of an intergovernmental conference on population by the UN in 1974 (ECOSOC Resolution 1484 (XLVIII)). According to this resolution, the objective of the WPC was to consider basic demographic problems, their relationship with economic and social development, and population policies and action programmes needed to promote human welfare and development.

Two years later, ECOSOC assigned to the UN Population Commission the task of serving as the intergovernmental preparatory body for the Conference (ECOSOC Resolution 1672 (LII), 2 June 1972). At the same time, it requested the Secretary General to appoint within the Department of Economic and Social Affairs a Secretary General for the Conference. In October 1972, Secretary General Kurt Waldheim appointed Antonio Carrillo Flores, former Foreign and Finance Minister of Mexico, to be Secretary General of the Conference.

The US gave the proposed Conference a lot of encouragement and support, because of individuals like William H Draper Jr and Philander Claxton. Mr Draper, who was a tireless campaigner for the cause of population, enjoyed a great deal of influence in the US administration in the late 1960s and early 1970s. He was designated by the US as its chief representative to the Population Commission, and it was mainly because of his efforts that the US actively supported the idea of a global intergovernmental population conference to be organized by the UN. I was told at the time that it was Mr Draper, along with Mr Claxton, who had persuaded the Population Commission to recommend the convening of an intergovernmental conference rather than a conference of demographers and experts along the lines of the Rome and Belgrade conferences. Furthermore, it was Mr Draper who suggested to Mr Waldheim the name of Mr Carrillo Flores, whom he had personally known for many years, for the position of Conference Secretary General. Mr Draper was also an active fund-raiser for the UN Population Fund

(UNFPA, known as the UN Fund for Population Activities until 1987). Mr Claxton, who was the senior State Department official in charge of population, demonstrated a great deal of official and personal interest in the Conference, and worked closely with Mr Draper in developing detailed organizational proposals for a global intergovernmental conference. Both of them also played an active role at the Conference itself.

The idea of an intergovernmental conference was also supported by many of the developed countries that had begun to contribute to population programmes, through UNFPA as well as bilateral channels. The developing countries went along with the idea, though one cannot say that in the beginning they were very enthusiastic. As the discussion on the Conference evolved over 1971–1972, Asian and European countries became more supportive.

Finding a host country for the proposed event was not easy. An attempt was made first to find a developing country which could host the event. But this did not prove possible. The persistent search finally produced an invitation from the Romanian Government and it was accepted by ECOSOC at its 54th Session in May 1973.

The Population Commission met three times as the intergovernmental preparatory body for the Bucharest Conference: first Special Session, 7–15 August 1972; second Special Session, 19–30 March 1973; and third Special Session, 4–15 March 1974. Also, at its 17th regular Session (29 October–9 November 1973), the Commission considered several aspects of the preparatory work for the WPC.

Four technical symposia were organized in preparation for the Conference: the Symposium on Population and Development (Cairo, 4–14 June 1973); the Symposium on Population and the Family (Honolulu, 6–15 August 1973); the Symposium on Population, Resources and the Environment (Stockholm, 26 September–3 October 1973); and the Symposium on Population and Human Rights (Amsterdam, 21–29 January 1974). The most important document for the Conference – the draft World Population Plan of Action (WPPA) – was prepared by the Population Division with the assistance of an Advisory Committee of Experts on the WPC, various UN bodies and a variety of technical studies. The Advisory Committee met three times, in June 1972, July 1973 and February 1974 (UN, 1975).

The draft Plan was also discussed with representatives of governments at a series of five regional consultative meetings held in 1974 at San José, Costa Rica (15–19 April), Bangkok (7–10 May), Addis Ababa (13–16 May), Damascus (21–23 May) and Geneva (29–31 May). Countries in the Asia and Pacific region had earlier organized a fully fledged Asian Population Conference in New Delhi (1971).

The primary responsibility for organizing the Bucharest Conference was given to a small Conference Secretariat (with 12–14 professional staff members and a similar number of support staff) within the UN. It on demographic issues. To the extent that these individuals knew of the controversy and acrimony between Western countries and members of the G77 over NIEO issues, they felt that these were not directly relevant to the preparations for a conference on population. The furious debate that erupted at the Bucharest Conference between supporters of population activities and the proponents of the NIEO thus came as a surprise to the technical advisers attached to many of the national delegations, as it did to many members of the UN staff involved in the organization of the Conference.

The Bucharest Conference was financed by an allocation of US$1.8 million from the UN regular budget and a contribution of US$2 million by UNFPA.* The WPC Secretariat received additional funds from some bilateral agencies for the travel of developing world participants to the Conference. UNFPA covered all the costs of the WPY secretariat and the activities organized by it or sponsored by it through UN agencies and NGOs. UNFPA and several bilateral agencies and foundations also supported the organization of an NGO Tribune at the 1974 Conference.

The negotiations with the Government of Romania on the host country arrangements required a certain amount of time and effort; but I understand the process did not encounter any serious problems. I was not involved in the main negotiations, but in October 1973 as the person in charge of NGO liaison, I participated in a mission to Romania fielded by the Conference of NGOs in Consultative Status with ECOSOC (CONGO), which was responsible for organizing the NGO Tribune. The same people who were in charge of host country arrangements for the Conference also dealt with NGO matters. The Government of Romania, with some prodding from the UN, agreed to provide conference facilities for the Tribune at the Faculty of Law of the University of Romania which proved quite adequate, although it was some distance from the Conference Centre.

The debates at the WPC were marked by the presentation of four different views on population. Asian and European countries, along with the US, took the position that rapid population growth intensified problems of economic and social development and therefore merited urgent attention. Bangladesh, which had become independent at the end of 1971 and as one of the poorest countries in the world was struggling with urgent and difficult problems of development, made one of the most forthright statements at the Conference: 'our demographic situation leaves us with no alternative but to try to contain and curb our population growth by all possible means and as quickly as possible'. India and Indonesia gave strong support to family planning programmes, justifying them within the overall context of development. On the other side, there were many Latin American and African countries

---

* Unless otherwise indicated, all figures quoted in the text are in US dollars.

remember that the relationship between these secretariats and units was not always free of tensions.

In his book *People: An International Choice*, Mr Salas makes a wry comment on this organizational arrangement:

> *This was a curious division of labour: the United Nations in designating previous Years and their accompanying conferences had entrusted the management of both events to one specific body. Normally, this was a special secretariat. But in 1972 the Fund already had worldwide visibility, and many participants in the preparatory committees thought it should be given a more definitive part in the celebration. Stanley Johnson, the IPPF representative, persuaded his Government's representative [UK] to propose an active role for UNFPA. What came out in the final ECOSOC resolution was an ingenious device of not giving total responsibility either to the Fund or the Population Division. The responsibility for the WPY was given to the Executive Director and the responsibility for the Conference to a Secretary-General staffed by the Population Division. A very unusual arrangement somehow obscured by the agreement that the World Population Conference was to be the highlight of the Year. (Salas, 1977: 101–2).*

What were the reasons for this 'very unusual arrangement'? I can think of two. The other major UN conference in the early 1970s – the UN Conference on the Environment (Stockholm, 1972) – had a full-time Secretary General (Maurice Strong) and its own Secretariat. This precedent might have been in the minds of those who finalized the secretariat arrangements during 1970–1972 for the WPC. Given the fact that the UN Population Division was the UN unit which had sponsored the two earlier population conferences, it would also have seemed logical to make it part of the WPC Secretariat and to give it the substantive responsibility for Bucharest. As regards UNFPA's role in the Conference, it had begun to attract a certain amount of attention among governments as well as NGOs as a funding organization and it may have been argued that it ought to have continued strengthening its role in this regard rather than taking on additional responsibilities for a world conference. In the end, because of WPY activities and Mr Salas's own efforts, UNFPA acquired much greater visibility in the period leading up to Bucharest.

The division of the preparatory activities into separate sectors – technical activities, organizational matters, external relations and coordination, and awareness creation and information activities – was perhaps one of the reasons why the political debates on economic and development issues (involving in particular the concept of a new international economic order (NIEO), the subject of two resolutions adopted over the strong objections of the US and several other industrialized countries at the sixth Special Session of the GA in 1973 (GA Resolutions 3201 and 3202 (S-VI)) did not receive appropriate attention at the technical or regional events. These meetings were attended mostly by technical and professional participants and focused was headed by Mr Carrillo Flores, Secretary General of the Conference. Leon Tabah, Director of the UN Population Division, was named as one of his deputies to take care of the substantive and technical preparations, while Ralph Townley was named as the other deputy to look after practical arrangements.

The third unit involved in the preparatory activities was the World Population Year (WPY) Secretariat set up by Rafael Salas, Executive Director of the UNFPA. A couple of years after the General Assembly (GA) had designated 1974 as WPY (the centrepiece of which was to be the WPC), ECOSOC gave the responsibility for organizing WPY-related activities to the Executive Director of UNFPA (ECOSOC Resolution 1672 (LII), 20 June 1972). Moving swiftly after the ECOSOC decision, Mr Salas set up a WPY Secretariat within UNFPA (with 10–12 professional staff and 12–14 support staff). Tarzie Vittachi, a well known Sri Lankan journalist and recipient of the Ramon Magsasy award for journalism, was appointed Executive Secretary. At about the same time, I was invited by Mr Salas to join the WPY Secretariat. As Secretary General of the World Assembly of Youth (WAY), I had met Mr Salas a couple of times in 1971–1972 in order to obtain UNFPA support for youth and population education projects in several countries. When he decided to establish the WPY Secretariat, he thought of me as someone who could help to promote WPY-related activities among NGOs. I was then about to finish my assignment with WAY and was very happy and honoured to accept Mr Salas's invitation. I came to UNFPA as the NGO Liaison Officer in 1972, and was appointed as Mr Vittachi's deputy in 1973.

Many separate units were thus in charge of various WPC–WPY activities. The four technical symposia were organized by the UN Population Division, and the regional consultations by the UN regional commissions. A large number of other preparatory events involving governmental authorities, academics, church and religious groups and NGOs, which sought to focus public and media attention on the urgency and importance of population issues, were organized by the WPY Secretariat. The WPC Secretariat, which was under the overall super-vision of Mr Carrillo Flores and the day-to-day supervision of Mr Townley, was responsible for negotiating the host country arrangements, mobilizing extra-budgetary contributions and managing external relations.

The ECOSOC resolution that gave the responsibility for the WPY to Mr Salas had urged the Secretary General of the Conference and the Executive Director of UNFPA 'to cooperate to the extent necessary to ensure that preparations for the WPC and WPY proceed smoothly, bearing in mind the complementary nature of the activities of the Year and the Conference' (ECOSOC Resolution 1672 (LII)). In this context, I recall regular meetings and consultations between the WPC Secretariat, including the Population Division, and the WPY Secretariat, but I also that expressed the view that population growth was not an important variable in development. Another group of countries argued that population growth was desirable for a variety of reasons: to fill empty land (Brazil), to defend the country (China) or to stimulate the economy (France). The USSR and other countries blamed the problems of development upon the inequities of the world economic system. They were supportive of overall development goals and of the NIEO concept, but saw no need for specific population policies. Romania, the host country, was part of this group, and the President of Romania, in his inaugural address, made this quite clear.

Finding common ground among these positions was not easy. The Working Group of the Conference entrusted with the task of considering the Draft WPPA did not make much progress on the first two days. Frustrated at this lack of progress, Carl Wahren, a delegate from Sweden (who later became Secretary General of the International Planned Parenthood Federation (IPPF)), called together 20–25 delegates on the evening of the second day to discuss what could be done to move the Working Group forward. This smaller caucus of delegates, with Mr Wahren as the convenor, was authorized by the Chairman of the Working Group to organize itself into an open-ended informal group in order to negotiate compromise solutions on difficult and unresolved issues confronting the main Working Group. As and when necessary, the informal group asked smaller groups of individuals to deal with specific paragraphs or phrases and to report back to it with their proposals. The informal group would then go back to the Working Group with consolidated amendments and revisions. Individual delegations still had the right to resubmit amendments that in their view were not accommodated during the informal consultations.

In total, the Working Group held 15 long meetings between 20 and 28 August 1974, and the record shows that more than 50 votes were taken in the Working Group to resolve intractable issues (UN, 1975: 134–141). Eventually, a composite compromise text emerged from the Working Group, and was adopted by the Conference on 30 August 1974.

The statements made by a number of delegations in the Working Group after the WPPA had been adopted recognized the compromises on several issues, but also reflected a diversity of opinions on other issues. France, Japan and the US recorded their reservations on the references in the WPPA to the concept of a NIEO, whereas Algeria and Czechoslovakia vigorously supported the call for the establishment of such a new order. Pakistan expressed the view (which was probably shared by a number of other Asian countries) that 'the Working Group which had prepared the Plan of Action had been dominated by countries where the problem of population did not exist with the intensity it did in Asia' (UN, 1975: 145). According to Toshio Kuroda, who served on the Working Group as a member of the delegation from Japan, the Asian countries did play an important role in working out compromises at Bucharest through a lot of behind-the-scenes negotiations (Kuroda, 1996).

While endorsing the Plan, Canada mentioned several specific themes and concerns that needed further attention: the full participation of women in all processes; the role of NGOs; the need to consider the problems of natural resources and the environment in the formulation of population policies; concern for the quality of life in rural areas and under conditions of rapid urbanization; and respect for human rights and minority cultures (UN, 1975). In retrospect, one can see that the Canadian delegate was prescient, for in the years following Bucharest all of these themes attracted increasing attention in the evolution of the debate on population and development.

On the other hand, the NIEO debate subsided with the lessening of the ideological confrontation between the proponents and opponents of a radical restructuring of the international economic system, and with the emergence of new disputes on trade, aid and structural adjustment issues between the G77, and the US and other industrialized countries. In 1984, the Recommendations for the Further Implementation of the WPPA, adopted at the Mexico Conference, made only a brief reference to the 1973 GA resolutions on the NIEO; and in this context, the US made a very brief statement simply reserving 'its position on all the international agreements mentioned in this document consistent with our previous acceptance or nonacceptance of them' (UN, 1984: 12). The topic did not come up at all for discussion during the ICPD process, and there is no reference to it in the ICPD Programme of Action.

WHAT WAS ACHIEVED AT BUCHAREST?

Immediately after Bucharest, I wrote an article for the UNFPA journal *Populi* summarizing the outcome of the Conference (Singh, 1974). At the time my view was that essentially three major agreements had emerged at the Conference, and more than two decades later I believe the view remains valid. The three agreements can be presented as follows.

(1) Population and development have an integral and mutually rein-forcing relationship. One of the major principles outlined in the WPPA is that

> *population and development are interrelated: population variables influence development variables and are also influenced by them; thus the formulation of a World Population Plan of Action reflects the international community's awareness of the importance of population trends for socio-economic development, and the socio-economic nature of the recommendations contained in this Plan of Action reflects its awareness of the crucial role that development plays in affecting population trends.* (UN, 1975, Para. 14(c))

10

Further on, Recommendation 95 suggests that:

> [p]opulation measures and programmes should be integrated into comprehensive social and economic plans and programmes and this integration should be reflected in the goals, instrumentalities and organizations for planning within the countries.

(2) Given varying national perceptions of and sensitivities on population issues, the Conference accepted the principle that '[t]he formulation and implementation of population policies is the sovereign right of each nation' (Para. 14), and that recommendations concerning the formulation of population policies 'must recognize the diversity of conditions within and among different countries' (Para. 14(i)).

(3) Agreement on the sovereignty issue was closely linked to an agreement on the human rights issue. The Plan invited countries 'to consider adopting population policies, within the framework of socio-economic development, which are consistent with basic human rights and national goals and values' (Recommendation 17). In this context, the WPPA recognized the basic right of all couples and individuals 'to decide freely and responsibly the number and spacing of their children and to have the information, education and means to do so' (Para. 14(f)). Most of this language came from the International Conference on Human Rights (Tehran, 1968), which had declared that 'parents have a basic human right to determine freely and responsibly the number and the spacing of their children' (UN, 1968: Para. 16). But the Bucharest Conference made an extremely significant change, substituting 'parents' with 'couples and individuals'. This broadened definition has stood the test of time and though repeated attempts have been made at subsequent UN conferences to alter it or to water it down, it has remained unchanged through the years.

Though the US had suggested in the Working Group on the WPPA the need to establish 'national goals together with a world goal of replacement level fertility by the year 2000',[2] the Bucharest Conference could not reach any agreement on quantitative global goals aimed at reducing fertility. Many developing countries, given national sensitivities, were unwilling or reluctant to endorse any global targets on the reduction of population growth or fertility. The Conference did agree that 'countries which aim at achieving moderate or low population growth should try to achieve it through a low level of birth and death rates' (Recommendation 18). It also recommended that 'countries wishing to affect fertility levels give priority to implementing development programmes and educational and health strategies which, while contributing to economic growth and higher standards of living, have a decisive impact upon demographic trends, including fertility . . .' (Recommendation 31).

Bucharest adopted a clearly defined goal: 'to reduce mortality levels, particularly infant and maternal mortality levels, to the maximum extent possible in all regions of the world and to reduce national and subnational differentials therein' (Recommendation 22). It also accepted a more specific goal for the countries 'with the highest mortality levels . . . to have an expectation of life at birth of at least 50 years and an infant mortality rate of less than 120 per thousand live births' (Recommendation 23).

MEXICO CONFERENCE

The proposal to organize another world conference on population ten years after Bucharest came from the Population Commission, as was the case with the Bucharest Conference. In 1979, ECOSOC asked the Population Commission, in consultation with appropriate UN bodies, to consider the possibility of holding an international conference to review developments in the first decade following the WPC.

In November 1981, ECOSOC reviewed the proposal put forward by the Population Commission for such a new world conference. Compared with Bucharest, this time there was a great deal of support from developing countries for an international conference on population. India, the Philippines and Mexico supported the proposal strongly. But many of the developed countries were not so keen. The experience at Bucharest had made them wary of the idea of a new population conference which might revive old controversies or generate new ones. Another group including the USSR and some of the Eastern European countries did not want the Bucharest consensus disturbed in any way. To satisfy them and many others, it was agreed early on that the proposed conference would take the WPPA as the guiding document and would only seek to formulate recommendations for further implementation of the WPPA. Also, the question of how much such a conference would cost was raised repeatedly by a number of delegations in informal discussions, and they wanted to make sure that if a conference were to be held, costs would be held down to a minimum.

ECOSOC finally decided to 'convene in 1984, under the auspices of the UN, an International Conference on Population open to all States as full members and to the specialized agencies' (ECOSOC Resolution 1981/87, 25 November 1981). It designated the Population Commission, meeting in an open-ended session which would be open to participation by all countries, to serve as the Preparatory Committee for the Conference. At the same time, it asked the UN Secretary General to name the

Executive Director of UNFPA as the Secretary General of the Conference and Director of the UN Population Division as the Deputy Secretary General. The appointment of Mr Salas, Executive Director of UNFPA, as Secretary General of the Conference was announced by Javier Perez de Cuellar, UN Secretary General, in January 1982. This recognized the emergence of UNFPA as the major actor in the area of population within the UN system. There was also the hope that the Executive Director of UNFPA would be in a position to raise most of the money needed for the Conference. The substantive responsibility for the preparation of the Conference was left, as in the case of Bucharest, with the Population Division of the Department for International Economic and Social Affairs (DIESA). Leon Tabah, Director of the Population Division, served as Deputy Secretary General until his retirement in February 1984. In March 1984, P Shankar Menon replaced him as Acting Director of the Division and as Deputy Secretary General of the Conference. I was appointed as the Executive Coordinator of the Conference in 1981, though I also continued to serve as Director of the UNFPA Information and External Relations Division. My assignment was to coordinate the Conference arrangements, including those in the preparatory phase.

Mexico offered to host the Conference at the ECOSOC session in April 1982. The Secretariat was told at the time that India was also willing to serve as the host country, but it did not present an offer in view of the Mexican announcement. ECOSOC, in Resolution 1982/7 of 30 April 1982, welcomed the offer from Mexico, but did not accept it immediately. The Secretariat was expected to find out more about the conference facilities available in Mexico City and other local arrangements before the approval of the offer by ECOSOC. Along with Luis Olivos, the chief of the Latin America programme unit at UNFPA, I was sent by Mr Salas to look at the facilities in Mexico City and to talk to Mexican officials. We came back with the impression that the facilities being offered were adequate, and through resolution 1982/42 of 27 July 1982 ECOSOC decided to accept Mexico's offer to host the Conference.

After the selection of Mexico as the host country, I led five 'planning' missions to Mexico during 1982–1984, to work out the host country arrangements. Manuel Bartlett Diaz, Mexico's Minister of the Interior, who also served as Chairman of the National Population Council of Mexico, took a great deal of personal interest in the preparatory arrangements for the Conference, and was chosen at the Conference to preside over its deliberations. Also, officials at the Ministry of Foreign Affairs were very helpful in working out various practical details. The host country agreement was finally signed in New York by the Permanent Representative of Mexico at the UN and the Secretary General of the Conference in June 1984. Though we suffered from limitations of space at the Ministry of Foreign Affairs, where the Conference was held, the Government provided excellent conference facilities, including office space, transportation and a media centre, and was a generous host.

The question of financing the Conference required intensive negotiations within ECOSOC. The USSR wanted the entire Conference, if it was to be held at all, financed by extra-budgetary funds. On the other hand, a majority of ECOSOC was willing to agree to a limited contribution from the regular budget, with additional funds being raised from extra-budgetary sources. The issue had to be brought to a vote at the ECOSOC session in July 1982 before it was resolved. The agreement was that up to US$800,000 out of the total budget of US$2.3 million would come from the regular budget. The rest of the funds were to come from extra-budgetary sources.

In January 1982, Mr Salas and I undertook a trip to Australia, where he was able to convince the Government to provide an extra-budgetary contribution of US$100,000 for the population conference. This set the ball rolling and eventually we were able to raise more than US$1.6 million in extra-budgetary contributions, including contributions from several developing countries ranging from US$25,000 to US$100,000. The total amount was sufficient for the organization of the four expert groups and the main Conference. But it did not allow for hiring of extra staff or any additional activities. The emphasis was on 'the utmost economy in costs' (ECOSOC Resolution 1982/27, 3 March 1982). Compared with Bucharest, Mexico was a rather modest affair.

The substantive preparations, entrusted to the Population Division of the DIESA, included the holding of four expert group meetings in the first half of 1983. These meetings were convened to review the major developments in each of the four thematic areas identified by the Population Commission as being of the highest priority: fertility and family (New Delhi, India, 5–11 January 1983); population distribution, migration and development (Hammamet, Tunisia, 21–25 March 1983); population, resources, environment and development (Geneva, Switzerland, 25–29 April 1983); and mortality and health policy (Rome, Italy, 30 May–3 June 1983). For the expert group meetings in India and Tunisia, we were able to obtain conference facilities and financial contributions from the governments concerned. The meeting in Geneva was supported by the Government of Germany through the Development Policy Forum of the German Foundation for International Development, and the meeting in Rome by the Government of Italy.

Preparatory activities at the regional levels included the Third Asian and Pacific Population Conference (Colombo, 20–29 September 1982), the European Meeting on Population (Sofia, Bulgaria, 6–12 October 1983), the Latin American Regional Preparatory Meeting for the International Conference on Population (Havana, Cuba, 16–19 November 1983), the Second African Population Conference (Arusha, United Republic of Tanzania, 9–13 January 1984) and the Third Regional

Population Conference in the Arab World (Amman, Jordan, 25–29 March 1984).

During the second half of 1982, members of the Secretariat met with many NGO representatives to discuss their role in the Conference and its preparatory process. A Planning Committee was established by the CONGO in November 1982 to formulate and coordinate NGO activities in support of the International Conference on Population. The first meeting of the Planning Committee took place in January 1983, involving population organizations as well as women's groups, church and religious groups and youth organizations. Participants in this meeting were generally of the view that it would be desirable to hold an international NGO consultation prior to the International Conference on Population, with September–October 1983 suggested as the most suitable time for such an event. Such a meeting at an early date, they felt, would have the advantage of enhancing NGO contributions to the process and substance of the Conference (UNFPA, 1983).

After consultations with Geneva-based NGOs, the Planning Committee decided to hold the proposed meeting in Geneva from 13 to 15 September 1983. Almost 200 participants from 62 international and 30 national NGOs took part in the meeting and a document containing a large number of recommendations, prepared at this meeting and signed individually by most of the participants, was circulated among government and NGO representatives prior to the meeting of the Preparatory Committee for the Conference. NGOs also contributed to the substantive preparation for the Conference through their participation in the four expert group meetings and in the briefing sessions and consultations on the Conference which were organized by the Secretariat.

The reports and recommendations of the expert group meetings, the regional conferences and the NGO consultations as well as the 1983 *Monitoring Report of Population Trends and Policies* and the results of the Fifth Population Inquiry among Governments (UN, 1985a), served as inputs for the preparation of the review and appraisal of the implementation of the WPPA and the draft recommendations for further implementation of the Plan of Action prepared for the consideration of the Preparatory Committee.

Initially, only one meeting of the Preparatory Committee was to be held (the Population Commission meeting in an open-ended session, ie with the participation of all member states that wished to attend) because of cost considerations. This meeting took place at the UN headquarters from 23 to 27 January 1984, to consider the draft recommendations for further implementation of the WPPA. But as the meeting could not complete its task, a resumed session was convened from 12 to 16 March 1984.

The Committee completed its consideration of the proposed recommendations at this session. However, an unexpected development at the resumed session later created a major problem at the Conference itself. In an article written for *Populi* soon after the Mexico Conference, Leon Tabah (who after leaving the UN served as a member of the official French delegation to the Preparatory Committee and the Mexico Conference) recalled 'a recommendation put forward by Senegal and adopted, amazingly enough without debate, condemning "the establishment of settlements in territories occupied by force", a reference to Israel's action in the Middle East' (Tabah, 1984: 14). This recommendation aroused much controversy at the Conference, and several attempts at finding a compromise, including one made by the UN Secretary General Mr Perez de Cuellar, were unsuccessful.

The issue was decided first by a vote in the Main Committee, and subsequently by two votes in the Plenary Session on 14 August 1984. The first was on the question of whether the Conference was competent to deal with Recommendation 36 on human settlements, which included the controversial recommendation formulated by Senegal. With 78 votes in favour, two against and 36 abstentions, the Conference decided that it had competence in the matter. The second was on an amendment proposed by the US which would have deleted from Recommendation 36 the controversial phrase on the relevance of the Geneva Convention on the Protection of Civilian Persons in Time of War to population distribution policies. The amendment was rejected by 77 votes to two, with 34 abstentions. The Recommendation as a whole was then adopted by a roll call vote, with 87 votes in favour, two against and 26 abstentions (UN, 1984).

The US, while joining the consensus, protested at the inclusion of the statement that population distribution policies must be consistent with the Geneva Convention.[3] But this was not the only issue on which the US was in disagreement with the majority. Under President Reagan, the US administration had begun to move away from the view held by previous US administrations that world population growth was an urgent issue. The alternative view first articulated by a few US academics, that population was a neutral phenomenon, found increasing acceptability within the US administration and became more pronounced in the first half of 1984. This shift was eventually reflected in a change of staff assignments on population within the Department of State and in the selection of official delegates to the Mexico Conference.

In July 1984, James Buckley, a well known conservative, was appointed to head the US delegation. Though the US delegation also included several proponents of family planning and international population assistance as advisers, the official position taken by the US on many controversial issues would demonstrate an almost complete reversal of the position it took at Bucharest. In his first statement to the Mexico Conference, Mr Buckley expressed the view that '[f]irst, and foremost, population growth is, of itself, neither good nor bad. It becomes an asset or a problem in conjunction with other factors such as economic policy, social constraints, and the ability to put additional men and women to useful work'. He also signalled that the US would not allow its assistance for population activities to finance or support abortion:

> *first, where US funds are contributed to nations which support abortion with other funds, the US will contribute to such nations through segregated accounts which cannot be used for abortion; second, the US will no longer contribute to separate non-governmental organizations which perform or actively promote abortion as a method of family planning in other nations; and third, before the US will contribute funds to the United Nations Fund for Population Activities, it will insist that no part of its contribution be used for abortion and will also first require concrete assurance that UNFPA is not engaged in, and does not provide funding for, abortion or coercive family planning programmes. Should such assurances not be possible, and in order to maintain the level of its overall contribution to the international effort, the US will redirect the amount of its intended contribution to other, non-UNFPA family planning programs.* (UN, 1985b: 539)

The radical change in the US position and the controversy over the settlements issue generated enormous media coverage for the Mexico Conference. An additional issue that caused a certain amount of controversy and generated a good deal of media coverage was the interrelationship between peace, disarmament and development. A more or less unexceptionable paragraph linking peace, security, disarmament and international cooperation became the subject of East–West confrontation, one side arguing in favour of giving the paragraph the status of a full recommendation, while the other wanted it to be placed in the preamble. Finally, Mr Tabah worked out a compromise acceptable to both sides: the paragraph in question would be placed in a section all by itself, between the preamble and the recommendations, under the title 'Peace, Security and Population'. The paragraph reads as follows:

> *Being aware of the existing close links between peace and development, it is of great importance for the world community to work ceaselessly to promote, among nations, peace, security, disarmament and co-operation, which are indispensable for the achievement of the goals of humane population policies and for economic and social development. Creating the conditions for real peace and security would permit an allocation of resources to social and economic rather than to military programmes, which would greatly help to attain the goals and objectives of the World Population Plan of Action.* (UN, 1984: Para. 12)

For the record, the Mexico Conference was significant in many additional ways. China reversed the position it had taken at Bucharest, and indicated its support for measures to reduce rapid population growth. Brazil announced that it had approved a set of guidelines, according to which family planning would be considered an integral part of public health activities. Mexico, the host country, which had adopted an official population policy in 1974, spoke of the priority and importance it had assigned to the implementation of its policy. Nigeria, Kenya and many other African countries demonstrated how far their positions had evolved since Bucharest. Quoting the Kilimanjaro Declaration adopted at the African Population Conference (Arusha, 1984), they all emphasized the importance of formulating and implementing population policies. Asian countries such as India, Pakistan, Bangladesh and Indonesia expressed their firm support for family planning and population programmes, under the rubric of general development objectives and policies.

Many of the developed countries, including Norway, Sweden and the UK, indicated their willingness to provide increasing support for population programmes, and complimented UNFPA on the success it had achieved thus far. This was particularly significant, given their increasing dismay over the new US position presented by Mr Buckley, which would later become known in US circles as the 'Mexico City policy'. This policy sought to deny US funds to all those overseas organizations that were regarded as being involved in abortion-related activities, even if no US funds were allocated for this purpose. It also led to the withdrawal of its voluntary contribution to IPPF in 1985 and to UNFPA in 1986.

MEXICO RECOMMENDATIONS

The Mexico Conference reaffirmed the three main principles adopted at Bucharest. On the provision of family planning that would in practice ensure 'the right of couples and individuals' to information and services, it was much more forthcoming than Bucharest. Reflecting the increasing experience gained by governments and NGOs in the 1970s and early 1980s in providing family planning services, it suggested that 'family planning services should be made available through appropriate and practicable channels, including ... community-based distribution ... Governments should bear in mind the innovative role which non-governmental organizations, in particular women's organizations, can play in improving the availability and effectiveness of family planning services' (UN, 1984: Recommendation 28).

Recommendation 27 maintained that '[g]overnments and intergovernmental and non-governmental organizations are urged to allocate, in accordance with national policies and priorities, the necessary resources to family planning services, where these services are inadequate and are not meeting the needs of a rapidly growing population of reproductive age'.

Two other recommendations bring up the themes of information and services for adolescents and the role of men in family planning. Recommendation 29 suggests that 'suitable family planning information and services should be made available to adolescents within the changing socio-cultural framework of each country'. Recommendation 9 says that '[g]overnments should promote and encourage, through information, education and communication, as well as through employment legislation and institutional support, where appropriate, the active involvement of men in all areas of family responsibility, including family planning, child-rearing and housework, so that family responsibilities can be fully shared by both partners'.

On the issue of abortion, which was not a topic for discussion at Bucharest, the Mexico Conference adopted a recommendation urging governments 'to take appropriate steps to help women avoid abortion, which in no case should be promoted as a method of family planning, and whenever possible, provide for the humane treatment and counselling of women who have had recourse to abortion' (Recommendation 18(e)). The draft proposed by the Preparatory Committee had the word 'illegal' before abortion, but it was deleted at the Conference. Though the final consensus on the abortion issue came close to the position taken by the Holy See, its representative did not join the consensus on the grounds that Mexico had agreed to support family planning services for adolescents and that insufficient attention had been paid to the concept of the family (Tabah, 1984).

Mexico updated the Bucharest goals on the reduction of general mortality as well as infant mortality. Countries with higher mortality levels were urged to 'aim for a life expectancy at birth of at least 60 years and an infant mortality rate of less than 50 per 1000 live births by the year 2000' (UN, 1984: Recommendation 14). Countries with intermediate mortality levels were urged to aim at achieving 'a life expectancy at birth of at least 70 years and an infant mortality rate of less than 35 per 1000 live births by the year 2000'. While Bucharest had adopted a general goal of reduction of maternal morbidity and mortality, Mexico called upon governments 'to reduce maternal mortality by at least 50 percent by the year 2000, where such mortality is very high (higher than 100 maternal deaths per 100,000 births' (Recommendation 18(a)).

Though Mr Salas, in his introductory statement, had called upon the governments and the international community to move towards the goal of population stabilization, the Mexico Conference did not adopt any specific language on the subject. It also did not adopt any quantitative targets on population growth.

In addition to family planning, the role and status of women and the role of NGOs were two other areas where Mexico represented a major advance over Bucharest. Two world conferences on women had taken place since Bucharest, the first in Mexico in 1975 and the second in

Copenhagen in 1980. The results of these conferences, and the follow-up action that had taken place at both national and international levels, had made the international community strongly conscious of the need to give increasing attention to women's rights issues. Furthermore, many more women's NGOs had emerged since 1974 to promote public awareness and understanding of a whole range of issues affecting women.

All this was at the back of the minds of those who formed an ad hoc Women's Caucus at Mexico (at the initiative of Dr Nafis Sadik, who was then Assistant Executive Director of UNFPA, Attiya Inyatullah, then minister in charge of family planning in Pakistan, Avabai Wadia, President of the Family Planning Association of India and Dr Esther Boohene, Executive Director of the National Family Planning Council of Zimbabwe). This Caucus pushed for and succeeded in getting the establishment of a separate chapter devoted to women's rights, covering such diverse issues as legal, economic and social equality, access to education and family planning and the delaying of marriage. Mexico recognized that achieving the full integration of women in society on an equal basis with men and removing all forms of discrimination against women were 'integral to achieving development goals, including those related to population policy' (Para. 7). It also accepted the proposition that 'the broadening of the role and the improvement of the status of women remain important goals that should be pursued as ends in themselves' (Para. 16).

The Mexico Conference also gave recognition to the increasingly important role of NGOs in population. Though NGOs did not organize a separate Tribune in Mexico City, as was the case in Bucharest, they were represented in large numbers at the official Conference, and many of them addressed the Conference. The Mexico Conference called on governments to encourage NGO activities and to draw upon NGO expertise, experience and resources in implementing national pro-grammes (Recommendation 84). It also supported the full participation of community groups and NGOs, including women's organizations, in all population and development activities (Recommendation 12) and invited donors to increase their support to NGOs (Recommendation 84).

The Mexico Conference also adopted, by acclamation, the Mexico City Declaration on Population and Development, which in 22 short paragraphs outlines the main characteristics of the global population issues and summarizes the outcome of the Conference. The idea of such a Declaration was first proposed by Bangladesh at the Preparatory Committee, but as no action could be taken there, Bangladesh came to the Conference with its own draft. Anawarul Karim Chowdhury, then Deputy Permanent Representative of Bangladesh at the UN, shared this draft with Dirk van der Kaa of the Netherlands, a Vice President of the Mexico Conference. The two of them prepared the final text, working with Mr Wahren of Sweden and a number of other delegates who felt that the Conference ought to produce a short, punchy document highlighting its major recommendations for use by the media and the general public.

THE AMSTERDAM FORUM

Five years after Mexico, UNFPA decided to organize an international meeting to coincide with its 20th anniversary, to review the operational experience in formulating and implementing population programmes. In February 1989, the Government of the Netherlands offered to host the meeting in Amsterdam. As the meeting was scheduled for November 1989, UNFPA had less than eight months to prepare for it. The responsibility for organizing the Forum fell on me, and a UNFPA task force that had been created to oversee UNFPA's 20th anniversary commemoration also looked after the coordination of the preparatory arrangements for the Forum.[4] Mr van der Kaa of the Netherlands helped to prepare the basic working document for the meeting and subsequently served as its Chairman. The meeting, called the International Forum on Population in the Twenty-First Century, took place in the spectacular setting of the Royal Tropical Institute, Amsterdam, from 5 to 9 November 1989, with the participation of senior ministers and government officials from 80 countries as well as representatives of a large number of UN agencies, NGOs and academic and research institutions.

The main product of the Forum was the Amsterdam Declaration entitled 'A Better Life for Future Generations'. The Declaration was noteworthy for outlining a blueprint for achieving the medium variant population projection of the UN and proposing, in this context, a number of quantitative goals and targets – an increase in contraceptive prevalence in developing countries so as to reach at least 56 per cent of women of reproductive age by the year 2000; a reduction in the average number of children born per woman commensurate with achieving, as a minimum, the medium-variant population projection of the UN; and the doubling of investment in population programmes in developing countries from around US$4.5 billion to US$9 billion by the year 2000 (UNFPA, 1989a).

Even though the Forum was not an official UN event, its Declaration was noted with appreciation by the GA, at the urging of the Netherlands and a number of developing countries (GA Resolution 44/210, 22 December 1989). The global funding estimate of US$9 billion became the benchmark for fund-raising efforts in the population field, until more comprehensive estimates were developed by the ICPD Secretariat in 1993. The background and implications of the major proposals included in the Amsterdam Declaration are discussed in further detail in several subsequent chapters (particularly Chapters 2 and 6).

THE CAIRO PROCESS: EXTENSIVE AND INCLUSIVE

The process for organizing the ICPD began in 1989, when the Population Commission discussed several options for a follow-up to the Bucharest and Mexico conferences and opted for what was then foreseen as a rather modest event called an International Meeting on Population. The proposal for such a meeting was formally endorsed by ECOSOC through Resolution 1989/91.

Follow-up action within the UN Secretariat took place a few months later. On 30 March 1990, at an interdepartmental meeting on follow-up to Bucharest and Mexico City chaired by Antonio Blanca, the UN Director General for Development Cooperation, it was proposed by Rafeeuddin Ahmed, Under Secretary General in charge of the DIESA, that following the formula adopted for Mexico City, the Executive Director of UNFPA should be appointed as the Secretary General of the proposed international meeting, with the Director of the Population Division serving as the Deputy Secretary General. The meeting agreed with the proposal and asked the Director General to transmit it to the Secretary General. The interdepartmental meeting also suggested that efforts be undertaken immediately to seek extra-budgetary contributions for the international meeting. Through a letter dated 29 June 1990 addressed to member states on the subject of the international meeting on population, the UN Secretary General announced these appointments and sought extra-budgetary contributions for the event. At the time of the announcement, Shunichi Inoue was Director of the Population Division and was therefore designated as Deputy Secretary General of the 1994 event. He was involved in the first session of the Preparatory Committee (1991) and the expert group meetings that took place during 1992 and early 1993. He was succeeded by Joseph Chamie in January 1993.

Soon after her designation as Secretary General of the 1994 event, Dr Sadik began discussing with the Department for Economic and Social Information and Policy Analysis (DESIPA, the former DIESA) how the Conference Secretariat should be organized. These discussions led to the understanding that the DESIPA (Population Division) and UNFPA would constitute a joint secretariat for the Conference. The joint secretariat would be responsible for initiating and coordinating the overall organizational and substantive preparations for the ICPD, including preparation of major Conference documents, promotion of international, regional and national activities, fund-raising and activities designed to raise awareness of ICPD-related issues.

I was named by Dr Sadik as Executive Coordinator for the Conference, while German Bravo-Casas of the Population Division was to serve as Deputy Executive Coordinator. As in the case of Dr Sadik and Mr Inoue, our assignments with regard to the Conference were to run concurrently with those relating to our regular posts. As I was then also the Director of the UNFPA Technical and Evaluation Division (TED), we were able to avail ourselves of the technical expertise of the TED staff on a continuing basis and seek the involvement and cooperation of other UNFPA divisions, as needed. With extra-budgetary funding and secondments from a number of UN organizations, we were also able to obtain additional staff fully dedicated to Conference-related tasks. We were fortunate to get the services of several talented and astute people to work in the ICPD Secretariat. I would like to mention especially David Payton (New Zealand) who joined us in 1992. Having worked in the Mission of New Zealand to the UN for several years, Mr Payton personally knew a very large number of delegates to ICPD-related meetings, and his contacts were immensely useful to us in sorting out a variety of questions with various delegations.[5]

There was a division of responsibilities between UNFPA and the Population Division, and frequent consultations and meetings chaired on many occasions by Dr Sadik herself enabled the two to work together very closely and harmoniously throughout 1990–1994. Mr Chamie, who succeeded Mr Inoue in January 1993, handled, with great distinction, substantive and technical responsibilities at the second and third sessions of the Preparatory Committee, as at the Cairo Conference. At each of these events, the Population Division and UNFPA staff members were paired together for drafting and reporting purposes, and this arrangement worked extremely well.

An interdepartmental Steering Committee consisting of senior departmental heads and, under its authority, a Working Group consisting of officials directly involved in day-to-day activities were set up at an early stage to coordinate inputs from various UN departments involved in the ICPD process. The Steering Committee met only a few times, but the Working Group met regularly to receive progress reports and to chart the future course of action on Conference-related matters. Many members of the Working Group participated in the planning missions sent to Egypt and also played highly significant roles at the Conference itself. For example, Margaret Kelley, who served on the Working Group as a representative of the ECOSOC Secretariat, was designated Secretary of the Cairo Conference.

An inter-agency Task Force under the chairmanship of Dr Sadik sought to involve all the UN agencies concerned in the Conference preparations. This Task Force met three times between 1992 and 1994. In addition, representatives of specialized agencies such as the World Health Organization (WHO), the International Labour Organization (ILO), the United Nations Educational, Scientific and Cultural Organization (UNESCO) and the Food and Agriculture Organization (FAO) participated actively in all the Preparatory Committee meetings and in a large number of ad hoc consultations on thematic issues.

The financing of the Conference, which was initially considered a difficult assignment for us, became easier as the interest in the Conference grew. The UN regular budget provided an allocation of US$1,485,000 in 1992–1993 and US$674,000 in 1994. More than US$6.5 million was raised in extra-budgetary resources over the same three-year period to support national activities, to provide travel assistance to delegates and NGO representatives to Preparatory Committee meetings and the Cairo Conference, and to meet additional costs for the ICPD Secretariat. The most generous donors were the US and Japan, which provided US$1 million each. Other countries and organizations that provided extra-budgetary support for the Conference were Australia, Austria, Belgium, Canada, Denmark, Finland, France, India, Italy, the Netherlands, New Zealand, Norway, Pakistan, Spain, Sweden, Switzerland, Thailand, the UK, the EU and the Hewlett Foundation.

Three governments – Egypt, Tunisia and Turkey – had initially expressed an interest in hosting the Conference. Ultimately, Tunisia and Turkey dropped out, leaving only the Egyptian offer on the table. ECOSOC accepted Egypt as the host country in 1992. The negotiations with the host government on local arrangements and the financing of the obligations of a host government, which began soon thereafter, were long and frequent over the next three years (1992–1994). I led six planning missions, including representatives of concerned departments and units of the UN, from New York to Cairo during this period. The host country agreement was finally signed in Geneva in July 1994 by Dr Maher Mahran, Minister of Population, on behalf of the Government of Egypt and Dr Sadik on behalf of the UN. Just before, during and after Cairo, we were able to settle many questions by referring to the agreement and, in retrospect, I can see that the very detailed negotiations we conducted on conference facilities, security and other issues proved essential to the smooth running of the Conference.[6]

The first Session of the Preparatory Committee (PrepCom I), which took place from 4 to 8 March 1991 (following a regular session of the Population Commission), proposed that the international meeting on population be called the International Conference on Population and Development (ICPD) and further defined its objectives and themes. On 26 July 1991, ECOSOC decided through Resolution 1991/93 to accept these proposals. The Preparatory Committee, which was open to participation by all member states, first served as a subsidiary body of ECOSOC, which had taken the formal decision to convene the ICPD. In 1993, under pressure from the G77, it was made subsidiary to the GA in order to make its status comparable to that of the UNCED (also a subsidiary body of the GA) and to give it a higher profile and greater visibility.

Subsequent to PrepCom I, six expert group meetings were organized by the Population Division in consultation with UNFPA, on the themes identified by ECOSOC as requiring the greatest attention in the forth-coming decade. These were: population, environment and development (New York, 20–24 January 1992), population policies and programmes (Cairo, Egypt, 12–16 April 1992); population and women (Gaborone, Botswana, 22–26 June 1992); family planning, health and family well-being (Bangalore, India, 26–29 October 1992); population growth and demographic structure (Paris, France, 16–20 November 1992); and population distribution and migration (Santa Cruz, Bolivia, 18–23 January 1993).[7] The sites for these meetings were chosen with a view to providing a geographical balance. In each case, the host government contributed to the costs of the event.

During 1992–1993, the five UN regional commissions in cooperation with UNFPA organized regional intergovernmental conferences with a view to reviewing the regional experiences and perspectives on population and to propose future action at the regional level. These were the Fourth Asian and Pacific Population Conference (Denpasar, Indonesia, 19–27 August 1992); with the Organization for African Unity (OAU), the Third African Population Conference (Dakar, Senegal, 7–12 December 1992); with the Council of Europe, the European Population Conference (Geneva, Switzerland, 23–26 March 1993); with the League of Arab States, the Arab Population Conference (Amman, Jordan, 4–8 April 1993); and the Latin American and Caribbean Conference on Population and Development (Mexico City, Mexico, 29 April–4 May 1993).[8]

Reports on the six expert group meetings and the five regional meetings were available to the Preparatory Committee at its second Session (PrepCom II) (10–21 May 1993). This session agreed in principle with the suggestion of the Secretary General of the Conference that a new programme of action be established to replace the WPPA and the Mexico recommendations for its further implementation. While incorporating many of the agreements reached in Bucharest and Mexico City, the new programme would propose specific goals, objectives and actions to meet the population and development challenges in the next 20 years. Cairo would thus mark a distinctly new phase in the chronology of world population events.

Subsequent to PrepCom II, Dr Sadik felt that a number of topics that were the subjects of discussion at the Committee needed further exploration. She therefore proposed that UNFPA, in consultation with the Population Division, organize round tables on these topics. Several governments and foundations came forward with offers to host or support such events and seven round tables were organized, in total. Five of these round tables, which were organized before the end of 1993, brought together in each case 20–25 experts and programme managers from all parts of the world. These were on women's perspectives on family planning, reproductive health and reproductive rights (Ottawa,

26–27 August 1993), Population Policies, Programmes and HIV/AIDS (human immunodeficiency virus/acquired immune deficiency syndrome) (Berlin, 28 September–1 October 1993), population and development strategies (Bangkok, 17–19 November 1993), population, environment and sustainable development in the post-UNCED era (Geneva, 24–26 November 1993) and population and communication (Vienna, 2–3 December 1993). Two events in 1994 – on population and food in the early twenty-first century (Washington, DC, 14–16 February 1994) and ethics, population and reproductive health (New York, 8–10 March 1994) – were also part of this series.

The reports and recommendations of these events, with exception of the last two, were available to the Secretariat in preparing the Draft Final Document. Subsequently, the reports of all the round tables were made available by the Secretariat to the Preparatory Committee at its third Session (PrepCom III) (New York, 4–22 April 1994) and served as valuable inputs into the discussion on specific sections of the draft Programme of Action. However, not all of their reports and recommendations could be taken into account. For example, food issues did not feature prominently in the Preparatory Committee debates, and discussion on ethical and moral issues was subsumed under the broader political debate on reproductive health. But, as the reports and recommendations of these meetings were also disseminated among a larger public audience, they helped to promote a greater awareness of the issues they were concerned with.

Several other international events also contributed to the ICPD preparations. UNFPA supported an Indonesian initiative to hold a Ministerial Meeting on the population of the non-aligned movement (of which President Suharto of Indonesia was then the Chairman) in Bali (9–13 November 1993). The Meeting adopted the Denpasar Declaration on Population, suggesting a number of topics and issues for discussion and providing strong support to the inclusion of the concept of South–South cooperation in population in the agenda for Cairo. UNFPA, in cooperation with the Government of Japan and the UN University, organized a meeting of eminent persons in Tokyo (26–27 January 1994), to examine population and development issues and to formulate proposals for inclusion in the Programme of Action. The meeting served an additional purpose, that of making the ICPD preparatory process better known in Japan.

The regional conferences in preparation for the ICPD had taken place in 1992–1993. In the post-PrepCom II period, several additional meetings at sub-regional levels were organized, with UNFPA support, to generate further support for the ICPD process. These were the Conference of Maghreb Countries (Tunis, Tunisia, 7–10 July 1993), the South Pacific Ministerial Meeting on Population and Development (Port Vila, Vanuatu, 9–10 September 1993), the South Asian Ministerial Conference on Women and Family Health (Kathmandu, Nepal, 21–23 November 1993), the Andean Conference on Population and Development (Lima, Peru, 1–3 December 1993) and the Caribbean Meeting of Experts for a Regional Plan of Action (Port of Spain, Trinidad and Tobago, 2–3 December 1993). For countries with economies in transition, the Population Institute, a Washington-based international NGO, organized a workshop involving both governmental and non-governmental representatives in Lillehammer, Norway, in July 1993. At the request of several countries, an additional meeting for this sub-region was organized with UNFPA support after PrepCom III – the Consultative Meeting of Countries with Economies in Transition (Budapest, Hungary, 19–20 July 1994). All of these were instrumental in deepening the understanding of ICPD-related issues in their respective areas. The meetings for the South Pacific, the Caribbean and the Eastern and Central European countries were, in my view, particularly effective in clarifying and consolidating the positions to be taken by the respective sub-regional groups at PrepCom III and the ICPD.

During 1993–1994, the ICPD Secretariat also supported a large number of NGO meetings at national, regional and international levels and participated in informal consultations organized by both governments and NGOs. Thus by the time we reached PrepCom III, we had had numerous consultations and meetings with governments, NGOs and international agencies across the spectrum; and these, in most cases, helped establish a clear understanding of the issues involved. The consultative process, including the organization of informal meetings, continued right up to Cairo.

The ICPD preparatory process was both extensive and inclusive. Systematic efforts were made to reach not only various departments, ministries and sectors concerned with the ICPD preparations but also all sectors of civil society – NGOs, community groups, women's organizations, academics, parliamentarians, the private sector and the media. All countries – developing and developed – were encouraged to establish national committees for the ICPD, involving not only government ministries and departments but also civil society organizations. Countries were also requested to prepare and disseminate national reports and in the months leading up to the Cairo Conference the ICPD Secretariat received a total of 168 such reports (UNFPA, 1995).[9] The aim was to get all of them to participate in the process and to encourage them to contribute to the evolution of consensus on various issues being debated. As the subsequent chapters show, we succeeded in a very large measure on both counts.

The ICPD process also benefited from several political developments in the early 1990s. The end of the Cold War meant that the East–West issues, some of which created tensions and difficulties at both Bucharest and Mexico, would not be a major factor in the discussions and negotiations leading up to Cairo. On the other hand, the emergence of a large number of new countries in Central Europe and Central Asia, following the dissolution of the USSR, brought in a new set of actors to the international arena whose claims for urgent, albeit temporary, technical and financial assistance had to be taken into account, in addition to those of the developing countries.

Another event which had a positive impact on the ICPD process was the election of Bill Clinton as President of the US at the end of 1992. The coming into office of a new US administration, the continuance of a Democratic majority in the US Congress and the keen interest and involvement in the ICPD process demonstrated by a very large number of US NGOs, including environmental and women's groups, enabled the US to play a strong and unequivocal role in formulating the substantive agenda for Cairo on such major issues as population, environment and resources, reproductive health and women's empowerment. The specific contributions the US made on these issues are discussed in some detail in subsequent chapters.

Information activities and media relations were considered an integral and important part of the work of the ICPD Secretariat. The *ICPD News* was issued in several languages during 1992–1994, and a large number of posters, brochures and media packages were issued to coincide with special events. The Secretariat worked closely with the UN Department of Public Information and the UNFPA Information and External Relations Division to ensure that the media had adequate access to senior officials and to relevant information at all times. In connection with all the regional conferences and Preparatory Committee meetings, UNFPA organized special media briefings involving both local journalists and selected media representatives from the regions concerned.[10] At PrepCom II and III and at the Cairo Conference, extensive facilities were provided to both print and electronic media and daily publications such as *The Earth Times*, *Terra Viva*, *Women's Watch* and *Vivre Outrement* (issued with the financial support of a number of international and bilateral agencies and foundations) kept the participants informed of developments on a day-to-day basis.

A clear sense of purpose and direction within the Secretariat under the strong and imaginative leadership of the Secretary General of the Conference, a set of dedicated and talented staff members, extensive use of the UNFPA field network, continuing and regular consultations with governments, NGOs and all others involved in the process, and the willingness on the part of the Secretariat to listen and react to new ideas and proposals, were the other major factors that contributed to the effectiveness of the ICPD process.

2   FROM FAMILY PLANNING TO REPRODUCTIVE HEALTH

The broadly based concept of reproductive health was adopted at the ICPD for the first time in a UN setting. The acceptance by the international community of this concept linking family planning with the treatment and prevention of sexually transmitted diseases (STDs), the reduction of maternal mortality and the promotion of maternal health, and sexual and reproductive health of both men and women, must be seen as one of the landmark achievements of the ICPD.

BASIC RIGHTS OF 'COUPLES AND INDIVIDUALS'

The link that connects Cairo with Bucharest and Mexico in this area is the definition, provided by Bucharest, of the basic right of all couples and individuals to decide freely and responsibly the number and spacing of their children and to have the information, education and means to do so. Para. 14(f) of the WPPA, which contains this definition, also outlines what is called 'the responsibility of couples and individuals':

> [a]ll couples and individuals have the basic right to decide freely and responsibly the number and spacing of their children and to have the information, education and means to do so; the responsibility of couples and individuals in the exercise of this right takes into account the needs of their living and future children, and their responsibilities towards the community. (UN, 1975: Para. 14[f])

This paragraph was not in the original draft presented to the Bucharest Conference, but was inserted as a new principle in the Working Group on the WPPA, after a certain amount of discussion, amongst other things on the question of whether only 'couples' should be mentioned instead of 'couples and individuals'. While many delegations were in favour of the second term, several others expressed unease or reservation about the reference to 'individuals', as this might imply the availability and provision of contraceptives to the unmarried. In order to determine the preference of the Group, the Chairman put the matter to a straw vote, and 'couples and individuals' carried the day, with 48 in favour of these two words, compared with 41 in favour of 'couples' and six abstentions. Having been adopted by a very thin margin, the definition of the basic right of couples and individuals has stood the test of time, and all efforts to change or revise it, including the efforts to drop the reference to 'individuals' at subsequent UN conferences, have failed.

Bucharest was not much concerned with operational activities, and it made only two references to family planning programmes. Para. 29(c) recommends that all countries

ensure that family planning, medical and related social services aim not only at the prevention of unwanted pregnancies but also at the elimination of involuntary sterility and subfecundity in order that all couples may be permitted to achieve their desired number of children, and that child adoption may be facilitated.

The second reference is in Recommendation 42: '[e]qual status of men and women in the family and society improves the over-all quality of life. This principle of equality should be fully realized in family planning where each spouse should consider the welfare of the other members of the family'.

The Mexico Conference, where many more programme managers were in attendance compared with Bucharest, went much further. Besides reiterating its support for the basic right of all couples and individuals (UN, 1984: Recommendation 30), Mexico approved several specific recommendations on family planning: active involvement of men in family planning (Recommendation 9); the resources required for family planning services (Recommendation 27); improving the quality and enhancing the effectiveness of family planning services (Recommendation 28); and suitable family planning information and services for adolescents, both boys and girls (Recommendation 29).

In the UN context, the concept of reproductive rights owes its origins to the Bucharest definition of the basic right of couples and individuals. The inclusion of family planning in a broader range of reproductive health services was first advocated at the International Conference on Better Health for Women and Children through Family Planning (Nairobi, Kenya, 5–9 October 1987), though, as the title of the Conference indicates, the primary focus was on family planning.[1] In the ICPD context, two of the expert group meetings (on women and population, and family planning, health and family well-being) paid considerable attention to the integration approach; and it was at PrepCom II that an intensive political debate began on the two interrelated issues – the concept of reproductive rights as derived from the Bucharest definition, and the integration of family planning and reproductive health.

DEFINITION OF REPRODUCTIVE HEALTH

WHO has used, for years, what it calls a 'working definition' of reproductive health. Mahmoud Fathalla, who served as the Director of the WHO Programme on Human Reproduction (HRP) from 1986 until 1992, wrote and lectured extensively on the linkages between safe motherhood, maternal and child health (MCH) services and family planning programmes, and on the evolving concept of reproductive health, arguing that it offers a more comprehensive approach to current health needs in human reproduction (Fathalla, 1989, 1991).

During the third session of the ICPD PrepCom III in 1994, WHO was asked by several delegations to explain what the term 'reproductive health' meant. This was the definition provided:

> *WHO defines reproductive health within the framework of the definition of health as a state of complete physical, mental and social well-being, and not merely the absence of disease or infirmity. Reproductive health addresses the reproductive processes, functions and system at all stages of life. Reproductive health implies that people are able to have a responsible, satisfying and safe sex life, and that they have the capability to reproduce and the freedom to decide, if, when and how often to do so. Implicit in this last condition are the right of men and women to be informed of and to have access to safe, effective, affordable and acceptable methods of fertility regulation of their choice, and the right of access to appropriate health care services that will enable women to go safely through pregnancy and childbirth and provide couples with the best chance of having a healthy infant.*[2]

WHO went on to say that 'the content of this definition of reproductive health [is] derived from nearly 30 years of policy established by WHO which enables the Organization to respond to the needs of, and demands for support by, Member States'. Implicit in this statement was the acknowledgment that this working definition was never brought to the attention of WHO's principal organ – the World Health Assembly – which meets once a year with the attendance of health ministers and senior health officials to define and update WHO's policies and strategies. One of the reasons given at the time by several former WHO officials was that a debate on the definition would have brought up such potentially divisive issues as reproductive rights, adolescent health and parental responsibilities, and abortion.

OPERATIONAL LINKAGES

Though the UN organizations concerned with family planning and other reproductive health issues were not always talking of the broad reproductive health approach in their official literature, it would be a mistake to assume that family planning and other reproductive health issues were seen as distinct and separate topics. There were well established operational linkages between family planning and MCH programmes. In several joint consultations, WHO, UNICEF and the UNFPA paid particular attention to the close relationship between these two types of programmes. UNFPA guidelines for this sector were called, for more than 20 years, *Guidelines on Maternal and Child Health/Family Planning*, and when they were revised and retitled in 1992 as *Guidelines on Family Planning* in order to sharpen the focus on UNFPA's own mandates, the linkage of family planning with MCH was reiterated (UNFPA, 1992a). A link between the provision of family planning services and the treatment of STDs was considered by many countries as not only desirable but necessary. Furthermore, as HIV/AIDS became a matter of increasing concern, particularly in several countries in Africa and Asia, it was generally the family planning clinics that were given the responsibility for the delivery of additional condoms, in the context of HIV/AIDS prevention programmes.

It would, however, be true to say that the integration of family planning and other reproductive health services was not initially on the ICPD agenda. The first meeting of the ICPD Preparatory Committee that took place in New York in 1991 did not take up the topic of reproductive health. The term in fact does not appear in the titles of any of the six expert group meetings that were originally proposed to the Committee by the UN (UN, 1991a). For that matter, nor does the term 'family planning'. The six clusters of issues proposed were (1) population, environment and development, (2) population growth and demographic structural change, (3) population distribution, (4) international migration, (5) women and population and (6) population policies and programmes.

The UN Population Division, which had prepared these proposals, felt that the 1994 event (which was at that juncture not even called a conference but a 'meeting', to denote its relatively modest character) would be prepared substantively in the same way as Bucharest and Mexico, the main focus being on demographic, policy and research issues. But at PrepCom I, many delegations expressed the view that more attention should be given to operational and programme issues and suggested treating family planning as a separate topic. To accomplish this, the proposed expert groups on population distribution and international migration were combined and the Committee agreed that the sixth expert group would be asked to deal with 'family planning programmes, health and family well-being'. The Expert Group on Women and Population was asked to look at 'the linkages between enhancing the roles and socioeconomic status of women and population dynamics, including adolescent motherhood, maternal and child health, education and employment, with particular attention to access of women to resources and the provision of services' (UN, 1991a: 5). Family planning was not listed specifically as one of the issues for this Group, presumably because it was to be dealt with by a separate expert group. The Preparatory Committee proposals were in due course authorized by ECOSOC, which also decided to give the 1994 event the title of the International Conference on Population and Development (ICPD) (ECOSOC Resolution 1991/93, 26 July 1991).

EXPERT GROUP MEETINGS

As a matter of fact, the first expert group that dealt with family planning and related reproductive health issues was the one on Population and Women (Gaborone, Botswana, 22–26 June 1992). This Group, which included many women's health advocates, took the working definition provided by the WHO as a starting point for its discussion and paid particular attention to the linkage between maternal health, family planning and other aspects of reproductive health services. In its view,

> *achieving positive reproductive health required policies and programmes that included but also looked beyond prevention of maternal death. However, given the paucity of statistical information about many aspects of reproductive health, attention had tended to focus on maternal mortality as an index of reproductive health conditions more generally.* (UN, 1992a: Para. 19)

Several recommendations of this Expert Group refer to family planning and reproductive health issues. Recommendation 9 invites governments to 'adopt measures to promote and protect adolescent reproductive health'; Recommendation 11 seeks to broaden the scope of family planning programmes by suggesting that these 'should also address infertility concerns and provide information on sexually transmitted diseases, including HIV/AIDS'. Recommendation 13 calls for 'the adoption of measures to promote the health of women and girls' to 'encompass the nutrition and health needs of young girls and women, women's reproductive health, and the implementation of the Safe Motherhood Initiative'. All of these recommendations anticipated the trend and direction that would be followed by the Preparatory Committee in its attempts to define the broad approach to reproductive health. On abortion, the Expert Group took the unequivocal position that 'women who wish to terminate their pregnancies should have ready access to reliable information, sympathetic counselling and safe abortion services' (Recommendation 8). The same position would be taken a few months later by the Expert Group Meeting on Family Planning, Health and Family Well-Being (Bangalore, 26–30 October 1992).

The participants in Bangalore were cognisant of the controversy surrounding abortion, but felt that 'as abortion played important roles in maternal mortality and fertility decline, the question of abortion could not be put aside' (UN, 1993b: Para. 15). They went on to recommend that 'women everywhere should have access to sensitive counselling and safe abortion services' (Recommendation 6).

Recommendation 4 of the Bangalore meeting urges governments and the international community 'to increase their investment in family planning and reproductive and maternal and child health (MCH) services. Governments are also urged to monitor the progress in safer motherhood and child survival and to take the necessary actions to enhance the effectiveness of the interventions'. The broader conceptual framework linking family planning, MCH and other reproductive health services was thus fully accepted by this meeting. As most of the participants in this meeting were health and family planning professionals, it formulated a very large number of recommendations of an operational nature; at the same time it also proposed two policy recommendations that would find widespread support in PrepCom II and III. Recommendation 10 says that 'family planning programmes should aim to help individuals to achieve their reproductive goals, and should be based on voluntary, free and informed choice'. Recommendation 11 states that

> governments should establish family planning goals on the basis of the unmet demand and need for information and services. Demographic goals, while legitimately the subject of government policies and programmes to achieve sustainable development, should not be imposed on family planning providers in the form of targets and quotas for recruitment of clients. Family planning services should be framed in the context of the needs of individuals, especially women. Over the long term, meeting unmet needs appears to be the best strategy for achieving national demographic goals.

The inputs from these two workshops, which sought to synthesize the views of three different groups of people (health professionals, family planning programme managers and women's groups), were very useful to the ICPD Secretariat in preparing the Proposed Conceptual Framework of the Draft Recommendations of the Conference (UN, 1993c). But while the workshops provided the views and suggestions of individual experts and programme managers, it was equally important for the Secretariat to take note of the governments' views expressed through the five regional conferences that were organized prior to PrepCom II during 1992–1993.

REGIONAL CONFERENCES

The first regional conference was organized in the Asia and Pacific region by the Economic and Social Commission for Asia and the Pacific (ESCAP) in cooperation with UNFPA and the Government of Indonesia in Bali

(Indonesia) from 19 to 27 August 1992. This was in keeping with the ESCAP tradition, as the Asia and Pacific regional conferences in preparation for the WPC, Bucharest, and the International Conference on Population, Mexico, were also the first in the series of regional meetings for those world events. As many Asian countries have officially adopted demographic goals, the Asian conferences have always had more of a population policy focus than the other regional meetings and the Bali Conference was no different. It formulated a number of demographic goals for the region, including the adoption of 'strategies to attain replacement level fertility, equivalent to around 2.2 children per woman, by the year 2010 or sooner' (UN, 1993d: 55). The Bali Conference also accepted several recommendations that took note of the continuing evolution of the thinking in the population community on maternal and child health, family planning and reproductive health issues.

Recommendation 29 of the Conference suggested that efforts be made 'to improve the accessibility and utilization of family planning and MCH services for men as well as women, taking into account the changing preferences and needs of clients and rapidly changing technologies'. Responding to the arguments put forward by many health professionals and women activists, the same Recommendation also stated that 'there is a particular need for women-centred and women-managed facilities to ensure that women and their family planning and MCH needs are fully taken into consideration'.

Recommendation 30 notes the emerging definition of reproductive health services: 'Reproductive health care should be improved considerably in the region. Policies and programmes should strive to incorporate the totality of reproductive health care and aim at reducing maternal morbidity and mortality, induced abortion, sterility, childlessness, STDs and spread of HIV and AIDS'.

Another topic that received attention at the Bali Conference was the role of men. Recommendation 33 suggests that sustained efforts be made 'to increase the involvement of males in family planning and to promote the use of family planning methods designed for males. Specific IEC [information, education and communication] strategies should be developed to inform and educate men about family planning and fertility regulation'. This theme would be taken up by many subsequent meetings and by the Cairo Conference itself.

The three recommendations cited above underscore the influence of the health professionals and programme managers who were members of national delegations. They also reflect many of the suggestions provided by the ICPD Secretary General Dr Sadik in her introductory statement. Though the ideas behind these recommendations were also being pursued around the same time by many NGOs, including women's groups, they were not yet fully active in the ICPD process and, in any case, only a few of them could afford to be represented at the Bali Conference. The involvement of international and national NGOs in the substantive debate grew as they became more active in the preparatory process in Asia, as in other parts of the world.

The second in the series of regional conferences was the African Population Conference, organized by the Economic Commission for Africa (ECA) in cooperation with UNFPA and the OAU in Dakar (Senegal). The conference was organized in two parts: a meeting of experts from 7 to 10 December 1992, and a ministerial conference on 11–12 December 1992. Speaking on behalf of Dr Sadik at the meeting of experts, I suggested that the Africa Conference should set goals for the subsequent two decades with regard to increased life expectancy, reduced infant mortality and morbidity, lower maternal mortality, education, particularly for women and girls, and a goal in the area of contraceptive prevalence, though this would not be based on 'rigid quotas' (UN, 1993e: 18). The meeting of experts did propose a number of goals until the year 2010, for adoption at the ministerial conference, and Dr Sadik in her statement at the conference commended these goals, while commenting that these could be achieved 'only if the whole international community made the necessary commitment' (UN, 1993e: 5).

The most important of these goals suggested the formulation of 'quantified national objectives for the reduction of population growth with a view to bringing down the regional natural growth rate from 3 percent to 2.5 percent by the year 2000 and 2 percent by 2010' (UN, 1993e: 32). For those who had attended the previous African Population Conference in Arusha (1984) and witnessed the debate between proponents and opponents of population policies, it was astonishing to see how far African countries had come since 1984 and how the formulation of population policies in the developmental context had become the accepted norm in Africa. Members of the ICPD Secretariat present were also happy to note the attendance of a large number of NGOs, particularly from Africa, at the conference, facilitated by grants from bilateral agencies, foundations and UNFPA field offices.

Concerned about the low rate of contraceptive prevalence in Africa, the Dakar Conference adopted the goal of ensuring the availability and promoting the use of all tested and available contraceptive and fertility regulation methods with a view to doubling the regional contraceptive prevalence rate (CPR) from about 10 to 20 per cent by the year 2000 and 40 per cent by the year 2010. While emphasizing the importance of MCH and family planning programmes, it also gave special attention to infant, child and maternal mortality, and prevention of HIV/AIDS. The Conference recommendations also emphasized the need to implement legal measures to improve the status of women and their reproductive health. Presumably this referred to the laws limiting or prohibiting access to contraception that still exist on the statutes of many French-speaking African countries following antiquated French colonial laws.

The third conference in this series was organized for European and North American countries by the Economic Commission for Europe (ECE) in cooperation with UNFPA and the Council of Europe in Geneva from 23 to 26 March 1993. The US delegation to this conference was appointed by the new US administration that took office following the election of President Clinton in November 1992 and, reflecting the views of the new administration, the US played a fairly active and vigorous role at the Geneva Conference on reproductive health issues. Through an Executive Order, President Clinton had, soon after his inauguration, overturned the so-called 'Mexico City policy' under which US assistance was barred for any international or non-governmental organization which provided support for abortion-related activities, even if that support came from non-US sources and was provided in accordance with the laws of the country concerned.

This dramatic change in the US position was reflected in the statements and negotiating positions of the US at the European Conference and at subsequent ICPD-related events, under the leadership of Senator Timothy Wirth who was named Counsellor (later confirmed as Under Secretary of State) at the Department of State to coordinate the US response to global issues such as population, the environment, refugees and the status of women. As a US senator for Colorado, he had been active on environmental and sustainable development issues for several years before his appointment at the Department of State. I happened to be with Dr Sadik when she met him and the then Senator Al Gore for the first time at an international conference on the environment and sustainable development in Moscow in January 1990. They met again at a parliamentarians' conference organized by Senators Gore and Wirth in Washington, DC, in May 1990, and became good friends. Throughout the ICPD process, the easy and informal interaction between Dr Sadik and Senator Wirth was extremely helpful to the ICPD Secretariat, as was its liaison with the US administration (including both the Department of State and the US Agency for International Development (USAID)).

The Geneva Conference paid a great deal of attention to the population situation in Eastern and Central Europe. Following the break-up of the Soviet Union and the change of regimes in almost all Eastern and Central European countries, UNFPA, WHO Europe and IPPF had undertaken visits to many of these countries to assess their contraceptive needs and were appalled to find the widespread use of induced abortion to regulate fertility, and a lack of availability of modern contraception. This issue aroused as much concern in Geneva among Western European govern-ments and NGOs as did the lack of adequate family planning services in many developing countries. The Geneva Conference suggested that 'counselling and quality family planning services should be provided and supported to reduce the number of induced abortions' (UN, 1993f: Recommendation 8). The Conference also suggested that 'in view of the current situation in countries in transition, Governments of these countries should strengthen their services in reproductive health, including family planning, and encourage NGOs in this field' (UN, 1993f: Recommendation 8). Another recommendation suggested that 'public authorities at national and local levels, non-governmental organizations and other institutions concerned should support non-coercive family planning services, which respect the values of recipients, together with maternal and child health programmes and related reproductive health services' (Recommendation 10).

The regional conference for the Arab world was sponsored by the Economic and Social Commission for Western Asia (ESCWA) in cooperation with UNFPA and the Arab League, and took place in Amman (Jordan) from 4 to 8 April 1993. The Conference had a number of articulate women among both government delegations and NGO observers who spoke up forcefully in support of family planning programmes and in favour of equal rights of women, even within the religious and sociocultural frameworks obtaining in the Arab world. Their views are reflected in a recommendation which says that

> programmes relating to MCH and family planning should be designed in such a way as to ensure: a) Acceptance of the question of family planning, in its broad sense, as a right of couples within the framework of its role in enhancing the various aspects of family health; b) the integration of family planning services into other family health services, including the expansion and streamlining of a system for the provision of MCH and family planning services, as well as health education programmes, within the framework of primary health care. (UN, 1993g: Para. 63)

Their more conservative colleagues, who were uncomfortable with the idea of unmarried individuals having access to family planning services, succeeded in quietly deleting the reference to 'individuals' in the phrase referring to the right of access to family planning.

The fifth and last conference in the series was the Latin American and Caribbean Regional Conference on Population and Development. It was organized by the Economic Commission for Latin America and the Caribbean (ECLAC), in cooperation with UNFPA, in Mexico City from 29 April to 4 May 1993. The documentation provided to it by the Latin American Demographic Centre (CELADE) gave the Conference even more of a demographic flavour than the Asia and Pacific Conference (UN, 1993h). Questions of economic and social inequality also figured high on its agenda. Debt relief and debt service constituted a major portion of the Consensus document adopted by the meeting. On family planning and other aspects of reproductive health, the regional conference followed the trend which was already in evidence at other regional conferences by recommending that family planning programmes should include reducing maternal and infant morbidity and mortality, lowering the risks of teenage pregnancy and abortion, and preventing STDs.

The issue of abortion received considerable attention at this Conference. A working paper prepared by UNFPA provided to the participants the latest data and analysis on the widespread prevalence of abortion in Latin America. Speaking at the opening session on behalf of Dr Sadik, I drew their attention to this information. However, the only agreement that could be reached on the issue of abortion was that it should be studied and followed up as a major public health problem. This is reflected in the following paragraph of the final document of the Conference, called the Consensus:

> [c]onsidering that abortion is a major public health issue in the countries of the region and that, while various views are held in this regard, none of them accepts abortion as a method of regulating fertility, generally speaking it is recommended that Governments devote greater attention to the study and follow-up of this issue, with a view to evaluating how prevalent abortion really is and its impact on the health of women and their families; Governments should also promote universal access to proper guidance on how to prevent unwanted pregnancies. (UN, 1993h: II–3–6)

NGO MEETINGS

In addition to the expert group meetings and the regional conferences, family planning and related reproductive health issues were discussed at several NGO meetings in 1992. One of the most important was the 40th Anniversary Congress of the IPPF held in New Delhi (23–25 October 1992). At the IPPF Congress, the challenge of meeting the unmet need for family planning among couples and individuals, providing a better rationale for future population policy, was brought up by a whole range of speakers including Dr Hafdan Mahler, Secretary General of IPPF, Dr Fred Sai, President of IPPF, and Dr Sadik.

It was at the IPPF Assembly that Steven Sinding, Director of Population Sciences at the Rockefeller Foundation, presented a rather important study comparing demographic targets adopted by 12 major developing countries (Bangladesh, Botswana, Dominican Republic, Egypt, Ghana, India, Indonesia, Kenya, Nigeria, Pakistan, Peru and Tunisia) with estimates of unmet need in those countries based on recent demographic and health surveys (see Table 2.1). His analysis, while of a preliminary nature, led him to the conclusion that

> a very significant demographic impact would result from family planning and reproductive health programme efforts that attempted no more than to satisfy the stated reproductive wishes of the women of the developing world. The analysis

strongly suggests that such an approach would equal or exceed what could be accomplished by achieving stated demographic targets of most countries.[3] (Sinding, 1993: 33)

Mr Sinding proposed abandoning the use of demographic targets and expressing the objectives of family planning programmes solely in terms of achieving a fully satisfactory response to the stated desires of women and couples. 'Family planning programmes still need quantitative objectives by which to assess their performance. But these objectives can and should be expressed in terms of satisfying people's stated needs rather than planners' notions of what a society's birthrate should be' (Sinding, 1993: 33).

The concept of the unmet need became the major theme for discussion at the IPPF Member Assembly held in conjunction with the 40th Anniversary Congress and, at the end, the Assembly adopted a bold strategic plan for the future called 'Vision 2000', outlining policies and measures to meet the challenge of the unmet need for family planing (IPPF, 1993). It also declared its firm adherence to the concept of sexual and reproductive health: 'sexual and reproductive health is becoming an integral part of the health culture in its full significance of physical, mental and social well-being, and not just the absence of disease or injury' (IPPF, 1993). With this end in view, IPPF set as its first objective 'to increase efforts to safeguard the individual's right to make free and informed choices in regard to reproductive and sexual health and advocate sound government policy in support of this right'. Several other objectives sought to respond to the unmet need for family planning, sexual and reproductive health services; while on the subject of abortion, IPPF committed itself to eliminating 'the high incidence of unsafe abortion', and to increasing 'the right of access to safe, legal abortion'.

In another important development on the NGO front, a group of women's health advocates, led by Joan Dunlop, President, and Adrianne Germain, Vice President of the International Women's Health Coalition (IWHC), met in London to draft a Women's Declaration on Population Policies. They asked a large group of individuals and organizations concerned with women's health issues to comment on the draft. The final text, which according to IWHC was revised in consultation with more than 100 women's groups, provided a strong affirmation of sexual and reproductive health rights for both men and women, and a stirring call for the recognition of these rights by the ICPD. This document was widely circulated before and during PrepCom II, and those NGO representatives present at PrepCom II who were involved in the drafting of the document engaged in intensive canvassing to gather support for the views articulated in the document.

PREPCOM II

The outcomes of the six expert group meetings, all the regional conferences (with the exception of the Mexico Conference which took place just a few days before the second Session of the ICPD Preparatory Committee, 10–21 May 1993) and major NGO events such as the IPPF Member Assembly and the IWHC meeting were available to the Conference Secretariat in preparing what was euphemistically called the 'Proposed Conceptual Framework of the Draft Recommendations of the Conference' (UN, 1993c).

By this time, it had become clear to Dr Sadik and her Secretariat colleagues that in view of the major changes that had taken place in the population field and the radical thinking that was emerging on such issues as the goals and objectives of population and related development policies, family planning and reproductive health, and equal rights and opportunities for women, it would be appropriate to ask the Cairo Conference to adopt a new plan or programme of action to replace the WPPA approved at Bucharest in 1974 and updated at Mexico in 1984. To this end, the Conceptual Framework proposed that

> the Conference adopt as its final document a new plan of action on population, sustained economic growth and sustained development. While the primary time-frame of such a document would be the ensuing decade, as decided by the Council, the recommendations could also take a longer perspective where appropriate. (UN, 1993c: 3)

A full year before PrepCom II, Dr Sadik had already begun to think of a 20-year time-frame on the grounds that the proposed goals and objectives could only be achieved in that period of time; this idea was conveyed by her and other members of the ICPD Secretariat to the regional conferences, beginning with Dakar. In line with her thinking, the Framework raised the possibility that a longer time-frame than that envisaged by ECOSOC would be needed.

The Conceptual Framework was expected to guide the Secretariat in drafting a new plan of action between PrepCom II and III. For this reason, it attached 'considerable importance to the holding of a substantive debate on the concept and structure of the proposed document for the Conference and to the agreement during the second session of the Preparatory Committee on its content and method of preparation' (UN, 1993c: Summary).

The Conceptual Framework was a very short document. It listed a large number of topics and issues, but did not elaborate on them, the idea being that the Preparatory Committee delegates themselves would provide the necessary definitions and explanations. The document suggested 'Reproductive Rights, Reproductive Health and Family

Table 2.1 . Comparison of Targets and Unmet Need[a]

Country	Target[c]	Year	TFR	CPR	Unmet need	CPR effect of achieving target vs meeting unmet need
Bangladesh	CPR 40 by 1990	1991	4.9	39.9	41.0[d]	−40.9
Botswana	CPR 15 by 1985	1988	4.9	33.0	26.9[d]	−26.9
Dominican Republic	CPR 57 by 1986	1991	3.3	56.4	15.0[e]	−14.4
Egypt	CPR 60 by 2000	1991	4.38	47.6	25.2[d]	−12.8
Ghana	TFR 4 by 2000 (CPR 45.8)	1988	6.41	12.9	26.6[e]	+6.2
India[b]	CPR 60 by 2000	1988–1989	4.2	40.1	18.3[f]	+1.6
Indonesia	CBR 23 by 1990 (CPR 54.8)	1991	3.02	49.7	13.0[e]	−13.5
Kenya	TFR 5.2 by 2000 (CPR 42.3)	1988–1989	6.50	26.9	28.9[e]	−13.5

Nigeria	TFR 4 by 2000 (CPR 45.8)	1990	6.01	6.0	20.8[d]	+19.0
Pakistan	CPR 16.6 by 1988	1990–1991	5.9	11.9	28.0[d]	–23.3
Peru	TFR 3 1995–2000 (CPR 60.9)	1991–1992	3.54	59.0	59.0[e]	–20.8
Tunisia	CPR 51 by 1991	1988	4.30	49.8	15.7[e]	–14.5

[a] The table is reproduced from Sinding (1993).
[b] Figure includes only those who want no more children and are not using contraception. It does not include respondents who wish to space or defer the next birth.
[c] Where the total fertility rate (TFR) was given as a target, the CPR was calculated using the formula (TFR=7.03–0.662 prevalence). Where the crude birth rate (CBR) was given as a target, the CPR was calculated using the formula (CBR=46–0.042 prevalence).
[d] Westoff and Ochoa (1991).
[e] Bongaarts (1991).
[f] Operations Research Group (1988–1989).

Planning' as the title for chapter IV of the final Conference document. The document did not define any of the three terms. But the assumption was that the concept of reproductive rights was embodied in the 'exercise of the rights of couples and individuals to decide the number and spacing of their children' (Para. 26). Family planning programmes were aimed at promoting this right as well as 'the health of women, children and the family', and constituted 'an important component of population programmes and development objectives' (Para. 26). The other major issue chapter IV was expected to deal with was adolescent fertility, because of 'the high and in some cases growing prevalence of preg-nancies among adolescents' (Para. 27). The following chapter on health and mortality would then take up the issues of AIDS and maternal mortality.

In her introductory statement at PrepCom II, Dr Sadik elaborated many of the ideas mentioned in the Conceptual Framework. She invited the participants to consider setting up a 20-year time-frame for achieving specific goals in such areas as 'maternal mortality, infant mortality, life expectancy, education especially for women and girls, gender equality, and availability of access to a full range of modern, safe and effective family planning services to enable the exercise of choice'.

Dr Sai, President of IPPF and a member of the Ghana delegation in his capacity as Chairman of the Government-sponsored National Popu-lation Council, was elected Chairman of the Preparatory Committee. This proved extremely fortuitous, as he knew first hand most of the issues brought before the Committee through his long experience in the health and medical profession. He had served with distinction as the Chairman of the Main Committee at the Mexico Conference (1984) and knew well how to run contentious UN meetings and how to strive towards compromise and consensus on difficult issues. He was elected to serve in the same capacity at the main Conference.

Dr Sai assigned Nicolaas Biegman, Dutch Ambassador to the UN, as Chairman of one of the two working groups, to tackle the chapters on reproductive health as well as health and mortality. Mr Biegman became greatly interested in the topics coming up before his Working Group and quickly acquired the reputation of being not only diplomatic in handling a variety of pressures but also extremely dexterous in moving the discussion along and resolving difficult issues as they arose. A cluster of other chapters was ably handled by Lionel Hurst, Ambassador of Antigua and Barbuda at the UN, as Chairman of the other Working Group.

One of the first questions to be resolved at PrepCom II was that of quantitative goals. While goals aimed at mortality reduction and an increase in life expectancy were never considered controversial and were adopted easily at both Bucharest and Mexico, these two previous conferences had ducked the question of setting up any goals in the area of fertility reduction or the provision of family planning services. Using assumptions of different levels of fertility, the UN Population Division prepares three projections for world population growth every two years – high, medium and low. Using the Division's 1992 projections as the point of departure in an informal Secretariat paper entitled 'Goals for 2015' (UN, 1993i, prepared in response to a request from Preparatory Committee), Dr Sadik proposed quantitative goals in three major areas: mortality reduction (infant, child and maternal mortality), access to and completion of primary education, and the availability of family planning information and services. Two of these sought to update the goals set by the Alma Ata Conference on Health for All, the World Summit for Children and the Jomtien Conference on Education for All. The third goal, on providing family planning information and services, was entirely new.

Dr Sadik also decided to bring up the implications of these quantitative goals for the rate of world population growth by suggesting that the world could arrive at the low population projection of the UN (approximately 7.27 billion) by 2015 if adequate family planning information and services were provided to all couples and individuals who needed them, and if policies were formulated and implemented to empower women to participate fully and equally in socioeconomic development.

This was a daring proposition. Its origins, however, can be found in the Amsterdam Declaration issued by the International Forum on Population in the Twenty-First Century in 1989. The Forum Declaration had proposed that 'at the very least, national population goals and objectives ... should include: a reduction in the average number of children born per woman commensurate with achieving, as a minimum, the medium variant population projection of the UN' (UNFPA, 1989a: Para. 1.13). This proposal was reiterated by Dr Sadik in her address to the UNCED (Rio, June 1992). But by the beginning of 1993 she had come to believe that the low variant projection itself could be reached if sufficient commitment were demonstrated at the local, national and international levels; and this is what she said in her statement to PrepCom II:

> [t]he needs and impact of a population of 7.27 billion in 2015, the low projection, are very different from the high projection of 7.92 billion, or even 7.6 billion, the medium projection. I believe that we must strive for the low projection. I believe that it can be achieved with sufficient commitment at the local, national and international levels. There is ample evidence that the currently unmet needs of couples and individuals make up the difference between the medium and the low population scenario.

Turning to the availability of family planning information and services, Dr. Sadik proposed that the delegates accept a target of 71 per cent for contraceptive prevalence by 2015, as this would ensure the achievement of the low variant projection.

The Conceptual Framework dealt with the subject of abortion very briefly. It stated that 'close to one third of maternal deaths are estimated to be due to unsafe and often illegal abortions, which represent one of the major health hazards confronting women' (UN, 1993c: Para. 30), but did not offer any recommendation on the subject. In her introduction, Dr Sadik suggested that the issue of abortion be addressed as a major health issue for women, and not as a means to family planning.

This view gathered widespread support in PrepCom II. Sweden and the US voiced their full support for the concept of reproductive choice, including access to safe abortion. Though not going as far as these two countries did, several other delegations supported the view that particular attention should be given to the issue of abortion, particularly in the context of women's health. A number of delegations did not want abortion to be considered as a method of family planning, but this was the view already reiterated by Dr Sadik.

On behalf of the Holy See, Archbishop Renato R Martino opposed voluntary abortion, because 'it violates the most fundamental right of any human being to life' (*Earth Negotiations Bulletin*, 2 June 1993). He was underscoring the view that the Holy See had also presented at many of the regional conferences. In numerous other interventions on family planning and reproductive health issues, the Holy See seemed to indicate that it would not totally oppose family planning, but wanted reaffirm-ation of the principle that abortion was not to be regarded as a method of family planning. It also wanted further clarifications on reproductive health and reproductive rights; and of course it was totally opposed to the legalization of abortion.

PrepCom II had a very large number of NGO observers compared with PrepCom I. More than 500 observers from 185 national, regional and international NGOs were at the meeting including representatives from developing countries whose travel had been supported by bilateral agencies, private foundations and the UNFPA field offices. Many of these representatives, including leaders of women's groups, were also included in national delegations appointed by the governments. The US delegation included several representatives from NGOs and the private sector as advisers, as did most delegations from Europe and from developing countries such as India and Bangladesh. These NGO representatives thus had the opportunity to influence the opinions and views formulated by the official delegations from their countries.

NGO representatives met almost daily in several caucuses including the Women's Caucus and regional caucuses. In a break with previous UN tradition, some of them were allowed to speak even during informal sessions. A great majority of the NGOs that participated in the Women's Caucus were pro-choice and pro-family planning. This became clear when at one of the informal sessions a representative of the Women's Caucus commented that 'women have the right to decide when and how to have children free from coercion and with universal access to safe abortion services' (*Earth Negotiations Bulletin*, 19 May 1993). Similar sentiments were expressed by many other NGOs in both formal and informal statements. On the other side, there were also several NGOs that strongly opposed not only abortion but also modern family planning methods. Some of them also had the opportunity to address the Preparatory Committee.

In the end, no agreement could be reached on abortion and many other issues, and PrepCom II simply ran out of time. As there was no way of negotiating a consensus resolution on the Conceptual Framework, it was agreed that the Chairman of the Preparatory Committee, Dr Sai (Ghana), would present his own summary of what transpired during the debate. As this Summary delicately pointed out, 'while many delegations suggested that all women should have access to safe abortion, others suggested that the best way to eliminate abortions was provision of effective, modern contraception information and services; a few delegations reiterated that abortion should not be promoted as a method of family planning' (UN, 1993j: 12).

More positively, the idea of a 20-year time-frame for implementation of the Conference recommendations was enthusiastically endorsed by many delegations and the Chairman's Summary indicated that 'there was general support for the proposal of the Secretary General of the Conference to include a set of quantitative goals in the Cairo document' (UN, 1993i: 16). The Committee asked the Secretary General of the Conference to be guided by the views of delegations and other participants at PrepCom II in preparing the final document. Inasmuch as many of these views were unclear or in some cases even contradictory, the Secretariat was left with the task of interpreting these views in such a way as to help the eventual emergence of a consensus.

ROUND TABLES AND OTHER MEETINGS

Following PrepCom II, five round tables were convened at the initiative of Dr Sadik to give her expert advice on those issues raised at PrepCom II which needed further elaboration or clarification. One of these – the Round Table on Women's Perspectives on Family Planning, Reproductive Health and Reproductive Rights – was asked to examine in depth the concepts of reproductive health and reproductive rights. The Round Table which took place in Ottawa (26–27 August 1993) was clear and forthright in its view that the Cairo Conference should adopt a strong recommendation on reproductive health. The meeting also gave special attention to the needs of adolescents within and outside marriage, and urged that the Conference address these needs and seek the removal of legal obstacles to family planning services to adolescents.

This view had received a great deal of support from several delegations during PrepCom II, but it was contrary to the view expressed by a number of other countries and the Holy See. In line with the recommendations of the Gaborone and Bangalore expert group meetings, the Round Table also endorsed 'safe abortion services and services for the management of the complications of unsafe abortion' (UNFPA, 1993: Recommendation 6). The Round Table was somewhat less successful in clarifying the concept of reproductive rights. While the preamble to its recommendations stated that 'all persons have inherent reproductive rights, including the right to have, or not to have, children' (UNFPA, 1993: 1), the Round Table did not provide any further explanation as to what this right implied in practice.

While the round tables were providing expert advice to the Secretariat, four sub-regional intergovernmental meetings held in the second half of 1993 sought to move forward the consideration of family planning and reproductive issues at the political level (UN, 1994b). The Maghreb Conference on Population and Development (Tunis, 7–10 July 1993) went much further than the Amman Regional Conference in calling upon governments to promote the role of women in development and to grant them the right to informed choice in the matter of family planning, with unimpeded access to necessary means. The South Pacific Ministerial Meeting on Population and Sustainable Development (Port Vila, 9–10 September 1993) agreed to broaden the scope of MCH/FP programmes by declaring that these programmes should address the following needs in the region: to reduce the high levels of maternal and infant mortality; to improve the information on and access to contraceptive methods; to improve adolescent health; and to increase the accessibility to and availability of safe, affordable, culturally and socially acceptable services. The third meeting – the South Asian Association for Regional Cooperation (SAARC) Ministerial Conference on Women and Family Health (Kathmandu, 21–23 November 1993) – had less specificity in its resolution, but it did call on governments to encourage through IEC and effective counselling the adoption of the small family norm as the ideal. The fourth regional meeting was organized by UNFPA in cooperation with the Government of Peru for the Andean countries (Bolivia, Colombia, Ecuador, Peru and Venezuela) in Lima, from 1 to 3 December 1993. The Declaration adopted at this meeting urged governments to increase the accessibility to information, education and family planning services. But it could not take any position on abortion. Instead, it echoed the call of the Mexico Regional Conference for further study on abortion as a public health problem. With varying degrees of success, all of these sub-regional meetings helped delegates from the countries concerned to arrive at a clearer understanding of the

ICPD preparatory process and of the substantive and political issues involved.

Reflecting its understanding of the conclusions reached at PrepCom II, the Secretariat prepared an Annotated Outline of the Final Document of the Conference (UN, 1993k), which was submitted to the 48th Session of the GA. The document suggested that the chapter on reproductive rights, reproductive health and family planning should include four sections: 1) reproductive health, 2) family planning, 3) human sexuality and gender relations, and 4) adolescents. These were the topics most frequently commented on during PrepCom II. Many of these would also be closely linked with the sections proposed for inclusion under the next chapter, on health and mortality: 1) maternal morbidity and mortality; 2) infant and child mortality; 3) STDs and AIDS; and 4) primary health care and the health-care sector.

The Annotated Outline and other documents relating to the preparations for the Cairo Conference were discussed by the Second Committee of the GA on 4–5 November 1993 (UN, 1994c). Forty-four countries (including the Holy See) spoke during the debate. Many of the speakers reiterated or re-emphasized the points made during PrepCom II. At the end, in summarizing the major points, Dr Sadik mentioned four that clearly illustrated the close links between reproductive health issues, the rights of the individual and the empowerment of women:

> [t]he interests and rights of the individual must be central to all population and development activities;
> personal integrity, the particular needs of women, and the freedom of choice must be extended in all population programmes;
> the empowerment of women in society must be championed in its own right; and
> the document should give more attention to sexuality and the family planning needs of youth and adolescents.

DRAFT FINAL DOCUMENT

Following the 48th Session of the UN GA, the main task before the Secretariat was to finalize the Draft Final Document for the Conference. Members of the Secretariat belonging to the UN Population Division and UNFPA worked together on this task during December 1993–January 1994. A two-day informal meeting with a dozen advisers including senior policy makers and experts, held at the Rockefeller Foundation in December 1993, was of special significance. The meeting offered rather critical but, at the same time, quite helpful comments and suggestions on many parts of the first draft prepared by the Secretariat. The Secretariat also reviewed and analysed voluminous documentation including statements, reports and documents from various meetings.

Furthermore, since PrepCom II, the Secretariat had received dozens of comments and suggestions from NGOs and all of these were also carefully reviewed.

The final text was ready by the end of January 1994 and was submitted to the UN Secretariat for processing in early February (UN, 1994d). In drafting the document, a serious attempt was made to use clear and succinct language, and many parts of the document which survived the scrutiny and review at PrepCom III and the Cairo Conference to become part of the Programme of Action read extremely well. Subsequently, Dr. Sadik and other members of the Secretariat also participated in several consultations and undertook a series of visits aimed at explaining and clarifying the proposed Draft.

Just prior to PrepCom III, Dr Sadik went to Rome to see Pope John Paul II. She was following a precedent set by the Secretary General of the 1984 Population Conference, Mr Salas, who had gone to see the Pope in June 1984. The Pope gave him a message for the 1984 Conference, which was eventually published by UNFPA in a volume containing messages from various heads of state and government (UNFPA, 1984).

There is no transcript available of the conversation that took place between Pope John Paul II and Dr Sadik on 18 March 1994;[4] but on her return to New York Dr Sadik told members of the Secretariat that the comments made by the Pope mostly focused on the definition of the family and the role of women in the context of moral and natural laws, and not so much on abortion. In her response, Dr Sadik referred to the health needs of poor women and made a personal appeal to the Catholic Church to provide special leadership to promote more responsible behaviour by men and to help ensure that among couples and the family the dignity and humanity of men, and women, boys and girls are respected.

It was Dr Sadik's understanding that there would be no press conference afterwards, but at the end of her visit the Holy See's Press Office gave to the media the text of the Pope's Message to the Cairo Conference. In his Message, the Pope said:

> [i]n defence of the human person, the Church stands opposed to the imposition of limits on family size, and to the promotion of methods of limiting births which seek the unitive and procreative dimensions of marital intercourse, which are contrary to the moral law inscribed on the human heart, or which constitute an assault on the sacredness of life. Thus, sterilization, which is more and more promoted as a method of family planning, because of its finality and its potential for the violation of human rights, especially of women, is clearly unacceptable; it poses a most grave threat to human dignity and liberty when promoted as part of a population policy. Abortion, which destroys existing human life, is a heinous evil, and it is never an acceptable method of family planning, as was recognized by consensus at the Mexico City UN International Conference on Population.

The Pope also expressed the view that this consensus was completely ignored in the Draft Final Document. He was probably reacting to Para. 8.21, which dealt with the question of abortion:

[a]ll Governments and intergovernmental and non-governmental organizations are urged to deal openly and forthrightly with unsafe abortion as a major public health concern. Governments are urged to assess the health impact of unsafe abortion, to reduce the need for abortion through expanded and improved family-planning services and to frame abortion laws and policies on the basis of a commitment to women's health and well-being rather than on criminal codes and punitive measures. Prevention of unwanted pregnancies must always be given the highest priority and all attempts should be made to eliminate the need for abortion. In case of rape and incest, women should have access to safe abortion services. Women who wish to terminate their pregnancies should have ready access to reliable information, compassionate counselling and services for the manage-ment of complications of unsafe abortions. (UN, 1994d)

This paragraph offered several proposals that certainly went far beyond Mexico. But it did not suggest in any way that abortion should be considered as a method of family planning. In numerous statements, Dr Sadik had made it clear that she did not regard abortion as a method of family planning, but that abortion, particularly unsafe abortion, was a major health concern and must be given urgent attention. Essentially this was the view reflected in the Document, which also took into account other major concerns such as the prevention of unwanted pregnancies through improved access to family planning, and compassionate counselling and services for the management of complications of unsafe abortions, which were brought to the fore at PrepCom II and after.

The Draft Final Document, which was made available to UN member states as well as NGOs towards the end of February 1994, followed the structure proposed in the Outline submitted to the 48th Session of the GA. It was provisionally given the subtitle of 'Programme of Action of the Conference', which after PrepCom III became the title of the Document. The Document was divided into 16 chapters and each chapter was organized under three major sub-headings: basis for action, objective/s and actions.[5]

Chapter VII of the Document entitled 'Reproductive Rights, Repro-ductive Health and Family Planning', had five sections: 1) reproductive rights and reproductive health, 2) family planning, 3) STDs, 4) human sexuality and gender relations, and 5) adolescents. While the section on STDs contained a brief reference to HIV/AIDS, a more detailed, separate section was included in chapter VIII, on 'Health and Mortality'. The Secretariat justified this on the grounds that while HIV/AIDS should be considered with other STDs, it was also a major pandemic with no known cure and thus needed to be considered with other health and mortality issues.

The basic definition of reproductive health was provided in Para. 7.4 of chapter VII:

> [a]ll countries should strive to provide through the primary health-care system reproductive health care to all individuals of child-bearing age as soon as possible, and in all cases no later than the year 2015. Reproductive health care in the context of primary health care should include: family-planning information and services; education and services for prenatal, normal delivery and post-natal care; prevention and treatment of infertility; prevention and treatment of reproductive tract infections and sexually transmitted diseases; prevention and treatment of other reproductive health conditions; and information, education and counselling, as appropriate, on human sexuality, sexual and reproductive health and responsible parenthood. Referral for further diagnosis and treatment should always be available, as required, for complications of pregnancy and delivery, infertility, reproductive tract infections, sexually transmitted diseases and HIV/AIDS. Active discouragement of traditional practices such as female genital mutilation should also be an integral component of reproductive health-care programmes.

Because abortion was considered a major public health concern, the proposed paragraph on abortion was placed in the next chapter, on 'Health and Mortality', as Para. 8.21 (quoted earlier). Para. 8.19 called upon all countries, with the support of the international community, to undertake measures 'to eliminate all unwanted births and all unsafe abortion', while Para. 8.22 cited the elimination of unsafe abortion as one of the 'effective ways to reduce high levels of maternal mortality'.

References to reproductive health and directly related topics were to be found in many other parts of the Draft, but very early on it was agreed that the Preparatory Committee would have to define its stand on reproductive health, including the sensitive and controversial topic of abortion in the context of the paragraphs mentioned above, before deciding on what to do with other references to these terms.

Chapter VII also contained the formulation of a new and specific goal to meet the 'unmet need for good-quality family planning, paying particular attention to the most vulnerable and underserved groups in the population' (Para. 7.13). With this objective in view, the Draft proposed that 'all countries should take steps to meet the expressed need of their populations as soon as possible and should, in all cases by the year 2015, seek to provide universal access to the full range of safe and reliable family-planning methods and to related reproductive health services'. In Para. 7.14, the Draft suggested that

> [i]t should be the goal of public and private family-planning activities to remove all programme-related barriers to family-planning use by the year 2005 through the redesign and expansion of information and services and in other ways to increase the ability of women to make free and independent decisions about contraceptive use.

Explicitly or implicitly, attempts were made throughout the Document to show the interrelationship between the concepts of freedom of choice, particularly for women, and the continuing importance of family planning in the broader framework of reproductive health. Most of the policy makers and programme managers who were involved in the ICPD preparatory process were knowledgeable about or directly involved in family planning programmes; while they understood and appreciated the need to integrate family planning with other health services they did not want references to it diluted in such a way as to de-emphasize its continuing importance. There was a continuing tussle between them and others who were so convinced of the validity of the overall framework of reproductive health that they wanted to see family planning totally submerged within it. These two groups would close ranks whenever family planning or freedom of choice were under attack. But between themselves they continued to argue on the relative weights to be assigned to family planning and other reproductive health services. This tension was reflected in the discussions at PrepCom III, as it was in the drafting of the Programme of Action.

PREPCOM III

Chapter VII was the subject of lengthy negotiations during PrepCom III. Except for the Holy See and Argentina, Guatemala, Venezuela, Ecuador, Honduras, Nicaragua and Malta, the delegates seemed to agree that the most effective way to deal with population questions was to address them in the context of providing good quality services to meet the challenge of unmet needs. Considerable progress was made towards acceptance of the need to shift from a narrow approach focusing on family planning to a broader reproductive health approach and towards defining family planning as an integral component of reproductive health services. But there was no agreement on several components of the definition of reproductive health. The Holy See had at one point placed brackets around all references to 'contraceptives' and 'couples and individuals'. Towards the end of the Session, it agreed to remove these brackets, but wanted its reservation placed on record. Brackets remained on 'unsafe abortion' and 'reproductive health services', and even 'safe motherhood' was bracketed on the grounds that it might include abortion. The Holy See called for written assurance in the document that 'safe motherhood programmes do not include abortion' (*Earth Negotiations Bulletin*, 25 April 1994). There was also no agreement on how to address the reproductive and sexual needs of adolescents.

The discussion on abortion was widely reported by the media throughout PrepCom III. Following the extensive international coverage of the meeting between the Pope and Dr Sadik on 18 March, the Pope addressed the subject of abortion again on 5 April, during his weekly 'audience' in Rome. This is how Reuters reported his speech in a news dispatch on 6 April 1994;

> [s]peaking to some 50,000 people in St Peter's Square at his weekly general audience, the Pope frequently raised his voice as he spoke in passionate defense of the rights of the family. 'We cannot accept the systematic death of the unborn,' he said. 'Every family must know how to resist the false sirens of the culture of death'.

In the same vein, the head of the Holy See delegation to the Preparatory Committee, Monsignor Diarmuid Martin, commented that the organizers of the ICPD did not grasp the 'cultural, ethical, spiritual and religious values' of developing countries and that the Draft Document lacked 'a clear vision' (*Inter Press Service*, 5 April 1994). This drew a sharp rejoinder from Preparatory Committee Chairman Dr Sai, who pointed out that the representatives of developing countries were quite capable of conveying their own moral and ethical values.

Interestingly, *The New York Times* quoted Monsignor Martin as saying, 'it would be very sad if this were to become a conference about abortion' (24 April 1994). Yet it was because of the unwavering focus placed on abortion-related issues by the Holy See and a small number of other countries that no consensus could be reached at PrepCom III on the reproductive health approach, and when the delegates left New York at the end of the Session, it was not clear to many of them how various controversies would be resolved at the Conference.

A great deal, however, did get accomplished at PrepCom III. Among its most important achievements was the near universal public acceptance of the integral relationship between reproductive health and the empowerment of women. Chapter IV of the Draft Final Document, 'Gender Equality, Equity and Empowerment of Women', emerged from PrepCom III virtually bracket-free (except for the phrases relating to reproductive health issues). As Robert Hirschfield pointed out,

> it has become increasingly apparent that the way to attain population stabilization is not just providing more information, services and devices relating to family planning. What is needed, rather, is a basic global change in the status of women ... With women present in unprecedented numbers at the PrepCom, serving on national delegations, as well as representing a record number of non governmental organizations, this call for change has been answered enthusiastically. (*The Earth Times*, 21 April 1994)

VIEWS ON ABORTION

Immediately after the closure of PrepCom III, the Holy See brought together the ambassadors accredited to it to meet with its Secretary of

State, Archbishop Sodano, to discuss the themes of the ICPD and the International Year of the Family.[6] In outlining its policy on the Conference, the Holy See continued to express sharp criticism of the Draft Programme of Action on proposals relating to reproductive health and abortion.

The international media reported on the growing controversy over abortion, focusing on the worldwide campaign undertaken by the Holy See and its envoys to convey to the international community as well as individual UN members its strong views against abortion. According to news reports, the Holy See worked especially hard to convince those countries that might be sympathetic to its point of view for religious or cultural reasons.

According to many media reports, every issue concerning abortion remained controversial at the end of PrepCom III. However, it appeared to members of the Secretariat who were deeply involved in PrepCom III that a consensus had been more or less reached on two of the three major issues: (1) abortion is not to be regarded as a method of family planning, and (2) special attention should be given to unsafe abortion as a major health concern. The issue that remained problematic was that of legal abortion. The Holy See maintained its vehement opposition to abortion, with Costa Rica, Argentina, Malta, Venezuela, Morocco and Ecuador continuing to insist that they would not agree to any definitions that could be construed as including access to abortion. It was clear to us that given the diametrically opposite views on the subject held by different member states, the Conference would not be in a position to endorse, on a global basis, the concept of legal abortion, even in case of rape or incest. At the same time, it was also well known that 174 countries around the world allowed abortion for a variety of reasons,[7] and for those countries, including India and China, where abortion was legal and easily accessible, it would be impossible to accept any international recommendation that would flatly condemn or rule out abortion under any circumstances. What the delegates essentially agreed on was to hold further consultations on the controversial aspects of those definitions that remained bracketed.

While the position of the Catholic Church on contraception and abortion received most of the media attention, theologians, thinkers and ethicists belonging to Protestant churches and several other religious faiths also sought to clarify their own positions on these matters, and it is a pity that their views did not receive much coverage. Many of them participated in a Round Table on Ethics, Population and Reproductive Health held in New York from 8 to 10 March 1994. This Round Table supported a broad definition of reproductive rights, including

the right to make a voluntary, informed choice of a family planning method, the
right to make the moral choice to undertake or terminate pregnancy, the right to

confidentiality in the relationship with a health provider, and the right of women not to be harmed or mutilated, even when such practices are carried out as part of traditional rituals. (Center for Population and Family Health, 1994: 6)

The Round Table also made a strong statement in favour of decriminalizing abortion:

[d]espite cultural and religious views that oppose abortion, women have always sought and will continue to seek an end to unwanted pregnancies. Maternal mortality and morbidity, as well as infertility, that can be traced to criminalization of abortion are preventable negative consequences of reproductive health policies. The separation of church and state that obtains in most nations throughout the world justifies, for the improvement of reproductive health, the decriminalization of a procedure officially condemned by some religions but accepted by many other religions and secular groups. (Center for Population and Family Health, 1994: 9)

Another thought-provoking statement was issued by a group of theologians and academics belonging to Buddhism, Christianity, Hinduism, Islam, Judaism and several other religious traditions who met in Genval, Belgium, under the auspices of the Park Ridge Center for the Study of Health, Faith, and Ethics, from 4 to 7 May 1994. The group took the position that

the ICPD, of course cannot and should not reach into particular religious communities and seek to impose its will on the consciences of individual believers. But international bodies could not achieve anything of importance for the larger world community if they were never permitted to challenge the religious outlook of one or more faiths or never allowed to develop programs that one or another of the religious communities might oppose. Religious groups themselves must respect the beliefs and values of others, because no single faith may claim final moral authority in international discourse. (Park Ridge Center, 1994: 4)

The group recognized that 'abortion is universally treated as a serious moral and religious concern' but it also noted that 'it is treated differently among and within religious communities'.

[w]hatever their stance on abortion, religious communities cannot disregard the fact that it occurs and that, in places where abortion is illegal or heavily restricted, it often poses risk to the life and health of the woman. Decriminalization of abortion, therefore, is a minimal response to this reality and a reasonable means of protecting the life and health of women at risk. (Park Ridge Center, 1994: 4)

In reviewing the available literature on what major religions and traditions other than the Catholic Church had to say about the reproductive health issues, the ICPD staff found confirmation of the view that scholars belonging to these religions were generally willing to endorse family planning. Islamic teachings have been interpreted in Indonesia, Bangladesh, Egypt, Iran and many other Islamic countries as demonstrating support for family planning; and there is already a large body of literature available in several languages that explains specific teachings from the Koran in this context. Not much written material is available regarding Buddhist and Hindu traditions, but what the Secretariat was able to find affirmed support for family planning. Similarly, many Protestant and Jewish groups and writers are supportive of modern family planning methods. There is a wide divergence of views and concerns on abortion, but it would seem that most of these traditions, as interpreted by various religious scholars, do not totally rule out abortion as the Catholic church does and are willing to accept justification for abortion under specific circumstances.[8]

For the media, all of this information was of course much less exciting than the controversy generated by the Holy See. Between May and August 1994, the media reported intensive efforts by the Holy See to seek new allies, in particular the support of a number of Islamic countries, for its campaign against abortion. There were reports of meetings between Papal Envoys and representatives of Iran and Libya. The Holy See acknowledged a meeting between the Papal Envoy in Tehran and Iranian officials on the subject of the Cairo Conference. It also acknowledged discussion with Libyan authorities, but it denied that there was any attempt at the coordination of views on the ICPD. Libya, in any case, did not come to Cairo, and Iran, to the surprise of many delegations, took essentially a pro-family planning line at Cairo. Many of us knew of the strong family planning programme in Iran, but were not quite sure, in view of the controversy over the Conference, of the final position the delegation from Iran would adopt at Cairo. To our delight, the position taken by Iran remained consistent with that taken by it at the Preparatory Committee – critical but constructive.

In the US, several Catholic organizations mounted a major campaign against the US stand on abortion and a number of related issues.[9] The Holy See spokesman, Joaquin Navarro-Valls, publicly criticized Vice President Gore for his defence of the ICPD Programme of Action and declared that the Programme 'in our reading is synonymous with abortion on demand' (Reuters, 31 August, 1994). This of course was a rhetorical statement, as the Programme of Action as it emerged from PrepCom III could not have been construed in any way as to supporting abortion on demand. In his response to the Holy See, the Vice President was quite conciliatory. He said the US 'has not sought, does not seek and will not seek to establish an international right to abortion'. He also asked for the cooperation of the Holy See in making the Cairo Conference successful: 'We must rather be co-laborers and friends in this historic effort to forge policies that affirm the dignity and worth of every human being on Earth'.[10]

Under Secretary of State Tim Wirth took a similar conciliatory approach when explaining the latest US position on abortion. Referring to his earlier statement at PrepCom II in favour of 'access to safe, legal and voluntary abortion', he said he was talking about access, and not about a universal human right. He further stated that the US was not seeking universal acceptance of abortion as a right but supported access to a full range of reproductive health services.[11]

Before the Conference opened in Cairo, newspapers in the Arab world reported statements by some Moslem clerics criticizing the proposed Programme of Action as a whole or in parts. Some of them even called upon Islamic states to boycott the Conference. Coming as it did in the wake of continuing criticism from the Holy See, those of us who were in the Secretariat began to worry about the potential impact of this crescendo of criticism on the success of the Conference. In the end, only two countries – Libya and Sudan – announced plans to boycott the Conference; two others – Saudi Arabia and Lebanon – simply informed the Conference Secretariat at the last minute that they were not coming. The Ministry of Foreign Affairs of the host country, Egypt, made a determined effort to encourage the participation of friendly countries in the Conference. The Secretary General of the Conference and other members of the Secretariat followed up on earlier contacts with UN member countries to ensure that they were going to be represented at the Conference. These efforts were quite successful, as can be seen from the final count of attendance at Cairo, which came to 179 countries.

CAIRO: MOVE TOWARDS A CONSENSUS

The Conference opened on 5 September 1994 in an atmosphere of high drama. Because of the publicity given to various controversies, more than 4000 journalists had descended on Cairo to cover the Conference – a record number for any UN Conference. The number of media representatives in fact slightly exceeded the number of official delegates from member countries. The opening session was addressed by Boutros Boutros-Ghali, Secretary General of the UN; the President of Egypt, Muhammad Hosni Mubarak; the Secretary General of the Conference, Dr Sadik; the Prime Minister of Norway, Gro Harlem Brundtland; the Vice President of the US, Al Gore; the Prime Minister of Pakistan, Benazir Bhutto; and the Prime Minister of Swaziland, Prince Mbilini.

The most forthright defence of the concept of reproductive health was provided by the Prime Minister of Norway, Gro Harlem Brundtland, in her statement:

> [i]t is encouraging that the Conference will contribute to expanding the focus of family-planning programmes to include concern for sexually transmitted diseases, and caring for pregnant, delivering and aborting women. But it is tragic that it

> had to take a disaster like the HIV/AIDS pandemic to open our eyes to the
> importance of combating sexually transmitted diseases. It is also tragic that so
> many women have had to die from pregnancies before we realized that the
> traditional mother-and-child health programmes, effective in saving the life of so
> many children, have done too little to save the lives of women.
>
> In a forward-looking programme of action, it therefore seems sensible to combine
> health concerns that deal with human sexuality under the heading 'reproductive
> health care'. I have tried, in vain, to understand how that term can possibly be
> read as promoting abortion or qualifying abortion as a means of family planning.
> Rarely, if ever, have so many misrepresentations been used to imply meaning
> that was never there in the first place. (UN, 1995a: 171)

Mrs Brundtland called unsafe abortion 'a major public health problem in most corners of the globe', and argued that Cairo 'should not accept attempts to distort facts or neglect the agony of millions of women who are risking their lives and health'.

She then turned to the subject of reproductive health services for adolescents:

> [r]eproductive health services not only deal with problems that have been
> neglected, they also cater to clients who have previously been overlooked. Young
> people and single persons have received too little help, and continue to do so, as
> family-planning clinics seldom meet their needs. Fear of promoting promiscuity
> is often said to be the reason for restricting family-planning services to married
> couples. But we know that lack of education and services does not deter adolescents
> and unmarried persons from sexual activity. On the contrary, there is increasing
> evidence from many countries, including my own, that sex education promotes
> responsible sexual behaviour, and even abstinence. Lack of reproductive health
> services makes sexual activity more risky for both sexes, but particularly for
> women.
>
> As young people stand at the threshold of adulthood, their emerging sexuality
> is too often met with suspicion or plainly ignored. At this vulnerable time in life
> adolescents need both guidance and independence, they need education as well
> as opportunity to explore life for themselves. This requires tact and a delicately
> balanced approach from parents and from society. It is my sincere hope that this
> Conference will contribute to increased understanding and greater commitment
> to the reproductive health needs of young people, including the provision of
> confidential health services for them. (UN, 1995a: 172)

Another important statement at the opening session was made by the Prime Minister of Pakistan, Mrs Bhutto. Her participation in the Cairo Conference as a Moslem head of government was especially significant in view of the fact that two other Moslem heads of government (Bangladesh and Turkey) had dropped out at the last minute, pleading the urgency of other tasks and responsibilities. In her statement, Mrs Bhutto criticized some aspects of the Draft Programme, suggesting that these needed to be revised. But she also spoke up strongly in support of family planning and reproductive health and against abortion 'except in exceptional circumstances':

> *[t]he followers of Islam have no conceptual difficulty in addressing questions of regulating population in the light of available resources. The only constraint is that the process must be consistent with abiding moral principles.*
>
> *Islam places a great deal of stress on the sanctity of life. The Holy Book tells us:*
>
> *'Kill not your children on a plea of want. We provide sustenance for them and for you.'*
>
> *Islam, therefore, except in exceptional circumstances, rejects abortion as a method of population control.*
>
> *There is little compromise on Islam's emphasis on the family unit. The traditional family is the basic unit on which any society rests. It is the anchor on which the individual relies as he embarks upon the journey of life.* (UN, 1995a: 181)

Explaining further her views on reproductive health issues, she said: 'Muslims, with their overriding commitment to knowledge, would have no difficulty with dissemination of information about reproductive health, so long as its modalities remain compatible with their religious and spiritual heritage. Lack of an adequate infrastructure of services and not ideology constitutes our basic problems'. (UN, 1995a: 181)

She also confirmed that the major objective of her own Government 'is a commitment to improve the quality of life of the people through provision of family planning and health services' (UN, 1995a: 181–82).

Mr Gore, while giving full support to the goals of the Cairo Conference, sought to further define the US position on abortion:

> *[w]e are all well aware that views about abortion are as diverse among nations as among individuals. I want to be clear about the US position on abortion so that there is no misunderstanding. We believe that making available the highest quality family-planning and health-care services will simultaneously respect women's own desires to prevent unintended pregnancies, reduce population growth and the rate of abortion.* (UN, 1995a: 177)

While stating that 'the US Constitution guarantees every woman within our borders a right to choose an abortion, subject to limited and specific exceptions', he re-emphasized the point he had made in press statements prior to the Conference: 'let us take a false issue off the table: the US does not seek to establish a new international right to abortion, and we do not believe that abortion should be encouraged as a method of family planning'.

Mr Gore went on to express his belief that 'policy-making in these matters should be the province of each Government, within the context of its own laws and national circumstances, and consistent with previously agreed human rights standards'. He condemned 'coercion related to abortion or any other matters of reproduction', and foreshadowing the view that would be eventually incorporated into Para. 8.25 he stated that 'where abortion is permitted, it should be medically safe and . . . unsafe abortion is a matter of women's health that must be addressed'. Finally, he put in a passionate plea to the delegates to resolve the remaining differences:

> as we acknowledge the few areas where full agreement among us is more difficult, let us strengthen our resolve to respect our differences and reach past them to create what the world might remember as 'the spirit of Cairo' – a shared and unshakable determination to lay the foundation for a future of hope and promise. (UN, 1995a: 177)

In his opening remarks, the President of Egypt, Mr Mubarak, obliquely referred to some of the controversies swirling around the Conference. He called for

> free dialogue ruled by a spirit of solidarity, a joint feeling of responsibility and a mutual desire to open up to the opinions of others and to maintain that no one alone can claim that he possesses all the facts. Our dialogue should be a matter of give and take, reflecting the interrelationship between cultures. We should guard against missing the objective and losing direction because our dialogue will then be confined to premeditated thoughts that some wish to impose on all. (UN, 1995a: 162)

Finally, speaking as a representative of the African continent, the Prime Minister of Swaziland, Prince Mbilini, gave full support to the proposed Programme of Action, pointing out that it was 'extremely consistent' with the earlier declarations adopted at Dakar and other regional meetings in Africa. He stated that '[t]he Dakar Declaration, which was further embraced by the OAU Heads of State and Government in Tunis . . . is emphatic about the responsibilities of member Governments with regard to the role of population in development', and 'with respect to actions which need to be taken'. (UN, 1995a: 183)

The five opening statements set the tone of the Conference and gave the Conference participants what they urgently needed – a sense of optimism about the eventual outcome of the Conference. Consideration of the Draft Programme of Action began in the Main Committee on the fifth afternoon, and one of the most important issues before it was how to define reproductive health and reproductive rights (under chapter VII). It seemed clear to most delegates that these definitions and their implications would not be cleared until they knew what the Conference would have to say on the subject of abortion (under chapter VIII). That was what eventually happened. There were also other issues and controversies that needed to be worked out in the context of 'Principles' (chapter II). All this required four days of both substantive and political negotiations.[12]

The text defining reproductive health that was finally adopted by the Main Committee on 9 September reads as follows:

> *7.2. Reproductive health is a state of complete physical, mental and social well-being and not merely the absence of disease or infirmity, in all matters relating to the reproductive system and to its functions and processes. Reproductive health therefore implies that people are able to have a satisfying and safe sex life and that they have the capability to reproduce and the freedom to decide if, when and how often to do so. Implicit in this last condition are the right of men and women to be informed and to have access to safe, effective, affordable and acceptable methods of family planning of their choice, as well as other methods of their choice for regulation of fertility which are not against the law, and the right of access to appropriate health-care services that will enable women to go safely through pregnancy and childbirth and provide couples with the best chance of having a healthy infant. In line with the above definition of reproductive health, reproductive health care is defined as the constellation of methods, techniques and services that contribute to reproductive health and well-being by preventing and solving reproductive health problems. It also includes sexual health, the purpose of which is the enhancement of life and personal relations, and not merely counselling and care related to reproduction and sexually transmitted diseases.*

> *7.3. Bearing in mind the above definition, reproductive rights embrace certain human rights that are already recognized in national laws, international human rights documents and other consensus documents. These rights rest on the recognition of the basic right of all couples and individuals to decide freely and responsibly the number, spacing and timing of their children and to have the information and means to do so, and the right to attain the highest standard of sexual and reproductive health. It also includes their right to make decisions concerning reproduction free of discrimination, coercion and violence, as expressed in human rights documents. In the exercise of this right, they should take into account the needs of their living and future children and their responsibilities towards the community. The promotion of the responsible exercise of these rights for all people should be the fundamental basis for government- and community-supported policies and programmes in the area of reproductive health, including family planning. As part of their commitment, full attention should be given to the promotion of mutually respectful and equitable gender relations and particularly to meeting the educational and service needs of adolescents to enable them to deal in a positive and responsible way with their sexuality. Reproductive health eludes many of the world's people because of such factors as: inadequate levels of knowledge about human sexuality and inappropriate or poor-quality reproductive health information and services; the prevalence of high-risk sexual behaviour; discriminatory social practices; negative attitudes towards women and girls; and the limited power many women and girls have over their sexual and reproductive lives. Adolescents are particularly vulnerable because of their lack of information and access to relevant services in most countries. Older women*

and men have distinct reproductive and sexual health issues which are often inadequately addressed.

7.4. The implementation of the present Programme of Action is to be guided by the above comprehensive definition of reproductive health, which includes sexual health.

Para. 7.2 includes a specific reference to 'the right of men and women to be informed and have access to safe, effective, affordable and acceptable methods of family planning of their choice, as well as other methods of their choice for regulation of fertility which are not against the law'. Para. 7.3 provides a definition of reproductive rights going back to the Bucharest formula, and includes a highly significant additional phrase, 'the right to attain the highest standard of sexual and reproductive health'.

The text did not use the term 'fertility regulation' mentioned in the working definition of WHO, since it had been strongly objected to by a number of countries on the grounds that it implied acceptance of abortion. WHO was consulted on the matter and its representative offered the explanation that according to the working definition, fertility regulation includes family planning, delayed child bearing, the use of contraception, the treatment of infertility, the interruption of unwanted pregnancies and breast-feeding. A working group was set up under the chairmanship of Hernando Clavijo, a delegate from Colombia who had played an active role in the Conference preparatory process, with the task of clearing up this and other related, controversial matters. Mr Clavijo's group turned the phrase around to read 'regulation of fertility' and this was accepted, with relief, by the delegates.

The attempt made by some Central American and Arab countries throughout the ICPD preparatory process to delete 'individuals' from the famous Bucharest phrase about 'the right of couples and individuals' continued at Cairo. However, support for retaining the phrase as part of the consensus established at Mexico and endorsed at the Preparatory Committee meetings remained strong and all attempts to change it were beaten back. The debate had its moments of humour. A statement during the debate made by Timothy Stamps, Minister of Health of Zimbabwe, pointed out that if the term 'individuals' was deleted, it would remove the right of individuals to remain celibate, and he did not think the Holy See would be happy about that.

The issue of adolescent sexuality also caused considerable dissension, as on similar previous occasions, between those who wanted to promote direct access for adolescents to both information and services and others who wanted parents or guardians to be included in the process. The first group included the Nordic countries and many African and Caribbean countries. In her statement, Mrs Brundtland had expressed the hope that the ICPD would 'contribute to increased understanding and greater commitment to the reproductive health needs of young people, including the provision of confidential health services to them' (UN, 1995a: 172). This sentiment was echoed by many speakers in both the plenary sessions and the Main Committee. Also, many population and youth NGOs were fully supportive of the right of adolescents to have direct access, without the involvement of parents or guardians, to both information and services. The second group included the Holy See and delegates from several Catholic and Moslem countries.

Ultimately it was agreed, with some reluctance on the part of members of the first group, that a vaguely worded reference to the rights, duties and responsibilities of parents would be brought into the text. This was accomplished by including the following revision in Para. 7.45:

> [r]ecognizing the rights, duties and responsibilities of parents and other persons responsible for adolescents to provide, in a manner consistent with the evolving capacities of the adolescent, appropriate direction and guidance in sexual and reproductive matters, countries must ensure that the programmes and attitudes of health-care providers do not restrict the access of adolescents to appropriate services and the information they need, including on sexually transmitted diseases and sexual abuse.

Para. 7.47 pointed out the need to provide sexually active adolescents 'special family planning information, counselling and services' and added that 'adolescents must be fully involved in the planning, implementation and evaluation of such information and services with proper regard for parental guidance and responsibilities'.

In addition to formulating these definitions, the Conference proposed a specific, time-bound framework for action:

> 7.6. All countries should strive to make accessible through the primary health-care system, reproductive health to all individuals of appropriate ages as soon as possible and no later than the year 2015. Reproductive health care in the context of primary health care should, inter alia, include: family-planning counselling, information, education, communication and services; education and services for prenatal care, safe delivery and post-natal care, especially breast-feeding and infant and women's health care; prevention and appropriate treatment of infertility; abortion as specified in paragraph 8.25, including prevention of abortion and the management of the consequences of abortion; treatment of reproductive tract infections; sexually transmitted diseases and other reproductive health conditions; and information, education and counselling, as appropriate, on human sexuality, reproductive health and responsible parenthood. Referral for family-planning services and further diagnosis and treatment for complications of pregnancy, delivery and abortion, infertility, reproductive tract infections, breast cancer and cancers of the reproductive system, sexually transmitted diseases, including HIV/ AIDS should always be available, as required. Active discouragement of harmful practices, such as female genital mutilation, should also be an integral component of primary health care, including reproductive health-care programmes.

DEBATE ON ABORTION

These definitions of reproductive health and reproductive rights were adopted only after long and hard-fought battles on abortion yielded a revised text of Para. 8.25. On 6 September, Ambassador Biegman opened the discussion on Para. 8.25 in the Main Committee by appealing to the delegates 'to move swiftly on this issue to show the world and the media that this Conference is not about abortion, but population. The purpose here, he said, is not to delve on the ethical or moral dimension of the question but, rather, to concentrate on the medical aspects of unsafe abortion' (*Earth Negotiations Bulletin*, 7 September 1994).

The delegates had before them two alternative texts of Para. 8.25.

Alternative A

8.25 [All Governments, intergovernmental organizations and relevant non governmental organizations are urged to deal openly and forthrightly with [unsafe abortion] as a major health concern. Particular efforts should be made to obtain objective and reliable information on the policies on, incidence of and consequences of abortion in every country. Unwanted pregnancies should be prevented through sexual health education and through expanded and improved family planning services, including proper counselling to reduce the rate of abortion. Governments are urged to assess the health and social impact of induced abortion, to address the situations that cause women to have recourse to abortion and to provide adequate medical care and counselling. Governments are urged to evaluate and review laws and policies on abortion so that they take into account the commitment to women's health and well-being in accordance with local situations, rather than relying on criminal codes or punitive measures. Although the main objective of public policy is to prevent unwanted pregnancies and reduce the rate of abortion, women should have ready access to quality health care services that include reliable information, counselling and medical care to enable them to terminate pregnancies in those cases where it is allowed by law, if they so decide, and that provide for the management of complications and sequelae of unsafe abortion. Post-abortion counselling, education and family planning services should be offered promptly so as to prevent repeat abortions.]

Alternative B

[Alternative 8.25. All Governments and intergovernmental and non governmental organizations are urged to deal openly and forthrightly with unsafe abortion as a major health concern. Governments are urged to assess the health impact of unsafe abortion and to reduce the need for abortion through expanded and improved family planning services. Prevention of unwanted pregnancies must always be given the highest priority and all attempts should be made to eliminate the need for abortion. In no case should abortion be promoted as a method of family planning. In circumstances where abortion is legal, women who wish to terminate their pregnancies should have ready access to reliable information and compassionate counselling and such abortion should be safe. In all cases, women should have access to services for the management of complications arising

from unsafe abortions. Any measures to provide for safe and legal abortion within the health system can only be determined at national level through policy changes and legislative processes which reflect the diversity of views on the issue of abortion.]. (UN, 1994e).

Both texts described unsafe abortion as a major health concern, and supported the provision of services for the management of complications of unsafe abortion. But there were also a number of significant differences between the two texts. Alternative A went further than Alternative B by urging governments to evaluate and review laws and policies on abortion and hinted at the need for changes in abortion-related laws and policies by suggesting that governments should pay attention to women's health issues rather than relying on 'criminal codes or punitive measures'. Alternative B, which was tabled by members of the EU towards the end of PrepCom III, did not include any of these proposals. It also included a statement desired by the Holy See and some others: 'in no case should abortion be promoted as a method of family planning'.

Most of the 85 delegations who spoke in the Main Committee supported the EU text with a view to finding a compromise acceptable to the other side. The Holy See and a few others were willing to accept Alternative B as a basis for discussion but had 'fundamental difficulties' with many parts of the text. After several hours of inconclusive discussion, consideration of these issues was postponed and the Committee moved on to another topic. But on the evening of 6 September, the Chairman proposed another 'compromise' text:

[i]n no case should abortion be promoted as a method of family planning. All Governments and relevant inter-governmental and non-governmental organizations are urged to strengthen their commitment to women's health, to deal with the health impact of unsafe abortion as a major health concern and to reduce the recourse to abortion through expanded and improved family planning services. Women who have unwanted pregnancies should have ready access to reliable information and compassionate counselling. Prevention of unwanted pregnancies must always be given the highest priority and all attempts should be made to eliminate the need for abortion. In circumstances in which abortion is legal, such abortion should be safe. Any measures or changes related to abortion within the health system can only be determined at the national or local level according to the national legislative process. In all cases women should have access to quality services for the management of complications arising from abortion. Post-abortion counselling, education and family planning services should be offered promptly which will also help to avoid repeat abortion.

This text seemed acceptable to most of the delegations that spoke, but the Holy See still had difficulties with it. The discussion was postponed and resumed on the seventh morning. After several more hours of statements, the Working Group agreed, at the suggestion of the Chairman, to set up a smaller group chaired by Muzzafar Quereshi (Pakistan) to negotiate a compromise. The setting up of this group turned out to be a masterly stroke on the part of Ambassador Biegman. The group (Iran, Egypt, the US, Norway, Indonesia, the EU, the Russian Federation, Barbados, South Africa, Nicaragua, Trinidad and Tobago, El Salvador, Benin and Malta) provided a balanced representation of all the major regions and tendencies, but most importantly, it included a number of delegates who were well versed in the intricacies and complexities of the issues involved and, at the same time, had considerable experience of the negotiation process. The small group worked through 8 September and by the evening, to the surprise of many, it was able to provide the Chairman with a consensus text. The text was distributed in English on the evening of 8 September and the following morning in the other main languages.

On the evening of Friday, 9 September, the Chairman asked the delegates to put this matter to rest so that the media could focus its attention on other population and development issues. He suggested that the debate should not be opened again at that time. After a few problems with translations of the text into French and Spanish had been noted, the Chairman invited brief expressions of support or dissent and it quickly became clear that the new text had overwhelming support cutting across all regions and groups. Forty-one countries (three of them speaking on behalf of a large number of other countries) offered their support for the consensus: Benin, the US, Senegal, Cameroon, Turkey, Turkmenistan, the Philippines, France, Uruguay, Zambia, Bolivia, Tunisia, China, Panama, Tanzania, Burkina Faso, Guinea, Cape Verde, Mali, the Central African Republic, India, Austria, Paraguay, Nicaragua, Israel, Mexico, Barbados (on behalf of the Caribbean states), Spain, Germany (on behalf of the EU), The Gambia, Venezuela, Congo, Norway, the Solomon Islands (on behalf of the Pacific Island States), Japan, South Africa, Colombia, Chile, Indonesia, Jordan, and Brazil. Egypt and Bahrain also accepted the text but said that it would be interpreted according to national and religious laws.

At this point, there remained only a handful of dissenting voices. The Holy See stated that it attached great importance to the issue of maternal death and was willing to endorse those parts of Para. 8.25 that addressed women's health issues. But for moral reasons it could not endorse legal abortion and would withhold its assent until the end of discussions on chapters VII and VIII. Argentina, Peru, Malta and the Dominican Republic expressed similar reservations (*Earth Negotiations Bulletin*, 10 September 1994).

The discussion finally came to an end with the formal adoption by the Main Committee on Saturday, 10 September of the following text as Para. 8.25:

8.25. In no case should abortion be promoted as a method of family planning. All Governments and relevant intergovernmental and non-governmental organizations are urged to strengthen their commitment to women's health, to deal with the health impact of unsafe abortion as a major public health concern and to reduce the recourse to abortion through expanded and improved family-planning services. Prevention of unwanted pregnancies must always be given the highest priority and every attempt should be made to eliminate the need for abortion. Women who have unwanted pregnancies should have ready access to reliable information and compassionate counselling. Any measures or changes related to abortion within the health system can only be determined at the national or local level according to the national legislative process. In circumstances where abortion is not against the law, such abortion should be safe. In all cases, women should have access to quality services for the management of complications arising from abortion. Post-abortion counselling, education and family-planning services should be offered promptly, which will also help to avoid repeat abortions. (UN, 1995a).

A footnote was added to explain unsafe abortion in WHO terminology: 'Unsafe abortion is defined as a procedure for terminating an unwanted pregnancy either by persons lacking necessary skills or in an environment lacking the minimum medical standards or both'.

A NEW CONSENSUS

Following the adoption of these definitions, brackets on phrases relating to these definitions in other parts of the document were removed. Thus concluded the contentious and sometimes acrimonious debate at the Cairo Conference on reproductive health, reproductive rights and abortion.

'Active discouragement of harmful practices, such as female genital mutilation', which is advocated in Recommendation 7.6 as one of the activities to be included in the broad framework of reproductive health services, was not the subject of much debate. But it is worth pointing out that the 'conspiracy of silence' on the issue of female genital mutilation was broken at Cairo, and those delegates and observers who addressed the issue strongly condemned the practice and urged that steps be taken immediately to eliminate it. An additional Recommendation proposed that

[g]overnments and communities should urgently take steps to stop the practice of female genital mutilation and protect women and girls from all such similar unnecessary and dangerous practices. Steps to eliminate the practice should include strong community outreach programmes involving village and religious leaders, education and counselling about its impact on girls' and women's health, and appropriate treatment and rehabilitation for girls and women, who have suffered mutilation. Services should include counselling for women and men to discourage the practice. (Para. 7.40)

To complete the picture, it should be pointed out that the adoption of the consensus texts on the reproductive health and reproductive rights issues was facilitated by another text, negotiated separately and placed as the umbrella paragraph under Chapter II ('Principles'):

> [t]he implementation of the recommendations contained in the Programme of Action is the sovereign right of each country, consistent with national laws and development priorities, with full respect for the various religious and ethical values and cultural backgrounds of its people, and in conformity with universally recognized international human rights. (UN, 1995a: 11)

The sovereign right of each country to implement the ICPD Programme of Action in accordance with its own national laws was mentioned by many of the delegations at the final Plenary Session on 13 September as a justification for their clarifications and reservations on the consensus. At an earlier stage, a group of developing countries had also wanted a reference to be made to 'religious beliefs, ethical values, cultures and traditions' that would be taken into account in determining the future course of action. But other developing countries, the US and members of the EU were not willing to accept this formulation, inasmuch as this would seem to condone or even justify the low status assigned to women in many societies. Hence, the juxtaposition of the 'sovereign right of each country' with the need for national action to be 'in conformity with universally recognized human rights'. At the same time, the proposed phrase regarding 'religious beliefs' and so on was changed to reflect a more pluralistic view, by advocating full respect for 'the various religious and ethical values and cultural backgrounds'.[13]

Some of the reservations recorded by individual countries were on the use of the term 'individual' in the phrase 'individuals and couples' (Afghanistan, Libya). Other countries stated that the Programme of Action would be applied in accordance with Islamic laws and moral values (Jordan, Kuwait). Several Latin American countries affirmed that life begins at conception, and recorded their reservations or clarifications on various words or concepts in the approved text (El Salvador, Honduras, Nicaragua, Paraguay, Ecuador, Guatemala and Peru). The Holy See submitted a long written statement joining the consensus on parts of the Programme of Action and expressing its reservations on others. This was the first time at a world population conference that the Holy See had agreed to join at least partially in the consensus. The following excerpts are taken from this statement:

> As you well know, the Holy See could not find its way to join the consensus of the Conferences of Bucharest and Mexico City, because of some fundamental reservations. Yet, now in Cairo for the first time, development has been linked to population as a major issue of reflection. The current Programme of Action,

however, opens out some new paths concerning the future of population policy. The document is notable for its affirmations against all forms of coercion in population policies. Clearly elaborated principles, based on the most important documents of the international community, clarify and enlighten the later chapters. The document recognizes the protection and support required by the basic unit of society, the family founded on marriage. Women's advancement and the improvement of women's status, through education and better health-care services, are stressed. Migration, the all too often forgotten sector of population policy, has been examined. The Conference has given clear indications of the concern that exists in the entire international community about threats to women's health. There is an appeal to greater respect for religious and cultural beliefs of persons and communities. (UN, 1995a: 143)

Having outlined the areas in which the Holy See agreed with the Programme of Action, the statement specified its concerns on abortion and adolescent health issues.

Since the approval of chapters VII and VIII in the Committee of the Whole, it has been possible to evaluate the significance of these chapters within the entire document, and also within health-care policy in general. The intense negotiations of these days have resulted in the presentation of a text which all recognize as improved, but about which the Holy See still has grave concerns. At the moment of their adoption by consensus by the Main Committee, my delegation already noted its concerns about the question of abortion. The chapters also contain references which could be seen as accepting extramarital sexual activity, especially among adolescents. They would seem to assert that abortion services belong within primary health care as a method of choice. Despite the many positive aspects of chapters VII and VIII, the text that has been presented to us has many broader implications, which has led the Holy See to decide not to join the consensus on these chapters. This does not exclude the fact that the Holy See supports a concept of reproductive health as a holistic concept for the promotion of the health of men and women and will continue to work, along with others, towards the evolution of a more precise definition of this and other terms.

The intention therefore of my delegation is to associate itself with this consensus in a partial manner compatible with its own position, without hindering the consensus among other nations, but also without prejudicing its own position with regard to some sections.

Nothing that the Holy See has done in this consensus process should be understood or interpreted as an endorsement of concepts it cannot support for moral reasons. Especially, nothing is to be understood to imply that the Holy See endorses abortion or has in any way changed its moral position concerning abortion or on contraceptives or sterilization or on the use of condoms in HIV/ AIDS prevention programmes. (UN, 1995a: 144)

The Holy See representative finally asked for the following specific reservations to be recorded.

1. Regarding the terms 'sexual health' and 'sexual rights', and 'reproductive health' and reproductive rights', the Holy See considers these terms as applying to a holistic concept of health, which embrace, each in their own way, the person in the entirety of his or her personality, mind and body, and which foster the achievement of personal maturity in sexuality and in the mutual love and decision-making that characterize the conjugal relationship in accordance with moral norms. The Holy See does not consider abortion or access to abortion as a dimension of these terms.

2. With reference to the terms 'contraception', 'family planning', 'sexual and reproductive health', 'sexual and reproductive rights', and 'women's ability to control their own fertility', 'widest range of family-planning services' and any other terms regarding family-planning services and regulation of fertility concepts in the document, the Holy See's joining the consensus should in no way be interpreted as constituting a change in its well-known position concerning those family-planning methods which the Catholic Church considers morally unacceptable or on family-planning services which do not respect the liberty of the spouses, human dignity and the human rights of those concerned.

3. With reference to all international agreements, the Holy See reserves its position in this regard, in particular on any existing agreements mentioned in this Programme of Action, consistent with its acceptance or non-acceptance of them.

4. With reference to the term 'couples and individuals', the Holy See reserves its position with the understanding that this term is to mean married couples and the individual man and woman who constitute the couple. The document, especially in its use of this term, remains marked by an individualistic understanding of sexuality which does not give due attention to the mutual love and decision-making that characterizes the conjugal relationship. (UN, 1995a: 145)

The agreement on definitions and implications of reproductive health, including FP and sexual health, and reproductive rights coupled with the support given to the broad variety of measures aimed at empowering women, were hailed by governmental delegates as well as the large number of NGO representatives present at the Conference as an extraordinary breakthrough (*The Earth Times*, 14 September 1994). On the 13th afternoon, as all of us sat in the Conference Hall listening to the congratulatory speeches being delivered by delegates representing regional groups, we were all aware and conscious of the profound significance of the agreements reached there and of the enormous impact the new definitions and paradigms adopted by the international community at Cairo would have on national priorities, laws and practices in the future.

This is how Dr Sadik, in her concluding remarks, described the achievements at Cairo.

Your achievements in this Conference have been historic. As one writer put it: 'Where else has the fundamental condition of all women, whatever their status or the state of their personal freedom, been so intensely debated, or seen to be so relevant to the next century?' The Programme of Action you are about to adopt places women and men, and their families, at the top of the international development agenda. It is a population action programme that puts people first.

Energetic and committed implementation of the Programme of Action over the next 20 years will bring women at last into the mainstream of development; it will protect their health, promote their education and encourage and reward their economic contribution; it will ensure that every pregnancy is intended, and every child is a wanted child; it will protect women from the results of unsafe abortion; it will protect the health of adolescents, and encourage responsible behaviour; it will combat HIV/AIDS; it will promote education for all and close the gender gap in education; and it will protect and promote the integrity of the family.

Prime Minister Brundtland advised: 'Let us turn from the dramatizing and focus on the main issues'. You have succeeded in doing that; although I see from the headlines that '8.25' has now become a synonym for controversy.

You have spent a long time discussing how the Programme of Action should deal with abortion. I think your conclusion is highly satisfactory. It fulfils the original intention of concentrating on unsafe abortion as a serious and preventable health problem. Abortion is not a means of family planning. There will be fewer abortions in future, because there will be less need for abortion.

Implementing the Programme of Action will encourage safer, more secure births, by providing information and services to enable women and men to plan for pregnancy. The Programme of Action recognizes that healthy families are created by choice, not chance. (UN, 1995a: 186)

WHAT DID CAIRO ACCOMPLISH ON REPRODUCTIVE HEALTH?

Millions of words that have been written since Cairo explaining and analysing what was new and significant in the ICPD Programme of Action broadly confirm and support the view that women's issues and concerns had taken the centre stage at Cairo and that the advance registered there on reproductive health and reproductive rights would contribute significantly to the empowerment of women.

It is within this broader perspective that we should look at the major achievements of the Conference in the areas of reproductive health and reproductive rights.

(1)   For the first time, a far-reaching, comprehensive definition of repro-
      ductive health was negotiated and approved by 179 UN member
      countries at a global intergovernmental conference. Though it
      is based on a 'working definition' used previously by WHO, it
      incorporates significant revisions of many of the concepts included

in the working definition and identifies the reproductive health services to be provided under primary health care. There is a clear and unambiguous recognition of 'the right of men and women to be informed and to have access to safe, effective, affordable and acceptable methods of family planning of their choice' (UN, 1995a: Para. 7.2). It also allows them access to 'other methods of their choice for regulation of fertility which are not against the law'. This would obviously include access to abortion in countries where it is legal. HIV/AIDS and female genital mutilation are two of the more important new topics that are covered under the ICPD definition.

(2)   The Conference clearly spelled out the linkage between family planning and other reproductive health activities. The agreement on this linkage was achieved during the ICPD process through a series of consultations and negotiations aimed at confidence-building and the evolution of a common understanding among three distinct groups: supporters of 'vertical' family planning programmes, supporters of fully integrated programmes in the health and medical professions, and feminist groups which were proponents of a 'quality of care' approach. NGO representatives who belonged to these groups played a crucial role in developing this understanding and the final agreement.

(3)   The Conference accepted a quantitative goal for the delivery of reproductive health services to 'all individuals of appropriate ages as soon as possible and no later than the year 2015' (Para. 7.6). At the same time, it specified qualitative goals aimed at improving the quality of family planning and other reproductive health services. It also provided a set of fairly precise estimates for the mobilization of domestic and international resources that would be needed to realize these goals.

(4)   The Conference signalled the unequivocal acceptance by the international community of the notion that targets and quotas should not be used for the delivery of family planning services and that coercion in any form is unacceptable. Principle 8 in Chapter II states that 'reproductive health care programs should provide the widest range of services without any form of coercion'. Further on, Para. 7.12 says that 'demographic goals, while legitimately the subject of government development strategies, should not be imposed on family planning providers in the form of targets or quotas for the recruitment of clients'.

(5)   A new definition of reproductive rights was adopted, going well beyond the formulation adopted by the WPC (Bucharest, 1974) on the right of 'couples and individuals'. Though many governments participating in the ICPD process continued to insist that no new rights were being formulated, the inclusion in Para. 7.3 of 'the right to attain the highest standard of sexual and reproductive health'

was highly significant. Acceptance of the concept of sexual health, and various specific references to 'sexuality', 'human sexuality' and 'high-risk sexual behavior' that are to be found throughout the Programme of Action brought in the notion that procreation was not the sole purpose of sexual relations, and that human beings, including adolescents, needed to be fully aware of the implications and consequences of various kinds of sexual behaviour. The Cairo Conference broke the taboo on open and frank discussion of sex-related topics at intergovernmental forums.

(6) The role and responsibilities of men in sexual and gender relations, the use of contraceptives and parenting were strongly emphasized throughout the Programme of Action. In a section of chapter IV entitled, 'Male Responsibilities and Participation', the Conference proposed 'the equal participation of women and men in all areas of family and household responsibilities, including family planning, child-rearing and housework' (Para. 4.26) and recommended that 'special efforts should be made to emphasize men's shared responsibility and promote their active involvement in responsible parenthood, sexual and reproductive behavior, including family planning; prenatal, maternal and child health; prevention of sexually transmitted diseases, including HIV; prevention of unwanted and high-risk pregnancies; shared control and contribution to family income; children's education, health and nutrition; and recognition and promotion of the equal value of children of both sexes' (Para. 4.27).

(7) The Conference crystallized the international community's growing concern with the pandemic of HIV/AIDS. Prevention of HIV is addressed in chapter VII, and an entire section in chapter VIII is devoted to HIV/AIDS. On moral and religious grounds, the Holy See and several UN member countries emphasized the importance of voluntary sexual abstinence in HIV/AIDS prevention; and while this was given appropriate recognition in the Programme of Action, the Conference called for urgent national and international action in the fight against the pandemic of HIV/AIDS, by providing information, counselling and condoms and drugs. Para. 8.35 says that

> *responsible sexual behavior, including voluntary sexual abstinence, for the prevention of HIV infection should be promoted and included in education and information programs. Condoms and drugs for the prevention and treatment of sexually transmitted diseases should be made widely available and affordable and should be included in all essential drug lists. Effective action should be taken to further control the quality of blood products and equipment decontamination.*

(8)   While reiterating the position taken at the Mexico Conference that abortion should not be regarded as a method of family planning, the Cairo Conference went far beyond Mexico by assigning high priority to action on unsafe abortion as 'a major health concern'. Mexico had urged governments 'to take appropriate steps to help women avoid abortion, which in no case should be promoted as a method of family planning, and whenever possible, provide for the humane treatment and counselling of women who have had recourse to abortion' (UN, 1984: Para. 18(e)). Instead of asking for 'appropriate steps', Cairo urged that recourse to abortion be reduced 'through expanded and improved family planning services' and that women should have access to 'quality services for the management of complications arising from abortion', 'in all cases' and not 'whenever possible'. Para. 7.6, which lists reproductive health services to be provided in the context of primary health care includes among these services 'abortion as specified in paragraph 8.25'. In practice, this would mean improving the quality of services and facilities so as to ensure safe abortion in countries where abortion is permitted by law.

(9)   The Conference emphasized the need to give particular attention to the sexual and reproductive health needs of adolescents. In a separate section on adolescents in chapter VII, it called for urgent action on a whole range of issues in this area, while recognizing the rights, duties and responsibilities of parents and guardians (Paras. 7.41–7.48). Para. 7.45 includes a key phrase asking countries to ensure 'that the programs and attitudes of health-care providers do not restrict the access of adolescents to appropriate services and the information they need, including on sexually transmitted diseases and sexual abuse'. Going further, one of the next paragraphs (Para. 7.47) urges governments, in collaboration with NGOs, 'to meet the special needs of adolescents and to establish appropriate programmes to respond to those needs'.

   While the provision of information and services to unmarried adolescents and young people remains a touchy and sensitive subject in a number of countries with Catholic and Islamic traditions, even these countries recognized at the Conference the need to pay special attention to the real problems facing this age-group in the areas of sexual and reproductive behaviour. The challenge before these and other developing countries is what specifically they are going to do, apart from engaging in moral exhortation, to help adolescents deal with these problems.

(10)   Accepting the argument that a large number of maternal deaths are caused by pregnancy-related complications, the Conference linked maternal mortality to other issues relating to family planning, women's health and safe motherhood. It called upon

countries to 'strive to effect significant reductions in maternal mortality by the year 2015' and for the provision of adequate maternal health services within the framework of primary health care. Safe motherhood was not to be regarded henceforth as a unique programme initiative, but as an activity closely related to family planning and other reproductive health services. Para. 8.26 states that 'programs to reduce maternal morbidity and mortality should include information and reproductive health services, including family planning services. In order to reduce high-risk pregnancies, maternal health and safe motherhood programmes should include counselling and family planning information'.

This is not a complete listing of Cairo's achievements. As the other chapters show, Cairo broke new ground in many other areas. While emphasizing the integral interrelationship between population and development, it underscored the importance and urgency of instituting and implementing population policies and programmes that would seek to meet the needs of individual men and women. It endorsed a holistic view of social development, and a whole range of quantitative and qualitative goals covering health care, education, particularly for girls, and a complement of legal and social measures aimed at promoting gender equality. It gave full and unequivocal support to the concept of 'partnership' between governments and civil society. But above all, it will be remembered for the clear links it established between women's right to choose and their empowerment.

3 POPULATION AND DEVELOPMENT

The Bucharest, Mexico and Cairo conferences were all concerned with the interrelationship between population and development issues. Each of them endorsed the importance of formulating population policies in a developmental framework, respect for national sovereignty in population matters and the centrality of human rights. Within the broad parameters of these principles, however, the governments and the international community have, since Bucharest, developed or modified their views on a large variety of issues, and these modifications and changes are reflected in the ICPD Programme of Action.

The concept of development was broadened at Cairo to include the strategies of sustainability (sustained economic growth and long-term sustainability in production and consumption) and a more integrated approach to population and environmental concerns. While urging the countries to give greater attention to population trends in relation to development, the Cairo Conference proposed a comprehensive package of policy measures: economic development and poverty alleviation; the improvement of women's status; universal access to quality primary education and primary health care, including reproductive health and family planning services; the reduction of infant, child and maternal mortality; and human resource development. By focusing attention on 'unmet needs' of couples and individuals and by criticizing the system of quotas and targets, the Conference clearly rejected the top–down approach in policy formulation and brought the concept of human rights, particularly those of women, to the fore. In taking these positions, Cairo marked a radical departure from the previous two population conferences.

The evolution of policy developments and issues from Bucharest to Cairo can be traced under four broad themes: (1) the integration of population and development strategies; (2) population growth and structure; (3) the reduction of mortality and morbidity; and (4) population distribution and migration. This chapter looks at the developments and controversies relating to these themes under four corresponding sections.

INTEGRATION OF POPULATION AND DEVELOPMENT STRATEGIES

Bucharest had emphasized the integration of population with development planning, mainly because development planning, in four- or five-year cycles, was at the time very much in vogue in many developing countries in Africa, Asia and Latin America. The WPPA suggested that '[p]opulation measures and programmes should be integrated into comprehensive social and economic plans and programmes and this integration should be reflected in the goals, instrumentalities and organizations for planning within the countries'. It went on to suggest that 'a unit dealing with population aspects be created and placed at a high level of the national administrative structure and that such a unit be staffed with qualified persons from the relevant disciplines' (UN, 1975: Recommendation 95).

The 1970s and 1980s were characterized by a widespread acceptance of this approach. UNFPA, as the major international funding organization in population, became a strong advocate and supporter of population planning units. It gave particular priority to setting up population units in the countries of sub-Saharan Africa, and more than 30 such units were set up in the region during this period. Often located in the ministries of finance or planning, they were expected to create better awareness of population issues, serve as the secretariats of national population commissions and help to integrate population considerations into development planning (Sadik, 1994). UNFPA and the UN also supported data collection and analysis in Africa, both technically and financially, including the first-ever censuses in around 20 countries.

The assistance provided by UNFPA and other organizations for data collection and analysis, demographic training and research and the establishment and maintenance of population units helped change the views of an increasing number of African countries regarding population issues. This became evident first at Arusha (African Population Conference, 1984) and then at Mexico, where more than 20 African countries emphasized the importance of population policies and their relevance to overall development efforts.

Mexico recommended continuing institutional support to population planning within the development process (UN, 1984: Recommendation 85). It also emphasized the training of personnel and human resource development by urging governments to develop an adequate corps of trained personnel and by supporting the inclusion of 'population studies [in] training curricula for policy-makers and executives who plan and implement development programmes' (Recommendation 75).

Theoretical and applied research on the integration of population processes with socio-economic development, the creation of better awareness of and support for policy issues among policy makers, parliamentarians and others in public life, and the full integration of women into all phases of the development process were other important policy-related recommendations adopted at the Mexico Conference.

The relevance of the environment to population was not a major topic at Bucharest, despite the fact that the first global UN Conference on the Environment (Stockholm, 1972) had taken place only two years before, and that one of the four technical meetings in preparation for Bucharest had reviewed several research papers on the subject. A partial explanation may be found in the fact that the members of official delegations to Bucharest came generally from ministries and institutions that were not that involved in Stockholm. Also, many developing countries, even after Stockholm, had not decided upon specific action to take on environmental issues, and the environmental NGOs were not represented at Bucharest in any significant number. However, the relationship of population to food, natural resources and the quality of the environment was among the many topics for further research listed by the Bucharest Conference.

Prior to the Mexico Conference, one of the four major expert group meetings examined the theme of Population, Environment and Development. The participants for this Meeting came from many different disciplines and I recall that several of them presented excellent papers on topics relating to the areas of their specialization. But it was difficult to see the connection between their individual presentations. At the end, the rapporteur of the Expert Group was asked to consult further with the participants before finalizing the report and the recommendations. The participants could only agree on very general conclusions and findings, and ended up emphasizing the need for more research.

The Mexico Conference was somewhat more specific in its recommendations on the interrelationship between population, environment and development.

> *In countries in which there are imbalances between trends in population growth and resources and environmental requirements, Governments are urged, in the context of overall development policies, to adopt and implement specific policies, including population policies, that will contribute to redressing such imbalances and promote improved methods of identifying, extracting, renewing, utilizing and conserving natural resources. Efforts should be made to accelerate the transition from traditional to new and renewable sources of energy while at the same time maintaining the integrity of the environment. Governments should also implement appropriate policy measures to avoid the further destruction of the ecological equilibria and take measures to restore them. (UN, 1984: Recommendation 4)*

At PrepCom I (1991), several delegations referred to the need for a sustainable relationship between human population, resources, development and the environment, and some of them expressed the hope that the 1994 Conference would address environmental issues within the context of sustainable development. As everybody knew that the UNCED would be taking place in June 1992, not much was said at PrepCom I on the topic of the environment.

The Expert Group Meeting on Population, Environment and Development, held in January 1992, also had an air of tentativeness about it, as its participants knew that their conclusions and recommendations would have to be revisited following the UNCED. Many of the participants expressed the hope that governments represented at the UNCED would pay adequate attention to population factors and trends, and this was reflected in one of the recommendations of the Expert Group:

> [g]overnments are urged, when formulating their social and economic policies, plans and programmes in any sector, to take fully into account the implications of projected demographic trends and of patterns of production and consumption, for the protection of the environment and the conservation of natural resources.
> (UN, 1992c: Recommendation 1)

The second Expert Group Meeting that took place prior to the UNCED (Cairo, 12–16 April 1992) was directly concerned with Population Policies and Programmes. After endorsing the need for 'a consistent policy framework that promotes balanced and sustainable development', it recommended that 'population considerations should be taken into account at all levels of decision-making and in resource allocation in all sectoral agencies and in those pertaining to education, health, labour, industry, agriculture and environment' (UN, 1992d: Recommendation 1). Many of the topics studied by these two expert group meetings would be revisited later in the year by the Expert Group Meeting on Population Growth and Demographic Structure.

Agenda 21, adopted by the UNCED, devoted a chapter to 'Demographic Dynamics and Sustainability' (chapter 5). This chapter began with the statement that '[d]emographic trends and factors and sustainable development have a synergetic relationship' (UN, 1993l: Recommendation 5.2). Reflecting the view that was negotiated as a compromise between the developed and the developing countries during the UNCED Preparatory Committee meetings, Agenda 21 further stated that the life-supporting capacities of our planet are under increasingly severe stress from the rapid growth of world population and unsustainable production and consumption. The action proposed included the formulation and implementation of 'comprehensive policies for sustainable development' that 'should address the linkages of demographic trends and factors, resource use, appropriate technology dissemination, and development' (UN, 1993l: Recommendation 5.3).

Agenda 21 offered recommendations on three major topics: (1) developing and disseminating knowledge concerning the links between demographic trends and factors and sustainable development; (2) formulating integrated national policies for environment and development, taking into account demographic trends and factors; and (3) implementing integrated environment and development programmes at the local level, taking into account demographic trends and factors. On the issue of how population, the environment and development should be integrated in practice, Agenda 21 left it to the ICPD to develop more specific recommendations. This was, in many ways, a desirable outcome, as the delegations to the UNCED Preparatory Committee meetings did not have too many population experts or officials to advise them, and the NGO community represented at these meetings included only a smattering of population organizations.

All the regional conferences held in preparation for the ICPD during 1992–1993 reiterated the proposition that population policies and programmes must be considered 'an integral part of national development plans aimed at sustainable socio-economic development' and that 'such policies and programmes should be fully formulated, implemented and integrated into all aspects of development planning and policy-making' (UN, 1994f: Para. 6). On the linkages between population, the environment and sustainable development,

> *there was widespread consensus among the countries participating in the regional conferences that population growth and distribution could reinforce and sometimes accelerate certain processes of environmental degradation. The recommendations stressed the need to bring population growth rates and spatial distribution into balance with natural resources and the environment without delay.* (UN, 1994f: Para. 16)

The Proposed Conceptual Framework of the Draft Recommendations of the Conference (UN, 1993c) proposed that chapter 1 of the Conference document be devoted to the topic of 'Integrating Population Concerns into Development'. Within this topic, three sub-themes would be developed: (1) population in the context of sustainable development; (2) population and socioeconomic development; and (3) population and the environment.

At PrepCom II there was general acceptance of the inextricable linkage among the three sub-themes. Sub-themes (1) and (2) above were taken together in the comments made by many delegations, and members of the G77 kept emphasizing that 'sustained economic growth' must be seen as part of the process of 'sustainable development' and that

> *achieving the objectives of sustained economic growth, sustainable development and effective population policies would require mobilization of substantial*

additional financial resources from the international community as well as within countries. It would not be useful to adopt objectives without considering the means of implementation and the resources required. (UN, 1993i: Para. 15)

On population, the environment and development, the responsibilities of the developed countries for changing wasteful patterns of production and consumption were emphasized by many. The overwhelming consensus on this topic was that:

the Conference should not run the risk of being too diffuse in its deliberation, but rather should focus most particularly on population-related issues, while taking note of complementary issues. In this regard, it was recognized that the Conference would build on existing international agreements, especially those adopted at the 1992 UN Conference on Environment and Development, including Agenda 21. Merely renegotiating these agreements would serve no purpose. (UN, 1993j: Para. 12)

Following the comments and suggestions made at PrepCom II and a number of round table meetings (especially on population and development plans and strategies at Bangkok, and on population, environment and sustainable development in the post-UNCED period at Geneva), the Secretariat regrouped the topics relating to population, sustained economic growth and sustainable development in the Draft Final Document as follows: integrating population, economic and development strategies; population, sustained economic growth, poverty alleviation and human resource development; and population, sustainable development and the environment (UN, 1994d).

The Draft Final Document presented to PrepCom III mentions as an objective the integration of population factors with the full range of development strategies. At PrepCom II and a number of subsequent meetings, there had been much less talk of development planning and much more about development strategies. This shift of emphasis was reflected in the Draft. Also, there were no specific references to the need for establishing or maintaining 'population units' to deal with population matters. Instead, the Draft suggested that 'Governments should establish the requisite internal institutional mechanisms to ensure that population factors are appropriately reflected by economists, planners and administrators within the decision-making processes of all those ministries and agencies responsible for economic and social development at all levels of Government' (UN, 1994d: Para. 3.7).

Chapter III underwent numerous changes at PrepCom III. There was further sparring between the G77 and the industrial countries on the relevance and importance of sustained economic growth for poverty reduction. Members of the G77 continued to insist that sustained economic growth must be regarded as essential to the alleviation or eradication of poverty, but they were willing to accept that such growth should be promoted in the context of sustainable development. 'Sustained economic growth within the context of sustainable development' emerged as the phrase everybody could agree on. Another area of disagreement between the G77 and the US and the EU was on whether the elimination of economic and social discrimination against women, who constitute the majority of the world's poor, should be mentioned in this chapter. This issue could not be resolved at PrepCom III, and was left for further discussion at Cairo.

In general, the G77, reflecting an internal understanding among its members not to reopen discussion on Agenda 21, wanted to keep the section on population, the environment and development as short as possible, by basically reiterating the commitments made in Agenda 21. The US, on the other hand, felt that Agenda 21 did not adequately reflect population concerns and that there was a need to present in this section of chapter III new and specific proposals for action. The US also pointed out that Agenda 21 had indeed left it to the ICPD to develop more detailed proposals on population, the environment and development. The compromise reached was that after referring to Agenda 21 other actions could be proposed, but these would have to be consistent with the Agenda. Para. 3.28, which outlines the objectives for integrating population and the environment, and Paras. 3.29–3.32, which propose a list of actions to promote and achieve such integration, reflect this understanding.

At Cairo, only a couple of important issues needed to be sorted out at the informal session of the Main Committee that met on Friday, 9 September to consider chapter III. Following earlier discussions at PrepCom III, the G77 proposed that Para. 3.16, which outlined the 'objective' for all actions on 'population, sustained economic growth and poverty', keep the reference to the right to development, but delete the reference to the elimination of discrimination against women, as a prerequisite of eradicating poverty. Their argument was that discrimination against women was not a problem confined to developing countries. Members of the EU were in favour of doing the opposite. They wanted to mention the elimination of discrimination against women, but saw no need to refer here to the right to development. Ultimately, a compromise proposal made by the US was accepted. This expanded the definition of the right to development to denote a universal and inalienable right and an integral part of fundamental human rights, and it included a statement that 'particular attention is to be given to the socio-economic improvement of poor women in developed and developing countries' (UN, 1995a: Para. 3.16).

The other issue was related to the part of Para. 3.21 which suggested that job creation in the industrial, agricultural and service sectors would be facilitated by, amongst other things, an end to corruption, good governance, democratic institutions, and the reorientation of budget priorities towards social sectors and resource development. There was a feeling among some members of G77 that this implied a sweeping criticism of all developing countries, and they wanted to delete this text, whereas the EU was strongly in favour of retaining it. Again, it was the US which put forward the compromise proposal. The revised text suggests that job creation could be facilitated through 'the establishment of more favourable climates for expanded trade and investment on an environmentally sound basis, greater investments in human resource development and the development of democratic institutions and good governance' (UN, 1995a: Para. 3.21).

POPULATION GROWTH AND STRUCTURE

All three of the global population conferences have looked at trends in population growth, on the basis of the high, medium and low variant projections prepared by the UN Population Division. The medium variant is considered the one providing the most likely scenario. In 1974, when the world population was growing at a rate of 2 per cent a year, little change was expected to occur in population growth rates, according to the medium variant projection, in either the developing or the developed regions by 1985 (UN, 1975: Para. 16). However, by 1984, when the International Conference on Population met in Mexico, it had become clear that the declines had been faster than expected. Taking into account the projections for the next decade, the Conference noted that 'the growth rate of the world population will decline more slowly than during the past 10 years' (UN, 1984: Para. 19). Cairo notes that 'world population grew at the rate of 1.7 percent per annum during the period 1985–1990, but it is expected to decrease during the following decades and reach 1.0 percent per annum by the period 2020-2025' (UN, 1995a: Para. 6.1).

The declines in the population growth rates have thus been faster than expected throughout this period due to economic and social development and the success of family planning programmes. The UN says that the current rate of population growth per year is around 1.5 per cent (see Table 3.1). This leads some people to argue that issues relating to population growth are being resolved. This is simply not true. The annual growth in absolute numbers was around 75 million in 1975 and around 87 million in 1985; for the mid-1990s the latest projection is that world population is increasing by around 81 million a year, more than 90 per cent of it in developing countries. Among the developing regions, the growth rate is highest in Africa (2.7 per cent), followed by Latin America (1.7 per cent) and Asia (1.5 per cent). Meanwhile, the growth rate in the developed world has come down to 0.4 per cent. The UN medium

Table 3.1 Population Growth Rates of the World, More Developed and Less Developed Regions, and Major Areas

Region	1950–1955	1990–1995	2045–2050
World	1.8	1.5	0.5
More developed regions	1.2	0.4	−0.2
Less developed regions	2.1	1.8	0.6
Least developed countries	1.9	2.6	1.1
Africa	2.2	2.7	1.1
Asia	1.9	1.5	0.3
Of which, China	1.9	1.1	−0.1
India	2.0	1.8	0.4
Europe	1.0	0.2	−0.4
Latin America and the Caribbean	2.7	1.7	0.5
North America	1.7	1.0	0.1
Oceania	2.2	1.4	0.4

Source: UN (1996).

variant projections indicate that the global population growth rate will continue to decline, from 1.48 per cent per annum in 1990–1995 to 1.37 per cent per annum in 1995–2000, and looking further into the future to perhaps 0.45 per cent in 2045–2050.

Despite the projected decline in the growth rate, the annual increase in world population will remain at the current level, around 80 million per annum until 2025. From 2025 onwards, the growth rate may come down to around 41 million per annum in 2045–2050. At the mid-point in the 21st century, the developed regions and China will have negative growth rates, but Africa will still have a growth rate of 1.1 per cent per annum. The ICPD Programme of Action endorses the objective of facilitating demographic transition as soon as possible in all regions of the world, indicating that such a transition would contribute to the stabilization of the world population (UN, 1995a: Para. 6.3). It goes on to recommend that the countries that have not completed their demographic transition should take effective steps 'within the context of their social and economic development and with full respect of human rights' (UN, 1995a: Para. 6.4). By putting forward the case for rapid demographic transition and eventual stabilization of the world population, Cairo goes much further than Bucharest and Mexico in dealing with issues relating to population growth.

In this context, it is worth noting that the perceptions and views of developing countries on population growth rates and fertility levels have undergone, in many respects, dramatic changes since Bucharest. One way this can be illustrated is by looking at the cases of the nine developing countries with the largest populations. In the mid-1970s, four of the five Asian countries with the largest populations – Bangladesh, India, Indonesia and Pakistan – had official population policies aimed at lowering fertility levels and population growth rates, but China did not. In the Arab world, Egypt had become concerned about high rates of population growth, but did not have a fully fledged population policy in place. In Africa, Nigeria had not pronounced itself on the matter, and in Latin America, while Mexico had changed its constitution in 1974 to guarantee the rights of its citizens to family planning services, Brazil was following a 'hands-off' policy in this regard. By the mid-eighties, China, Nigeria and Brazil had changed their views and policies to favour a lower population growth rate. In fact, more than 25 African countries, in addition to Nigeria, had pronounced themselves on the urgency and importance of population issues.

According to the UN, between 1976 and 1993 the percentage of countries intervening to lower fertility increased from 26 to 41 per cent. During the same period, the proportion of countries with a policy of non-intervention declined from 51 to 33 per cent (UN, 1994g).

Most of the countries with population policies aimed at lowering fertility and growth rates belonged to Asia and Africa. It was, therefore, not surprising that the regional conferences for Asia and the Pacific (Denpasar, 1992) and Africa (Dakar, 1992) set specific regional goals in this regard. The Asia and the Pacific Conference urged the adoption of 'strategies to attain replacement level fertility, equivalent to around 2.2 children per woman, by the year 2010 or sooner' (UN, 1993d: 55). The African Population Conference recommended the formulation of 'quantified national objectives for the reduction of population growth with a view to bringing down the regional natural growth rate from 3 percent to 2.5 percent by the year 2000 and 2 percent by 2010' (UN, 1993e: 32). Furthermore, it adopted the goal of ensuring the availability and promoting the use of all tested and available contraceptive and fertility regulation methods with a view to doubling the regional CPR from the rather low current level of about 10 per cent to 20 per cent by the year 2000 and 40 per cent by the year 2010. The population conferences for the Arab world and Latin America and the Caribbean did not adopt any goals on the reduction of fertility or growth rates. However, all of the regional conferences were supportive of policies in favour of family planning.

In formulating and implementing national objectives for the reduction of fertility or population growth rates, several developing country governments have experimented with incentives and disincentives. However, there is no evidence to show that such schemes have achieved any significant success. On disincentives and penalties, in particular, almost all research findings point out that these do not work. They have also been criticized almost universally as being morally repugnant. On the other hand, the provision of adequate information and services to couples and individuals who need them has proven to be a much better way of reducing fertility and, thus, reducing population growth rates.

This was the line of thinking reflected in the Proposed Conceptual Framework on the Draft Recommendations of the Conference, which was presented to PrepCom II. The Conceptual Framework listed several 'fundamental concerns and issues which must be at the centre of all action on population and development' and 'should set the context for all subsequent recommendations and observations' (UN, 1993c: Para. 15): (1) individual rights and responsibilities; (2) societal rights and obligations; (3) gender equality and the empowerment of women; (4) choice and the protection of reproductive rights; (5) intergenerational equity and responsibility; (6) opposition to coercion; (7) the interrelationship of population and sustainable development; (8) the protection of vulnerable groups, particularly women and children, in times of disaster, civil unrest, war, and so on; and (9) moral and ethical perspectives on population and development. All of these are clearly linked to the issues of freedom of choice, human rights and women's empowerment, as they are also to the nature and extent of government intervention in seeking the reduction of fertility.

Statements by delegations commenting on the Conceptual Framework generally emphasized 'the central importance of the human being in all questions of population and development and the need for population policies and programmes to be based on the fundamental rights and freedoms of individuals and couples' (UN, 1993j: Para. 9). This view was also strongly supported by a large number of population and women's NGOs. Most delegations were in favour of including these concepts in a set of principles which would be placed at the beginning of the final document emerging from the Conference and thus be seen as guiding and motivating all the recommendations for action, including those relating to population growth and structure. While agreeing with these concepts, several other delegations insisted that no new rights should be created at Cairo. It was therefore suggested that the principles guiding future action should be drawn from existing sets of commitments and agreements.

It was on this basis that the Conference Secretariat drew up chapter II, 'Principles', in the Draft Final Document of the Conference. Every principle was attributed to a previous document; many of the principles were direct quotes, while others were adapted from previous documents, on the basis of the Secretariat's understanding of what the delegations had suggested at PrepCom II (UN, 1994d).

PrepCom III did not manage to reach a final agreement on the principles. In the view of some, the proposed text included too many principles; they wanted a smaller number in more succinct language.

Others saw a clear linkage between the principles and the issues that were still to be resolved in other chapters. They preferred, therefore, to finalize the principles only after other principal issues had been resolved. In the end, there was simply no time left for further discussions on this topic and the ICPD Secretariat was asked to submit a revised, shorter text of the principles to the Conference.

The 15 principles and the three preambular paragraphs preceding the principles that were finally adopted by the Conference are drawn from previous international declarations and agreements. However, taken together they provide a coherent and updated rationale for the entirety of the ICPD Programme of Action. They include the highly significant statement that 'while development facilitates the enjoyment of all human rights, the lack of development may not be invoked to justify the abridgement of internationally recognized human rights' (Principle 3). Opposition to coercion is clearly stated in another principle which suggests, amongst other things, that '[r]eproductive health-care programmes should provide the widest range of services without any form of coercion' (Principle 8).

Four other topics that were dealt with under the rubric of population growth and structure were (1) children and youth, (2) elderly people, (3) indigenous people, and (4) persons with disabilities. The needs of children and youth received attention at both Bucharest and Mexico, but in the preparatory process for Cairo several new themes and issues were brought up. These reflected changing national concerns as well as the emergence of new activist groups that focused on and advocated specific action on these themes and issues. They included street children, child exploitation across national boundaries and children as victims of war and armed conflict. On youth, Cairo urged countries 'to meet the needs and aspiration of youth, particularly in the areas of formal and non-formal education, training, employment opportunities, housing and health' (UN, 1995a: Para. 6.13) and to actively involve youth 'in the planning, implementation and evaluation of development activities that have a direct impact on their daily lives' (Para. 6.15). In this context, Cairo paid particular attention to 'information, education and communication activities and services concerning reproductive and sexual health, including the prevention of early pregnancies, sex education and the prevention of HIV/AIDS and other sexually transmitted diseases' (Para. 6.15). Though both Bucharest and Mexico had supported raising the age at marriage, Cairo made a much stronger statement against child marriages and early marriages (Para. 6.11).

The issues relating to the elderly or the ageing are no longer confined to the developed countries but also affect an increasing number of developing countries. Cairo suggested that 'all levels of government in medium- and long-term socio-economic planning should take into account the increasing numbers and proportions of elderly people in the population' (Para. 6.18). Provision of adequate social security measures to enable elderly people to lead self-determined, healthy and productive lives, and the strengthening of formal and non-formal support systems for the elderly, were some of the other recommendations made by the Cairo Conference.

The Cairo Conference adopted several specific recommendations on the distinctive needs and requirements of indigenous populations and persons with disabilities, and on the measures needed to prevent discrimination against them. NGOs representing these segments of the population played an active role at the sessions of the Preparatory Committee and the Conference, and with the help of several governments were able to get their proposals included in the Programme of Action.

THE REDUCTION OF MORBIDITY AND MORTALITY

Each of the three population conferences emphasized the importance of policies aimed at providing basic health services to all and further reducing morbidity and mortality, particularly infant and maternal mortality. The Bucharest Plan of Action affirmed that 'it is a goal of this Plan of Action to reduce mortality levels, particularly infant and maternal mortality levels, to the maximum extent possible in all regions of the world and to reduce national and subnational differentials therein' (UN, 1975: Recommendation 22). It also endorsed specific goals in two areas: the reduction of general mortality so that countries with the highest mortality levels might achieve an expectation of life at birth of at least 50 years and an infant mortality rate of at most 120 per 1000 live births (Recommendation 23).

Mortality reduction is one area where developing countries, with the exception of sub-Saharan Africa, have achieved significant successes since the early 1970s. Reflecting this development, the Mexico Conference recommended raising the crossbar:

> [c]ountries with higher mortality levels should aim for a life expectancy at birth of at least 60 years and infant mortality rate of less than 50 per 1000 live births by the year 2000. Countries with intermediate mortality levels should aim to achieve a life expectancy at birth of at least 70 years and infant mortality rate of less than 35 per 1,000 live births by the year 2000. (UN, 1984: Recommendation 14)

The World Summit for Children (New York, 1990), which attracted the participation of more than 70 heads of state or government, helped to raise global awareness of issues relating to infant and child mortality as well as maternal mortality. The Summit proposed the reduction of infant

Table 3.2 . Life Expectancy at Birth (Years), by Major Area and Region, 1970–1995

Major area and region	1970–1975			1980–1985			1990–1995		
	Both sexes	Males	Females	Both sexes	Males	Females	Both sexes	Males	Females
World	57.9	56.4	59.4	61.3	59.4	63.3	64.3	62.2	66.5
More developed regions	71.2	67.6	74.7	73.0	69.2	76.7	74.2	70.4	78.0
Less developed regions	54.7	53.9	55.4	58.6	57.3	59.9	62.1	60.6	63.7
Least developed countries	43.6	42.8	44.5	47.1	46.1	48.1	49.7	48.7	50.8
Africa	46.0	44.5	47.6	49.4	47.8	51.1	51.8	50.4	53.3
Eastern Africa	44.8	43.2	46.4	43.9	42.3	45.6	51.3	50.0	52.6
Central Africa	53.4	50.6	56.3	42.9	41.4	44.4	46.8	45.2	48.4
Northern Africa	48.1	46.3	49.9	56.6	55.3	57.9	57.6	54.8	60.4
Southern Africa	46.2	44.7	47.8	46.7	45.4	48.0	51.0	49.3	52.7
Western Africa	62.1	60.8	63.4	62.1	59.3	64.9	49.5	48.0	51.1
Asia	56.3	55.8	56.8	60.5	59.5	61.6	64.5	63.2	66.0
Eastern Asia	64.2	63.2	65.2	67.6	66.3	69.0	69.7	67.6	71.9
South-Central Asia	57.9	56.1	59.9	50.2	50.8	49.6	51.9	50.3	53.5
South-Eastern Asia	58.1	56.2	60.0	62.8	60.9	64.8	55.1	54.9	55.3
Western Asia	60.4	59.9	60.8	63.7	61.7	65.6	66.3	64.4	68.4
Europe	70.8	67.1	74.2	71.9	67.8	75.7	72.7	68.5	76.9
Eastern Europe	69.4	64.8	73.4	72.4	69.2	75.5	71.5	68.7	74.2
Northern Europe	71.8	68.4	75.0	69.0	64.1	73.6	74.1	70.8	77.3
Southern Europe	74.0	70.9	77.1	74.3	70.7	77.7	68.2	63.0	73.6
Western Europe	75.8	72.8	78.8	76.0	72.7	79.3	76.7	73.2	80.2

Latin America	61.1	58.7	63.5	65.2	62.2	68.4	68.5	65.3	71.8
Caribbean	63.1	61.4	65.0	61.3	59.0	63.7	60.7	58.3	63.3
Central America	66.4	64.4	68.5	66.0	62.7	69.4	64.8	61.8	68.1
South America	68.5	66.4	70.8	70.5	67.6	73.4	67.8	64.4	71.4
North America	71.5	67.7	75.4	74.7	71.0	78.4	76.2	72.8	79.5
Oceania[a]	66.6	64.0	69.4	70.1	67.2	73.1	72.9	70.3	75.6
Australia/New Zealand	71.7	68.4	75.1	75.0	71.7	78.3	77.4	74.5	80.3

Source: UN (1996b).
[a] Includes Melanesia, Micronesia and Polynesia.

and under-five mortality rates by the year 2000 by one-third, or to 50 and 70 per 1000 live births respectively, whichever is less. The Summit also proposed the reduction of maternal mortality rates by half by the year 2000.

According to the UN, the continuing decline in mortality has helped raise life expectancy at birth at the global level from around 58 years in the early 1970s to around 64 years in the early 1990s. But there is a gap of 12 years in life expectancy at birth between developed and developing countries – 74 years and 62 years respectively. For the least developed countries, the average life expectancy is around 50, which is 12 years lower than the life expectancy for the developing countries taken together. Africa as a region has the largest number of countries with a life expectancy of below 50 years (see Table 3.2).

The infant mortality rate at the global level in the early 1990s was around 62 per 1000 live births. But this figure hides an enormous disparity between developed and developing countries. Whereas in the developed countries the infant mortality rate is 11 per 1000, in the developing countries the corresponding rate comes to 68 per 1000. Among the regions, Africa, with 94 deaths per 1000 live births, and Asia, with 62 deaths per 1000 live births, have the highest rates of infant mortality (see Table 3.3).

Against this background, Dr Sadik, in her introductory statement at PrepCom II, proposed the reduction of infant, child and maternal mortality as one of three major quantitative goals within a 20-year framework (1995–2015). This meant updating the goals set by the World Summit for Children by going beyond the year 2000 up to the year 2015. After discussions between the UN Children's Fund (UNICEF) Executive Director James Grant and the Conference Secretary General Dr Sadik, Mr Grant became a strong and enthusiastic proponent of all the three quantitative goals within the proposed 20-year framework.

For obvious reasons, no arguments were needed to convince the participants at PrepCom II to agree to update the goals relating to infant and child mortality. However, the issues relating to 'the unacceptably high levels of maternal mortality and morbidity in many developing countries', particularly the subject of unsafe and illegal abortion, attracted many comments:

> [u]nsafe and illegal abortion, which in many countries was an important cause of maternal morbidity and mortality, constituted one of the most neglected problems affecting women's lives. It was seen . . . as a major public health issue which the Conference needed to recognize and address as such. While many delegations suggested that all women should have access to safe abortion, others suggested that the best way to eliminate abortions was provision of effective, modern contraception information and services; a few delegations reiterated that abortion should not be promoted as a method of family planning. (UN, 1993j: Para. 37)

Several delegates asked members of the Secretariat why the global estimates for maternal mortality (500,000 deaths per year) had not changed since 1985. The reply the Secretary General gave was that given the paucity of adequate data on maternal mortality in many developing countries, the figure of 500,000 deaths was a rounded estimate and both WHO and UNICEF, which had continued to collect and analyse whatever limited data on the subject were available, felt that this was still the best available estimate, as not much progress had been achieved in the preceding decade in reducing maternal mortality rates.

Table 3.3 Infant Mortality Rate (per 1000 Births), by Major Area and Region, 1970–1995

Major area and region	1970–1975	1980–1985	1990–1995
World	93	78	62
More developed regions	21	15	11
Less developed regions	104	87	68
Least developed countries	147	130	109
Africa	130	112	94
Eastern Africa	137	135	132
Central Africa	81	129	125
Northern Africa	113	100	66
Southern Africa	113	108	97
Western Africa	67	55	98
Asia	98	83	62
Eastern Asia	56	132	101
South-Central Asia	111	48	107
South-Eastern Asia	78	79	41
Western Asia	78	54	60
Europe	25	18	13
Eastern Europe	28	16	31
Northern Europe	18	23	10
Southern Europe	18	10	19
Western Europe	7	11	7
Latin America	80	56	40
Caribbean	72	74	84
Central America	57	52	58
South America	43	37	41
North America	18	11	9
Oceania[a]	41	30	26
Australia/New Zealand	17	10	7

Source: UN (1996).

[a] Includes Melanesia, Micronesia and Polynesia.

Following the acceptance, in principle, by PrepCom II of the idea of the three major quantitative goals within a 20-year framework, the Conference Secretariat consulted with several governments as well as UN agencies, in particular WHO and UNICEF, on the wording of the updated goals on the reduction of infant, child and maternal mortality. The following wording, which was included in the Draft Final Document (UN, 1994d), was formulated on the basis of these consultations:

8.13. Over the next 20 years, the gap between average infant and child mortality rates in the developed and the developing regions of the world should be substantially narrowed, and major differences among socio-economic and ethnic groups should be eliminated. Countries should strive to reduce their infant and under-five mortality rates by one third or to 50 and 70 per 1000 live births, respectively, whichever is less, by the year 2000, with appropriate adaptation to the particular situation of each country. By 2015 all countries should aim to achieve an infant mortality rate below 35 per 1000 live births and an under-five mortality rate below 45 per 1000. Countries that achieve these levels earlier should strive to lower them further.

8.17. Countries should strive to effect a reduction by one half of the 1990 levels of maternal mortality by the year 2000 and a further reduction by one half by 2015. The realization of these goals will have different implications for countries with different 1990 levels of maternal mortality. Countries with intermediate levels of mortality should aim to achieve by the year 2015 a maternal mortality rate below 60 per 100,000 live births. Countries with the highest levels of mortality should aim to achieve by 2015 a maternal mortality rate below 75 per 100,000 live births.

Further elaboration of these goals took place at PrepCom III. Several delegates were of the view that intermediate benchmarks for the year 2005 should be introduced in both of these texts. The text regarding the reduction of infant and child mortality was thus amended to include the following: '[b]y 2005, countries with intermediate mortality levels should aim to achieve an infant mortality rate below 50 deaths per 1000 and an under-5 mortality rate below 60 deaths per 1000 births' (UN, 1994e: Para. 8.16). A maternal mortality rate below 100 per 100,000 live births was proposed for the countries with intermediate levels of mortality and a maternal mortality rate below 125 per 100,000 for the countries with the highest levels of mortality (UN, 1994e: Para. 8.21).

While there was no major disagreement at PrepCom III on these revised goals, controversy on the issue of abortion and its relevance to 'safe motherhood' initiatives prevented the adoption of the goals, including that on maternal mortality. The Holy See, which expressed its reservations on safe motherhood initiatives because some of them might include access to abortion, finally withdrew its objection at Cairo to the adoption of the goal on maternal mortality, after the issue of abortion was settled. In Para. 8.19, the Conference also agreed that 'safe mother-hood has been accepted in many countries as a strategy to reduce maternal morbidity and mortality'.

POPULATION DISTRIBUTION AND MIGRATION

The Programme of Action devotes two chapters to this area: chapter IX, entitled 'Population Distribution, Urbanization and Internal Migration', and chapter X, entitled 'International Migration'. On a wide range of population distribution questions, one can observe a continuity of thinking from Bucharest to Cairo. The reduction of rural–urban inequities, the development of small and medium-size cities to relieve the pressure on large cities, increasing support for rural development, and the avoidance of policies that may infringe upon the human rights of migrants are among the recommendations adopted by both Bucharest and Mexico, and were included in the Draft Final Document on the basis of the recommendations formulated by the Expert Group Meeting on Population Distribution and Migration (UN, 1993m). They were duly included in the Draft Programme of Action and adopted at Cairo.

Noteworthy among the new actions proposed by Cairo are: strength-ening the capacity of city and municipal authorities to deal with social development and environment issues, and specific measures to integrate migrants in urban areas, including special programmes for women and street children.

REFUGEES AND DISPLACED PERSONS

Problems of refugees and displaced persons also received attention at all three Conferences. The Bucharest Conference recommended that

problems of refugees and displaced persons arising from forced migration, including their right of return to homes and properties, should also be settled in accordance with the relevant Principles of the Charter of the UN, the Universal Declaration of Human Rights and other international instruments. (UN, 1975: Recommendation 53)

At Mexico, one of the flashpoints concerned the rights of refugees and displaced persons in the territories occupied by Israel since the 1967 war. In fact, some observers felt that 'the recommendation on the settlements issue (Recommendation 34, later 36) provoked the most heated encount-ers of the conference' (Finkle and Crane, 1985: 10). As I have mentioned in Chapter 1, the final text on the settlements issue, which follows, required voting in both the Main Committee and the Plenary Session:

population distribution policies must be consistent with such international instruments as the Geneva Convention relative to the Protection of Civilian Persons in Time of War (1949), wherein article 49 prohibits individual or mass forcible transfers from an occupied territory and forbids the occupier from transferring parts of its own civilian population into the territory it occupies. Furthermore, the establishment of settlements in territories occupied by force is illegal and condemned by the international community. (UN, 1984: Recommendation 36)

The political climate had changed by the time this topic came up for consideration during the Cairo process. The Oslo agreement brokered by Norway between Israel and Palestinian representatives, and the resulting reduction in tension between Israel and the Palestinians, enabled Prepcom III to adopt a much shorter statement, qualifying the reference to the Geneva Convention by adding the words 'when applicable': 'Population distribution policies should be consistent with such international instruments, when applicable, as the Geneva Convention relative to the Protection of Civilian Persons in Time of War (1949), including article 49.' (UN, 1995a: Para. 9.11)

The Conference itself dealt with one unresolved issue, left over from PrepCom III, relating to Para. 9.25. This said that '[m]easures should be taken, [nationally and internationally,] to find lasting solutions to questions related to internally displaced persons, including their right to voluntary and safe return to their home of origin' (UN, 1994e). A few delegations, including India, felt that if the word 'internationally' were left in the text, it might be interpreted in such a way as to justify interventions in the domestic affairs of a country by other countries. To avoid this interpretation, the Conference adopted the following language: 'at the national level with international cooperation, as appropriate, in accordance with the Charter of the UN'.

INTERNATIONAL MIGRATION

International migration which is the subject of a separate chapter (chapter X) in the Programme of Action, attracted far greater interest and attention during the ICPD process than did internal migration. One of the immediate reasons was the publicity given to the massive dislocation of hundreds of thousands of foreign workers brought about by the Gulf War of 1991 and its after-effects. But there were also other major developments increasing the level of concern on issues of international migration in both 'sending' and 'receiving' countries: migration from the former USSR and former Yugoslavia into Western Europe, the rising number of refugees in the African region, and an increasing preoccupation with asylum seekers in Europe and undocumented and illegal workers in the US.

As the estimates of international migration prepared by the UN show, the rate of growth in international migration went up from 1.2 per cent per annum in 1965–1975 to 2.2 per cent during 1975–1985 and to 2.6 per cent during 1985–1990 (see Table 3.4). While migration across borders has occurred in both developed and developing countries, the proportion of international migrants constitutes only 1.6 per cent of the total population of developing countries, whereas in the case of developed countries it comes to 4.1 per cent. By 1990, there were 25 million international migrants in Europe and 24 million in North America (including 20 million in the US alone).

In the light of increased global interest in the issues of international migration, the Conceptual Framework presented to PrepCom II proposed that a separate chapter be devoted to international migration, and that particular attention be given to three specific topics: documented migrants, undocumented migrants and refugees. Following a suggestion made by several delegations at PrepCom II, the Draft Final Document added a general section on international migration and development at the beginning of the chapter and expanded the title of the section on refugees to include asylum seekers. Another sub-category of migrants – displaced persons – was added under this section at PrepCom III.

The Chairman's Summary on the Conceptual Framework noted that the discussion on international migration at PrepCom II had a generally positive tone and, in many circumstances, migration was considered 'beneficial to both countries of origin and receiving countries' (UN, 1993j: Para. 42). Some of the issues discussed at this session were: the need for bilateral or multilateral negotiations on particular aspects of international migration, the need to protect female migrant workers from exploitation, the provision of adequate health services to refugees, particularly female refugees, and an interchange of information between receiving and sending countries. All of these were eventually incorporated in the Draft Final Document and Programme of Action.

The Draft Final Document attempted to provide a comprehensive overview of the current issues in international migration and made a number of general proposals addressed to both sending and receiving countries. The most important of these suggested redressing the causes of emigration in order to alleviate the massive and uncontrolled international migration flows:

> *The redressing of these causes would require increased effort to achieve sustainable economic and social development, avoid international and internal conflicts, respect the rule of law, promote good governance, strengthen democracy, promote human rights, support education, nutrition, health and population-relevant programmes, and ensure effective environmental protection. This may require financial assistance, reassessment of commercial and tariff relations and full access to world markets, and stepped-up efforts on the part of developing countries to create the framework for a market-oriented economy and a liberal trading system.*
> (UN, 1994d: Para. 10.3)

Table 3.4 Key Indicators of Trends in Migrant Stock, by Region, 1965, 1975, 1985 and 1990

Region	Estimated foreign-born population (thousands)				As percentage of total population				Annual rate of change				Percentage distribution by region			
	1965	1975	1985	1990	1965	1975	1985	1990	1965–1975	1975–1985	1985–1990	1965–1990	1965	1975	1985	1990
World total	75,214	84,494	105,194	119,761	2.3	2.1	2.2	2.3	1.2	2.2	2.6	1.9	100.0	100.0	100.0	100.0
Developed countries	30,401	38,317	47,991	54,231	3.1	3.5	4.1	4.5	2.3	2.3	2.4	2.3	40.4	45.3	45.6	45.3
Developing countries	44,813	46,177	57,203	65,530	1.9	1.6	1.6	1.6	0.3	2.1	2.7	1.5	59.6	54.7	54.4	54.7
Africa	7952	11,178	12,527	15,631	2.5	2.7	2.3	2.5	3.4	1.1	4.4	2.7	10.6	13.2	11.9	13.1
Northern Africa	1016	1080	2219	1982	1.4	1.1	1.8	1.4	0.6	7.2	-2.3	2.7	1.4	1.3	2.1	1.7
Sub-Saharan Africa	6936	10,099	10,308	13,649	2.9	3.2	2.5	2.8	3.8	0.2	5.6	2.7	9.2	12.0	9.8	11.4
Asia	31,429	26,662	38,731	43,018	1.7	1.3	1.4	1.4	-0.6	2.7	2.1	1.3	41.8	35.1	36.8	35.9
Eastern and South-Eastern Asia	8136	7723	7678	7931	0.7	0.5	0.5	0.4	-0.5	-0.1	0.6	-0.1	10.8	9.1	7.3	6.6
China	266	305	331	346	0.0	0.0	0.0	0.0	1.4	0.8	0.9	1.0	0.4	0.4	0.3	0.3
Other Eastern and South-Eastern Asia	7870	7419	7347	7586	1.9	1.5	1.2	1.2	-0.6	-0.1	0.6	-0.1	10.5	8.8	7.0	6.3
South-Central Asia[a]	18,610	15,565	19,243	20,782	2.8	1.9	1.8	1.8	-1.8	2.1	1.5	0.4	24.7	18.4	18.3	17.4
Western Asia	4683	6374	11,810	14,304	7.4	7.6	10.4	10.9	3.1	6.2	3.8	4.5	6.2	7.5	11.2	11.9
Latin America and the Caribbean	5907	5788	6410	7475	2.4	1.8	1.6	1.7	-0.2	1.0	3.1	0.9	7.9	6.9	6.1	6.2
Caribbean	532	665	832	959	2.4	2.5	2.7	2.9	2.2	2.2	2.8	2.4	0.7	0.8	0.8	0.8
Central America[b]	445	427	948	2047	0.8	0.6	1.0	1.8	-0.4	8.0	15.4	6.1	0.6	0.5	0.9	1.7
South America	4930	4695	4629	4469	3.0	2.2	1.8	1.5	-0.5	-0.1	-0.7	-0.4	6.6	5.6	4.4	3.7

North America	12,695	15,042	20,460	23,895	6.0	6.3	7.8	8.6	1.7	3.1	3.1	2.5	16.9	17.8	19.5	20.0
Europe and former USSR	14,728	19,504	22,959	25,068	2.2	2.7	3.0	3.2	2.8	1.6	1.8	2.1	19.6	23.1	21.8	20.9
Countries with economies in transition[c]	2835	2394	2213	2055	2.4	1.9	1.6	1.7	-1.7	-0.8	-1.5	-1.3	3.8	2.8	2.1	1.7
USSR (former)	140	148	156	159	0.1	0.1	0.1	0.1	0.6	0.5	0.5	0.5	0.2	0.2	0.1	0.1
Other Europe	11,753	16,961	20,590	22,853	3.6	4.9	5.8	6.1	3.7	1.9	2.1	2.7	15.6	20.1	19.6	19.1
Oceania	2502	3319	4106	4675	14.4	15.6	16.9	17.8	2.8	2.1	2.6	2.5	3.3	3.9	3.9	3.9

Source: Derived from *Trends in Total Migrant Stock*, Rev. 3, a database maintained by the Population Division of the DESIPA Secretariat.

[a] Excluding Armenia, Azerbaijan, Georgia, Kazakstan, Kyrgzstan, Tajikistan, Turkmenistan and Uzbekistan

[b] Including Mexico.

[c] Including Albania, Bulgaria, former Czechoslovakia, the former German Democratic Republic, Poland, Romania and the former Yugoslavia, and excluding the former USSR.

Governments have always asserted the right to control their borders and to decide who is allowed to come into their territory. The Draft Final Document recognized this reality:

> [g]overnments of countries of destination have the right to control access to their territory and adopt policies that shape immigration flows. Such measures should conform with universally recognized international standards. As movements of persons are part of the process of development of free societies and market economies, host countries should also adopt policies that allow legal migrants the option of remaining, either on a temporary or on a permanent basis. (UN, 1994d: Para. 10.4)

Chapter X of the Draft Final Document underwent numerous changes at PrepCom III. Addressing the root causes of migration, especially those related to poverty, became one of the principal objectives under the section entitled 'International Migration and Development'. The recommendations were extensively redrafted to add a number of details and nuances. In the end, brackets still remained on a number of words and phrases, to be negotiated finally at the Conference.

The right of family reunification was one of these bracketed phrases. The International Convention on the Protection of the Rights of All Migrant Workers and Members of Their Families, which was adopted by the GA in 1990, after 10 years of negotiations, enumerates several rights for the families of migrant workers in a documented or legal situation, but does not go so far as to guarantee the right to family reunification. In any case the Convention has not yet come into force, as the required number of ratifications (20) has not been received.[1] The attempt made by a number of 'sending' countries at PrepCom III to establish an unequivocal right of family reunification ran into a major difficulty that was to be expected: there was no agreement on what constituted a family or the family. The US, as one of the major receiving countries, referred to the lack of a standard definition of the family and registered its concern that family reunification, if interpreted broadly, could require the inclusion of cousins and in-laws.

This debate continued at Cairo. Many developing countries re-emphasized their support for a clear and unequivocal recognition of the right to family reunification. On the other side, the countries that receive large numbers of immigrants on a regular basis, such as Australia, Canada and the US, stated their commitment to the concept of family reunification, but pointed out that their governments could not give up the right to determine what categories of family members would be provided immigrant visas.

As the Main Committee was unable to resolve the debate on this issue, a Working Group chaired by Soliman Awad (Egypt) was established for further negotiations. When the Working Group came back to the Main

Committee on 10 September with a compromise text which did not refer to the right of family reunification, an unexpected uproar followed. One after another, 35 representatives of developing countries got up to register their dissent, dissatisfaction or disappointment: the Dominican Republic, Zambia, Mali, Benin, Zimbabwe, The Gambia, Cuba, Senegal, Tunisia, Algeria, China, Cameroon, Swaziland, Ecuador, Nicaragua, Guatemala, Mexico, Mauritania, Honduras, Libya, Liberia, Chile, the Philippines, Bangladesh, Bolivia, Uganda, Malawi, Botswana, Peru, El Salvador, Paraguay, Suriname, the Congo, Chad and Haiti. The Holy See also made a statement criticizing the compromise text (*Earth Negotiations Bulletin*, 14 September 1994).

The Chairman asked the working group to reconvene and renegotiate. Finally, on 12 September, the Group came up with a new text, which explicitly mentioned article 10 of the Convention on the Rights of the Child, dealing with several specific aspects of the family reunification issue. The Committee accepted the incorporation of this text in Para. 10.12, which now reads as follows.

> *In order to promote the integration of documented migrants having the right to long-term residence, Governments of receiving countries are urged to consider giving them civil and political rights and responsibilities, as appropriate, and facilitating their naturalization. Special efforts should be made to enhance the integration of the children of long-term migrants by providing them with educational and training opportunities equal to those of nationals, allowing them to exercise an economic activity, and facilitating the naturalization of those who have been raised in the receiving country. Consistent with article 10 of the Convention of the Rights of the Child and all other relevant universally recognized human rights instruments, all Governments, particularly those of receiving countries, must recognize the vital importance of family reunification and promote its integration into their national legislation in order to ensure the protection of the unity of the families of documented migrants. Governments of receiving countries must ensure the protection of migrants and their families, giving priority to programmes and strategies that combat religious intolerance, racism, ethnocentrism, xenophobia and gender discrimination and that generate the necessary public sensitivity in that regard (UN, 1995a).*

The compromise text adopted by the Main Committee did not satisfy all the interested parties. The Philippines, which had campaigned hard for the acceptance of the right to family reunification, recorded, at the final Plenary Session on 13 September, its regret that

> *in paragraph 10.12 of the Programme of Action the originally proposed wording, recognizing 'the right to family-reunification' was toned down to just recognizing 'the vital importance of family reunification'. In the spirit of compromise, we agreed to the revised wording based on the argument forwarded by other delegations that there have been no previous international conventions or declarations proclaiming such a right, and that this is not the appropriate*

conference to establish this right. For this and other worthy reasons, we wish to reiterate the recommendation made in the Main Committee, supported by many delegations and received positively by the Chairman, that an international conference on migration be convened in the near future. We trust that this recommendation will be part of the record of this Conference and will be formally referred to the Economic and Social Council and the General Assembly for proper consideration. (UN, 1995a: 137–38)

Cairo did not adopt an official position on the proposal for an international conference on migration, which was mooted by the Philippines. The idea was brought up again in the Second Committee of the UN GA, when the Report of the Cairo Conference was being discussed and at the initiative of several countries, including the Philippines, a separate resolution on the subject (GA Resolution 49/127, 19 December 1994) was adopted.[2] Reflecting a lack of enthusiasm for the convening of an international conference on migration, the Resolution asked for a report on various possibilities and options, based on further consultations, to be submitted to the subsequent session of the GA.

All told, Cairo represented a considerable advance over previous UN conferences on many aspects of international migration. It advocated a comprehensive set of strategies in order to reduce the need for large-scale international migration (UN, 1995a: Para. 10.3). It proposed the ratification of the International Convention on the Protection of the Rights of All Migrant Workers and Members of Their Families (Para. 10.6). This Convention, if ratified by the major receiving countries, will take care of most of the concerns and issues raised at the ICPD. The protection of migrant women and children from abuse, sanctions against those trafficking in undocumented migrants and equitable sharing of the refugee burden by the international community are some of the other important issues covered by the ICPD Programme of Action.

DATA, RESEARCH AND TRAINING

Chapter XII of the Programme of Action contains fairly long lists of proposals on basic data collection and analysis, reproductive health research and social and economic research. The UN and UNFPA efforts, complemented by support provided by several other agencies, have over the last two decades succeeded in building up national capacity, particularly in sub-Saharan Africa, for the collection, analysis and dissemination of population and related development data that would provide a sound basis for the formulation, application and evaluation of population and related development policies. But as the Programme of Action points out, 'many gaps remain with regard to the quality and coverage of baseline information, including vital data on births and deaths, as well as the continuity of data sets over time' (Para. 12.1). It therefore recommends that '[g]overnments of all countries . . . should strengthen their national capacity to carry out sustained and comprehensive programmes on collection, analysis, dissemination and utilization of population and development data' (Para. 12.3). The proposed agenda for action includes 'the monitoring of population trends and the preparation of demographic projections and . . . the monitoring of progress towards the attainment of the health, education, gender, ethnic and social-equity goals, and of service accessibility and quality of care'. (Para. 12.3). This is in tune with the proposals for the development and utilization of adequate databases, with quantitative indicators, to measure progress towards Cairo's goals.

The Programme of Action also proposes, in the section on basic data collection and analysis, training programmes in statistics, demography and population and development studies, particularly in developing countries (Para. 12.8). Most of the support for such training programmes at the international level has in the past come through UNFPA, and it is now in the process of assessing future training needs in the context of its programme priorities based on the ICPD Programme. Training needs are also identified under many other chapters.

In the area of reproductive health, governments, assisted by the international community, NGOs, the private sector and the academic community, are urged to increase support for basic and applied biomedical, technological, clinical, epidemiological and social science research. Research on sexuality and gender roles, the development of new methods for the regulation of fertility for men and research on the determinants and consequences of induced abortion are some of the other important topics covered in this section.

The agenda for social science research updates the agenda proposed at the earlier conferences by proposing research to fill existing gaps in knowledge in practically all the major themes: fertility, mortality, migration, changes in family structures, the linkages between women's roles and status and the demographic and development process, and the linkages between poverty alleviation, the environment, sustained economic growth and sustainable development. No attempt was made at Cairo to establish research priorities, and it is to be assumed that governments, international organizations, academic institutions and foundations which fund or sponsor social science research will establish priorities, in accordance with their own work programmes.

THE ROLE OF POPULATION SPECIALISTS AT CAIRO

Cairo has come in for some criticism from a number of population specialists who felt that the Conference did not give adequate attention to demographic objectives. In a speech given in early 1995, Professor Dirk van de Kaa, who has participated in all three population conferences, decried the smaller number of people with a background in demography or population studies attending Cairo, compared with those who attended the previous population conferences.

> *Moreover, those population experts who were there, had – with very few exceptions – only minor roles to play. My uneasiness stemmed from the fact that the conference was ready to deal with everything as long as it did not relate directly to the mundane issues of population growth and the need to generate the financial resources necessary to enable people everywhere to plan their families responsibly.* (van de Kaa, 1996: 22)

Actually, the number of demographers or population specialists who attended Cairo may not have been that much smaller than the number at previous conferences. But it is true that diplomats, government officials and policy makers were more numerous and played a much more important role in the ICPD. Also, compared with the previous conferences there were many more NGOs involved in the process, at all levels. There are many who feel that the broad involvement of so many people from both governmental and non-governmental sectors achieved during the ICPD process, and the experience and perspectives they gained as a result, may actually help to ensure that the implementation of the ICPD Programme of Action will be given serious attention at various levels of policy and decision making. Issues relating to population growth did not feature in several of the plenary statements, but as far as I can recall it, we had a similar situation at the previous two conferences. As I have pointed out earlier, Cairo went much further than Bucharest and Mexico, by recommending that effective steps be taken to achieve demographic transition. The issue of financial resources received, in my view, a great deal more systematic and careful review at Cairo than was the case in the past.

Alison McIntosh and Jason Finkle, who share the view that demographers and population specialists played a somewhat limited role in the ICPD process, argue that at Cairo 'the demographic objective was subordinated to other social goals' (McIntosh and Finkle, 1995: 252). The 'demographic objective' is not to be found in the Bucharest WPPA or in the Mexico Recommendations for its Further Implementation; and there was no expectation at any stage during the ICPD preparatory process that Cairo would discuss or accept a global policy goal or a quantitative global goal on the reduction of population growth rates.

However, Cairo did accept the objective of facilitating demographic transition and to this end proposed a package of comprehensive measures including family planning and reproductive health services within a primary health-care framework, universal access to quality primary education, educational strategies regarding responsible parent-hood and sexual education, the improvement of women's status and economic development and poverty alleviation (UN, 1995a: Para. 6.4). It also signalled a major shift away from demographic goals and policies that emphasized government intervention based on pre-determined planning concepts and estimates, to human-centred goals and policies that would be defined on the basis of an assessment of what individuals and couples need. According to the ICPD Programme of Action, '[g]overnmental goals for family planning should be defined in terms of unmet needs for information and services' and '[d]emographic goals, while legitimately the subject of government development strategies, should not be imposed on family-planning providers in the form of targets and quotas for the recruitment of clients' (Para. 7.12).

While maintaining the concept of national sovereignty, Cairo provided strong momentum to the efforts to apply internationally recognized human rights in the formulation and implementation of population policies and programmes. Freedom of choice and reproductive rights are strongly emphasized throughout the Programme of Action.

The reduction of maternal mortality was given an extremely high priority by Cairo. In adopting a quantitative goal in this regard, as in adopting other quantitative and qualitative goals, the Conference was strongly influenced by women's concerns and perspectives.

Cairo adopted a set of fairly specific recommendations on international migration pertaining to the rights of different types of migrants. If implemented, these could go a long way towards meeting the concerns of both sending and receiving countries.

4   THE EMPOWERMENT OF WOMEN

Cairo was as much about the empowerment of women as about population policies and programmes. The debates and controversies on reproductive health and reproductive rights, which attracted so much public and media attention during the ICPD process, were of great interest and concern not only to policy makers, programme managers and technical experts but also to women's groups and individual women all over the world. In shaping the ICPD Programme of Action, the delegates agreed that women's concerns and women's rights must be given priority, as women constituted the most profoundly affected and interested parties.

Cairo used gender equality as its guiding principle in dealing with a wide range of population and development issues. It also paid particular attention to the reduction of maternal mortality, education for young girls, the elimination of discriminatory laws and practices against women and the creation of better economic and social opportunities and options for women.

The ICPD Programme of Action justifies its focus on women by stating quite unequivocally that '[a]dvancing gender equality and equity and the empowerment of women, and the elimination of all kinds of violence against women, and ensuring women's ability to control their own fertility, are cornerstones of population and development-related programmes' (UN, 1995a: 12). It also declares that '[t]he empowerment and autonomy of women and the improvement of their political, social, economic and health status is a highly important end in itself' (UN, 1995a: Para. 4.1).

BUCHAREST AND MEXICO

Compared with Cairo, the approach taken by Bucharest to women's issues was rather perfunctory. In fact these issues were brought up at

Bucharest only after some of the female delegates made the point that the draft WPPA had paid no attention to such issues. Bucharest urges governments to ensure the 'full participation of women in the educational, social, economic and political life of their countries on an equal basis with men' and to

> make a sustained effort to ensure that legislation regarding the status of women complies with the principles spelled out in the Declaration on the Elimination of Discrimination Against Women and other United Nations declarations, conventions and international instruments, to reduce the gap between law and practice through effective implementation, and to inform women at all socio-economic levels of their legal rights and responsibilities. (UN, 1975: Recommendation 41(d))

Ten years later, the Mexico Conference reiterated these general recommendations, but also went further by asking governments to 'pursue more aggressively action programmes aimed at improving and protecting the legal rights and status of women through efforts to identify and to remove institutional and cultural barriers to women's education, training, employment and access to health care'. (UN, 1984: Recommendation 5)

Two UN world conferences on women (Mexico City, 1975 and Copenhagen, 1980), which had taken place in the interval between the Bucharest (1974) and Mexico (1984) population conferences, had helped generate a great deal of public attention on women's issues. At the Mexico Conference an ad hoc caucus working on family planning and women's rights proved highly effective in getting official delegations to accept major recommendations on both of these issues.

The Mexico Conference also accepted the proposition that 'demographic policy or cultural tradition' or for that matter 'the biological role of women in the reproductive process' should not be used in any way to limit women's right to work (UN, 1984: Recommendation 6). Governments were further asked to undertake positive measures to enlarge the options and opportunities available to women simultaneously on many fronts. Recommendation 7 of the Mexico Conference says:

> [g]overnments should provide women, through education, training and employment, with opportunities for personal fulfillment in familial and non-familial roles, as well as for full participation in economic, social and cultural life, while continuing to give due support to their important social role as mothers. To this end, in those countries where child-bearing occurs when the mother is too young, Government policies should encourage delay in the commencement of child-bearing.

The Third UN Conference on Women, which took place in Nairobi (Kenya) in 1985, revisited many of the issues which were considered at the International Conference on Population the previous year. The presence of many delegates from the population conference in the official delegations for Nairobi and the highly effective lobbying done by many population-related and women's NGOs resulted in the Nairobi Conference paying much greater attention to population and family planning issues than was the case at the previous UN conferences on women (Mexico City and Copenhagen). The Nairobi Conference declared that 'the ability of women to control their own fertility . . . forms an important basis for enjoyment of other rights' (UN, 1986: Para. 156).

The UNCED, the first UN conference to be held in the 1990s, did not give much time or attention to population issues. However, several NGO representatives meeting in Rio at the same time prepared what was called the NGO Treaty on Population, Environment and Development. After pledging 'to expose and oppose any coercive population control programmes', the Treaty demanded

> *women-centred, women-managed and women-controlled comprehensive health care, including pre- and post-natal care, safe and voluntary contraceptives and abortion facilities, sex education and information for girls and boys, and programmes that also educate men on male methods of contraception and their parental responsibilities.* (Pollard et al., 1992)

As I have noted earlier, all of these issues became important topics for discussion in the subsequent ICPD process. Also, UNFPA had organized a seminar on women, population and the environment during the Rio Conference, and those members of the ICPD staff who were at Rio had the opportunity at the seminar and several NGO events to listen to a diverse set of views, all of which proved pertinent to their substantive tasks in preparing for the ICPD.

EXPERT GROUP MEETING ON POPULATION AND WOMEN

One of the events that helped to formulate and clarify the thinking of the Secretariat on many women's empowerment issues was the Expert Group Meeting on Population and Women which took place in Botswana in June 1992, soon after the Rio Conference. A deliberate attempt was made by the Secretariat to bring together at this event technical experts who held diverse views on these issues. The interaction that took place between them for five days in Gaborone enabled them and members of the Secretariat to engage in a frank and open discussion and ultimately agree on a series of important recommendations that would help us with the drafting of the Final Document, in particular the chapter on women's empowerment.

Dr Sadik, in her introductory remarks at the five-day meeting, chose to focus on practical actions that recognize women's rights and autonomy and that enhance women's participation in the development process. Her list of such actions included the removal of the remaining legal barriers to women's full equality, policies to improve the education of girls and programmes to provide reliable information about reproductive rights and reproductive health, high-quality family planning services and whatever health care services were needed to combat disease and promote healthy childbirth. The Expert Group formulated a series of detailed recommendations on these and other related topics, and over the next few months the Secretariat received several submissions and proposals from governments, NGOs and individuals that were very similar in content. Many of these themes were also commented upon by other expert group meetings and the regional conferences that took place during 1992–1993.

The Expert Group also suggested a comprehensive research agenda

on the linkages between women's roles and status and demographic processes. Among the vital areas for research are changing family systems and the interaction between women's, men's and children's diverse roles, including their use of time, access to and control over resources, decision-making and associated norms, laws, values and beliefs. Of particular concern is the impact of gender inequalities on these interactions and the associated economic and demographic outcomes. (UN, 1992a: Recommendation 29)

PREPCOM II

Prior to PrepCom II, WEDO decided to organize a cooperative effort with like-minded activists and organizations aimed at influencing the ICPD process in a manner similar to that used in the Rio process. WEDO also made a conscious effort to contact a very large group of NGOs in developing countries and to help them find the means to attend the second Session of the Preparatory Committee, where a fully fledged Women's Caucus was launched.

The Women's Caucus played a critical role in ensuring that women's empowerment became the most important cross-cutting theme in the ICPD Programme of Action. As its members belonged to NGOs as well as to official delegations, they were in a position to ensure that the proposals made by them were given adequate attention and consideration at the second and third sessions of the Preparatory Committee.

In addition to the Women's Caucus, there were several other groups that met regularly during the Preparatory Committee sessions to focus, amongst other things, on women's issues. The Center for Development and Population Activities (CEDPA) and IPPF held regular briefings for their own constituents, and the regional groups that met from time to time also discussed these issues. Their interaction with the delegations on these issues was instrumental in broadening the understanding of many delegations on how important and urgent these issues were.

As I have mentioned in Chapter 3, the Conceptual Framework presented to PrepCom II had listed nine fundamental concerns and issues that were central to all actions on population and development. One of these was gender equality and the empowerment of women. But the other issues and concerns also had a direct bearing on women's empowerment issues, inasmuch as they dealt with human rights, including reproductive rights. Part II of the Conceptual Framework proposed a specific chapter devoted to 'The Role and Status of Women', conveying the expectation 'that the full spectrum of issues involving women and population concerns will be in the final document adopted by the Conference' (UN, 1993c: 8).

As the Chairman's Summary of the discussions on the Conceptual Framework indicates, all those delegations which spoke on the topic endorsed the view that the empowerment of women was an essential factor in achieving population and development objectives.

Existing gender inequalities and barriers to women should be eliminated and their participation in all levels of policy-making and implementation should be increased. Opportunities should be enhanced for leadership roles and for greater access to education, jobs and improved health services, including sexual and reproductive health and family planning. The role and responsibility of men in bringing about gender equity, policy and value changes was repeatedly emphasized. (UN, 1993j: Para. 21)

Sweden and Malaysia proposed during the discussion that the title of the chapter dealing with women's issues and concerns should be expanded to include a reference to gender equality for women. The same proposal was also put forward by the Women's Caucus. Proposals were made to examine in the next round of discussions at PrepCom III a whole host of specific concerns and strategies to deal with them. These included women as victims of aggression during war, prostitution, female genital mutilation, the minimum age at marriage, empowerment of the girl child, population and breast feeding, gender equality in school attendance, pornography, violence against women, the negative stereotyping of women in society and contraceptive research (*Earth Negotiations Bulletin*, 2 June 1993). Colombia, speaking on behalf of the G77, proposed that a separate chapter be devoted to the family.

There was not enough time at PrepCom II to discuss any of these issues in depth. But it was clear that delegates saw gender issues as cutting across most of the chapters, including those relating to health and reproduction, and they were of the opinion that those issues that could not be dealt with adequately in other chapters should be addressed in a chapter to be entitled 'Gender Equality and Empowerment of Women'.

In between the second and third sessions of the Preparatory Committee, the IWHC, in cooperation with a local NGO called Citizenship, Studies, Information, Action (CEPIA), organized the International Women's Health Conference in Rio de Janeiro which put together many of the proposals and strategies later used by the IWHC at PrepCom III.[1] The Rio Statement adopted at the Conference voiced 'the need to design social development policies starting from the concerns and priorities of women' (IWHC and CEPIA, 1994: 5). The Statement put forward the view that '[c]entral to fundamentalists' attempts to gain political power is the control of women's lives and in particular of female sexuality, including the right to self-determination and reproductive decisions' (IWHC and CEPIA, 1994: 5). In another major comment on the 'fundamentalist' position, the Statement said that '[a] major site of the fundamentalist war against women is over the meaning of "families"'. The participants at the conference agreed that a definition of 'family' that is limited to a model with a male 'head' of household, wife and children, does not reflect the life situation of all of the world's people. Instead, it was agreed that all those who voluntarily come together and define themselves as a family, accepting a commitment to each other's well-being, should be respected, supported and affirmed as such (IWHC and CEPIA, 1994: 6).

DRAFT FINAL DOCUMENT AND PREPCOM III

The Draft Final Document prepared by the Secretariat for discussion at PrepCom III took into account these suggestions as well other suggestions made by the Round Table on Women's Perspectives on Family Planning, Reproductive Health, and Reproductive Rights and the comments made by several delegations during the 1993 GA. The Secretariat had also reviewed a large number of written suggestions and proposals on these topics from both governments and NGOs.

The Draft Final Document proposed a chapter (chapter IV) on gender equality and the empowerment of women with three sections: the empowerment and status of women, the girl child and male responsibilities, and participation. The Document also proposed a separate chapter on the family, its roles, composition and structure, with two sections: the diversity of family structures and composition, and socio-economic support to the family (UN, 1994d).

PrepCom III discussions on chapter IV brought up three issues. First, there was a debate on gender equity versus gender equality. Canada was in favour of gender equality, whereas Norway argued for including both terms, as they were complementary to each other. Several Islamic countries argued that Islamic law and tradition provided for equitable treatment of women, but the concept of equality between men and women could not be applied in their societies in matters of inheritance and succession. In the end, it was agreed that the title of the chapter should include both the terms, and Para. 4.3 sets the following objectives aimed at empowering women and eliminating inequalities between men and women.

> (a) *To achieve equality and equity based on harmonious partnership between men and women and enable women to realize their full potential;*
> (b) *To ensure the enhancement of women's contributions to sustainable development through their full involvement in policy- and decision-making processes at all stages and participation in all aspects of production, employment, income-generating activities, education, health, science and technology, sports, culture and population-related activities and other areas, as active decision makers, participants and beneficiaries;*
> (c) *To ensure that all women, as well as men, are provided with the education necessary for them to meet their basic human needs and to exercise their human rights.* (UN, 1994e: Para. 4.3)

Second, the application of the concept of equality to inheritance and succession was not acceptable to Malaysia and many other countries that follow Islamic law. They favoured 'equity' over 'equality'. The final text refers to 'equitable inheritance rights' (UN, 1995a: Para. 4.17).

The third issue was more procedural than political. The EU members did not want to agree to any reference in this chapter to the goal of universal primary education for all by 2015, until such time as an overall agreement could be reached on all the quantitative goals. The goal was therefore put in brackets, as was the term 'reproductive and sexual health'. At the end of PrepCom III, these were the only two items left in brackets in chapter IV.

The agreement on virtually the entire chapter on gender equality, equity and the empowerment of women was perhaps the most solid accomplishment of PrepCom III, though it was overshadowed at the time by continuing controversy over reproductive health, reproductive rights and abortion, three issues also directly related to women's status and rights. The adoption of this chapter clearly demonstrated the acceptance by the delegates of the centrality of women's empowerment to population and development issues.

The chapter urges the ratification of the UN Convention on the Elimination of All Forms of Discrimination against Women and the promulgation and implementation of national laws that would protect women against economic discrimination and sexual harassment. It also asks for the implementation of the Declaration on the Elimination of Violence against Women, which had been adopted by the UN GA in December 1993 (GA Resolution 48/104), at the urging of the UN World

Conference on Human Rights (Vienna, 1993). Reports of mass rapes and other acts of violence against women in the former Yugoslavia had led the UN Human Rights Conference in Vienna to strongly condemn violence against women in situations of armed conflict as a human rights violation and to state unequivocally that 'all violations of this kind, in particular murder, systematic rape, sexual slavery, and forced pregnancy, require a particularly effective response' (UN, 1995b: Para. 38).

The Declaration on the Elimination of Violence against Women provides a broad definition of violence, including violence within the family, the actions of the community and actions undertaken by the state. While recommending the full implementation of the Declaration, chapter IV also took note of the crimes being committed against women in the former Yugoslavia and other similar situations by urging countries to

> *identify and condemn the systematic practice of rape and other forms of inhuman and degrading treatment of women as a deliberate instrument of war and ethnic cleansing and take steps to assure that full assistance is provided to the victims of such abuse for their physical and mental rehabilitation. (UN, 1995a: Para. 4.10)*

Chapter IV also lists a whole series of specific actions needed to eliminate discrimination and economic and social inequities and inequalities. These include appropriate measures to improve women's ability to earn income beyond traditional occupations and achieve economic self-reliance, and to ensure women's equal access to the labour market and social security systems (UN, 1995a: Para. 4.4(d)), the elimination of discriminatory practices by employers against women, such as those based on contraceptive use or pregnancy status (Para. 4.4(f)) and making it possible, through laws, regulations and other appropriate measures, for women to combine the roles of childbearing, breast-feeding and child-rearing with participation in the workforce (Para. 4.4(g)).

The section on the girl child urges countries to go beyond the achievement of universal primary education for all by the year 2015. It asks them to ensure the widest and earliest possible access by girls and women to secondary and higher levels of education as well as vocational education and technical training (Para. 4.18). It recommends an integrated approach to the special nutritional, general and reproductive health, education and social needs of girls and young women (Para. 4.20). It recommends that governments

> *strictly enforce laws to ensure that marriage is entered into only with the free and full consent of the intending spouses. In addition, Governments should strictly enforce laws concerning the minimum legal age of consent and the minimum age at marriage and should raise the minimum age at marriage where necessary. Governments and non-governmental organizations should generate*

*social support for the enforcement of laws on the minimum legal age at marriage,
in particular by providing . . .. educational and employment opportunities. (Para.
4.21)*

Governments are urged to prohibit female genital mutilation (Para. 4.22)
and to take the necessary measures to prevent infanticide, prenatal sex-
selection, trafficking in girl children and the use of girls in prostitution
and pornography (Para. 4.23).

On male responsibilities and participation, the objective is 'to promote
gender equality in all spheres of life, including family and community
life, and to encourage and enable men to take responsibility for their
sexual and reproductive behavior and their social and family roles' (Para.
4.25). This should be pursued by means of 'information, education,
communication, employment legislation and by fostering an econo-
mically enabling environment, such as family leave for men and women'
(Para. 4.26). Governments are urged to enforce child-support laws and
to ensure the safety of women in abusive relationships (Para. 4.28). In
general, '[n]ational and community leaders should promote the full
involvement of men in family life and the full integration of women in
community life' (Para. 4.29).

DEFINITION OF FAMILY

The debate that took place on the definition and the roles of the family
in the context of chapter V was essentially part of the broader debate on
women's issues. While many delegations at PrepCom II had asked that
a separate chapter in the Final Document be devoted to the family
emphasizing its centrality in society, their views and perceptions on what
constituted a family or the family covered a very wide range of views.
There were those who wanted to emphasize the traditional notion of a
nuclear family (parents and children) or an extended family (parents,
children, grandparents and other relatives). Others pointed out that
family structures had evolved in many societies to denote single parent
families, couples without legal links living together and other types of
family structures. Much of this debate focused on the use of the term
'other unions' to describe relationships outside the framework of legal
marriage. The members of the EU and the Caribbean and Pacific
countries favoured the use of this term to describe families that did not
fit the traditional mould. On the other side, many countries which
followed traditional Islamic or Catholic personal laws objected to the
term on the grounds that this might signal the acceptance of homosexual
unions.

The Draft Final Document recognized the diversity of family structures
by proposing that 'the objective is to develop policies and laws that better
support the plurality of family forms, including the large number of

households headed by single parents, and to address the social and economic factors behind the increasing costs of child-rearing to women' (UN, 1994d: Para. 5.2).

The measures proposed for achieving these objectives gave special attention to single parent households (which are in most cases headed by women) and to poor women. A considerable amount of time was devoted to definitional issues, which were finally resolved by adopting a text used by the GA in its resolution on the International Year of the Family in 1993. This is how Chapter V begins now: '[w]hile various forms of the family exist in different social, cultural, legal and political systems, the family is the basic unit of the society and as such is entitled to receive comprehensive protection and support' (UN, 1995a: Para. 5.1).

The rest of the chapter was rewritten to reflect agreements on women's issues that were emerging with regard to other chapters. Para. 5.3 recommends that

> [g]overnments, in cooperation with employers, should provide and promote means to facilitate compatibility between labour force participation and parental responsibilities, especially for single-parent households with young children. Such means could include health insurance and social security, day-care centres and facilities for breast-feeding mothers within the work premises, kindergartens, part-time jobs, paid parental leave, paid maternity leave, flexible work schedules, and reproductive and child health services.

Para. 5.5 emphasizes measures recommended in other parts of the Final Document as well, for the elimination of child marriages and female genital mutilation. At the urging of several NGOs, assistance to persons with disabilities was also recommended in the same paragraph.

The one issue that was not settled at PrepCom III was that regarding 'other unions'. The Main Committee of the Cairo Conference spent a considerable amount of time negotiating about this term, which was to be found in the first sentence of Para. 5.5 of the Draft from PrepCom III: '[g]overnments should take effective action to eliminate all forms of coercion and discrimination in policies and practices related to marriage, other unions and the family'. The final compromise was to delete the words after 'practices'. This was the last contentious point to be settled with regard to chapter V.

The second section of the chapter, entitled 'Socio-Economic Support to the Family', brings up such issues as sexual exploitation, unwanted pregnancies and STDs, and asks governments to assist single parent families and to pay special attention to the needs of widows and orphans (Para. 5.13). The chapter taken as a whole manages to accommodate many of the concerns of those who value and cherish traditional family structures, but it is also clear and forthright on many current and emerging issues that are of special concern to women's groups.

OTHER ISSUES AND CONCERNS

Chapter XI, 'Population, Development, and Education' should also be mentioned here in the context of women's empowerment issues. The elimination of gender disparities is part of the overall objectives outlined in this chapter (Para. 11.5). Para. 11.6 urges countries to strive to ensure complete access to primary school or an equivalent level of education for both girls and boys as quickly as possible, and in any case before the year 2015. Further on, it pays special attention to the needs of young girls:

> *11.8. Countries should take affirmative steps to keep girls and adolescents in school by building more community schools, by training teachers to be more gender sensitive, by providing scholarships and other appropriate incentives and by sensitizing parents to the value of educating girls, with a view to closing the gender gap in primary and secondary school education by the year 2005. Countries should also supplement these efforts by making full use of non-formal education opportunities. Pregnant adolescents should be enabled to continue their schooling.*

Women's issues and concerns are thus reflected not only in the specific chapter on Gender Equality, Equity and the Empowerment of Women, but also in many other chapters. Chapters VII ('Reproductive Rights and Reproductive Health') and VIII ('Health, Morbidity and Mortality', which includes the much discussed paragraph on abortion) are two obvious examples. If we go to the first part of the Programme of Action, four of the five goals and objectives mentioned in Preamble 1.12 and Principles 5 and 13 relate to the need to improve the status of women. Taken together, the Programme of Action has 243 recommendations for action, and approximately one-third of them mention women or girls. Other recommendations that focus on the role of the family or of men are also of direct relevance in this context.

It should be pointed out, however, that the adoption by consensus of these positions by the Conference did not necessarily imply their acceptance by each and every individual country. At the final plenary, 15 countries recorded their own interpretations of the term 'various forms of the family' and six countries stated that they would implement the Programme of Action in accordance with Islamic law. For example, Paraguay stated that

> [o]n chapter II, principle 9, and chapter V, paragraph 5.1, our national Constitution considers that the family is the basic unit of society and is based on the union of a couple – man and woman – recognizing as well single-parent families. It is only from this perspective that we can include the term 'various forms of the family', respecting the various cultures, traditions and religions. (UN, 1995a: 137)

On the implementation of the Programme of Action in conformity with Islamic law and on the interpretation of the term 'individuals', Jordan said that

> [t]he delegation of Jordan understands that the final document, particularly chapters IV, V, VI and VII, will be applied within the framework of Islamic Sharia and our ethical values, as well as the laws that shape our behaviour. We will deal with the paragraphs of this document accordingly. Therefore, we interpret the word 'individuals' to mean couples, a married couple. (UN, 1995a: 135)

WAS WOMEN'S EMPOWERMENT OVEREMPHASIZED?

The emergence of women's empowerment as a central theme of the ICPD Programme of Action, though widely acclaimed by women's groups and many governments, also has its share of critics. In a statement made in 1995, Professor van de Kaa does not question the importance of the empowerment of women as a valuable goal in its own right, but he does not quite see the need for a separate chapter on this topic in the Programme of Action as 'the effects of improving the status of women upon population dynamics have not been sufficiently specified and quantified' (van de Kaa, 1996: 33). In the same vein, John Cleland, a British demographer says that

> [o]f course problems of gender inequity and inequality are an important component of the population debate and need to be addressed. But the dominance of this theme at Cairo has some unfortunate consequences and is all the more regrettable because the 1995 Beijing Conference on Women offered a more appropriate forum for detailed consideration of gender issues. (Cleland, 1996: 107)

The ICPD Programme of Action accepted the view that the empowerment of women is not only essential for the success of population policies and programmes, but is also an important end in itself. The record shows that this view was not challenged by anybody during the entire ICPD process. Nor did anybody argue against the incorporation in the Programme of Action of the themes and issues that are covered by chapter IV. Not only women's groups but also a very large number of governments argued strongly at PrepCom II that these should be included in the final outcome of the Cairo Conference, and more specifically that a separate chapter should be devoted to many of these themes and issues.

Even those countries that hold traditional views on the status and role of women chose, perhaps tactically, not to argue against the proposal to devote a chapter to women's empowerment. Instead, many of them sought to defend and justify their positions on such specific issues as the definition of the family, reproductive health, reproductive rights and adolescence, by rising in defence of 'sociocultural values' and systems and reaffirming the concept of national sovereignty in population matters. The encouraging point to note with regard to this group of countries is that they represent a wide spectrum of policies and views on women's issues and while some of them may have had no intention of taking any action on relevant ICPD recommendations, many others, in recognition of new pressures and realities, have already begun to move towards appropriate policy changes that would be needed.

The special attention given by the Programme of Action to the educational needs of the girl child comes under criticism from John Knodel and Gavin Jones (1996), who argue that the emphasis almost exclusively on closing the gap between boys and girls by promoting girls' education may divert attention from the gap in access to education that is caused by socioeconomic status:

> *while the strong emphasis on eliminating gender inequality in schooling is appropriate educational policy in some regions and countries, it is far less pertinent across a wide swathe of countries where such a gender gap is modest or nonexistent. Moreover, the gender gap in education appears to be in the process of closing everywhere, in some cases so rapidly that strong policy emphasis on closing the gap is no longer needed. At the same time, there is another gap, with serious implications for development and for equality of opportunity, as well as for demographic outcomes, that is largely ignored in the new population policy paradigm. This is the gap in access to education by socioeconomic status. In most developing countries, the lack of access for children from poor families, whether boys or girls, to good-quality primary education or to secondary or higher education of any kind is a much more urgent issue than the gender gap in education.* (Knodel and Jones, 1996: 684)

Socioeconomic factors are indeed very important, and most of the developing countries that are aiming at providing at least primary education to both boys and girls take these into account in their policies. But, at the same time, they have also come to recognize the need to give particular attention to the education of the girl child, given the discriminatory treatment she suffers from in her family and community. These include the nine major countries with the largest populations in the developing world.[2] It should not therefore be seen as an either/or situation.

Professor Nathan Keyfitz (1995) put all of this in a broader perspective in an article published soon after the Cairo Conference, in which he commented that

> *the central proposition recognizing birth control was unexceptionable, and had been anticipated in documents drafted before the conference: the way to get birth*

control into use is education, and particularly the education of women. From there it was an easy move to equality of the sexes not only in schooling but all decision-making. (Keyfitz, 1995: 86)

Professor Keyfitz says the move towards affirmation of the equality of the sexes is what 'accounted for the fierceness of the opposition. Brundtland said it frankly: male fear of change in the status of women played a significant role in opposition to the Conference's agenda' (Keyfitz, 1995: 86).

All of these comments and views are discussed in some detail by Harriet Presser in a highly interesting and provocative article entitled 'Demography, Feminism and the Science–Policy Nexus' (Presser, 1997). She argues that personal and institutional ideologies play a major role in determining policy and research agendas, and offers the view that

demographers need to study gender systems in all their complexity as they relate to population processes, and to view this effort as a two-way relationship whereby the consequences of population change for gender relations are given concentrated study, along with the effects of gender relations on population change. Moreover, the study of gender relations is the study of power relations, and the multiple dimensions of dominance and submission need to be quantified. (Presser, 1997: 321)

It is worth noting that the research agenda proposed by the ICPD in chapter XII of the Programme of Action, which is based on a recommendation of the Expert Group on Population and Women cited earlier, already includes an extensive list along these lines:

[g]overnments, intergovernmental organizations, non-governmental organizations concerned, funding agencies and research organizations are urged to give priority to research on the linkages between women's roles and status and demographic and development processes. Among the vital areas for research are changing family structures; family well-being; the interactions between women's and men's diverse roles, including their use of time, access to power and decision-making and control over resources; associated norms, laws, values and beliefs; and the economic and demographic outcomes of gender inequality. Women should be involved at all stages of gender research planning, and efforts should be made to recruit and train female researchers. (UN, 1995a: Para. 12.24)

For the many thousands of us who were in Cairo, the Conference has come to symbolize a watershed for the movement to empower women and for population policies and programmes in general. Most likely some of that feeling has percolated down to millions more who were not there but who read about it in newspapers or heard about it from the electronic media. Professor Keyfitz did not get to Cairo, but learned about it through detailed reports on the internet. To quote him again,

Cairo was a genuine 'happening', not a mere bureaucratic routine. It was news on the media and news in the bazaars in a way that few such international meetings have been. Because it came at the same time as many other smaller incidents in the awakening of women, the time was ripe for it; it fitted into the historic moment. (Keyfitz, 1995: 90)

The adoption of the ICPD Programme of Action registered a significant advance in the international consensus on women's empowerment and its direct relevance to population policies and programmes. It established a number of significant goals and signposts, which an increasing majority of countries have agreed to follow. These were further reinforced by the Fourth UN World Conference on Women in Beijing (1995). It is now the task of the international community and NGOs to ensure that countries strive to implement the agreements they reached at Cairo and Beijing.

There is also the continuing need to change public perceptions and views on a large number of issues that affect and influence women's status and roles, because the implementation of the international agreements, which advocate radical social change, requires not only legislative action but also a transformation of public opinion and social behaviour. This is indeed an urgent need in many societies and governments, NGOs and the international community – all must play an active and coordinated role in meeting this need.

5 PARTNERSHIP WITH THE NON-GOVERNMENTAL SECTOR

The ICPD Programme of Action devotes an entire chapter (Chapter XV) to the non-governmental sector. Rather than advocating cooperation or collaboration, the chapter talks about 'partnership' between governments, NGOs (comprising not-for-profit groups and organizations at local, national and international levels) and the private, profit-oriented sector. NGOs are also mentioned elsewhere in the Programme more than 40 times.

The major reasons for this new approach towards NGOs are spelled out in the Programme of Action itself (UN, 1995a: Paras. 15.1–15.7).

> *In many areas of population and development activities, non-governmental groups are already rightly recognized for their comparative advantage in relation to government agencies, because of innovative, flexible and responsive programme design and implementation, including grass-roots participation, and because quite often they are rooted in and interact with constituencies that are poorly served and hard to reach through government channels. (Para. 15.2)*

Furthermore,

> *[m]any of them have . . . a long history of involvement and participation in population-related activities, particularly family planning . . . Formal and informal organizations and networks, including grass-roots movements, merit greater recognition at the local, national and international levels as valid and valuable partners for the implementation of the present Programme of Action. (Para. 15.4)*

The unambiguous recognition of the crucially important role of NGOs and the concept of partnership in the Cairo Programme of Action came about because of the extraordinarily active participation of NGOs in the Cairo process and the clear acceptance by most of the governments of the NGO contribution and potential in the population sector. But seen from a historical perspective, NGOs have had to work very hard to reach this level of recognition.

NGOs IN THE BUCHAREST
PREPARATORY PROCESS

The NGOs which were most active in the Bucharest preparatory process were those directly involved in population issues. These included well known organizations such as IUSSP, IPPF, and the Population Council, and several others, like the Population Crisis Committee and the Population Institute, which had been established in 1969 following the beginning of the active US involvement – governmental and non-governmental – in population issues worldwide. Many of these NGOs were associated with a committee created by the CONGO to organize the Population Tribune, an NGO activity parallel to the Bucharest Conference.

The IUSSP was the cosponsor with the Population Division of the earlier international population conferences in Rome (1954) and Belgrade (1964). Given the intergovernmental character of the Bucharest Conference, it was not involved in organizing the Conference; its status there was that of an observer. But many of its members participated in their individual capacity in expert group meetings and other preparatory activities and were on national delegations as members and advisers. IUSSP also organized a series of 'distinguished' lectures at the Population Tribune. Their influence can be seen in the very large number of recommendations in the WPPA relating to technical and research issues. But when it came to the overriding political concerns and issues at the Conference, obviously it was the ministers, the political officials and the diplomats who had the greater say. IPPF was another international organization, several of whose national officials were included in official delegations, especially those from Asia and Europe. Family planning, however, did not figure as a major topic for public discussion and is rarely mentioned in the WPPA.

One of the more interesting events in Bucharest was the International Youth Population Conference, which took place prior to the opening of the official Conference (11–15 August 1974). The Conference was attended by approximately 250 participants, including many from developing countries. It foreshadowed the debate on population *vs* development at the main conference. After three days of intense and lively deliberations, it adopted an Appeal to the Youth of the World and a Statement from the International Youth Population Conference to the UN World Population Conference, which emphasized the integral inter-relationship between population, poverty alleviation and development.

The two documents include views coloured by the strong political and ideological orientations of some of the participating organizations. Referring to 'abject poverty, malnutrition, widespread disease, massive unemployment and shameful iniquity and injustice', the statement says that 'the primary causes of these conditions are the exploitative and repressive social, economic, and political structures and institutions, often the legacy of prolonged colonial oppression. The primary cause is not over-population, as some people falsely claim' (Angel, 1995: 622).

The paragraph that follows was added at the insistence of youth organizations actively involved in population activities such as WAY and the Young Women's Christian Association (YWCA):

> *a high rate of population growth in some countries adds to their existing social and economic problems. Measures to reduce a high rate of population growth in these respective countries will only be effective if they are part of a comprehensive and integrated strategy for rapid social and economic development.* (Angel, 1995: 622).

The Youth Conference designated a ten-person delegation to the main Conference and its statement was presented to the Conference by a representative of this delegation. His was one of the few NGO statements at the Conference. One cannot say that this statement had much of an impact on the Conference, but it did reflect fairly accurately many of the themes and issues that would come up for intensive discussion at the Conference.

The Population Tribune, which ran from 18 to 30 August 1974 was a bigger affair. It attracted 1350 participants, including both representatives of NGOs and individuals. 109 NGOs, with about 300 representatives, were accredited to the main Conference, and seven of them were given the opportunity to speak at the plenary sessions.

The Population Tribune, which was organized on the model of the parallel NGO activity at the Stockholm UN Conference on the Environment, had a full roster of activities, including lectures, panels and exhibitions. One of the widely publicized lectures at the Tribune was given by John D. Rockefeller III. He made the point that 'family planning alone was not enough and that it should be integrated with modern economic and social development that emphasizes an overriding moral purpose – to improve the lives of all the people to combat poverty, hunger and disease' (Harkavy, 1995: 66). The speech dismayed many of the supporters of family planning as such, but received a favourable response from those at the Conference who were pushing for an integrated approach to population and development.

NGOs also sponsored a daily newspaper called *The Planet*, which was widely distributed at the Conference. But as the Conference organizers had agreed before the Tribune was conceived, the Tribune did not take a common position on any issues before the Conference. Its objective was to provide a forum for the presentation and discussion of a variety of opinions and viewpoints, and in the view of Rosalind Harris, who was President of the CONGO at that time, this was fully accomplished.

The WPPA mentions NGOs in what would today be regarded a somewhat condescending manner. It says that '[t]he success of this Plan of Action will largely depend on the action taken by national Governments. To take action, Governments are urged to utilize fully the support of intergovernmental and non-governmental organizations' (UN, 1975: Recommendation 96). Another recommendation urges international NGOs

> to respond to the goals and policies of this Plan of Action by coordinating their activities with those of other non-governmental organizations, and with those of relevant bilateral and multilateral organizations, by expanding their support for national institutions and organizations dealing with population questions, and by cooperating in the promotion of widespread knowledge of the goals and policies of the Plan of Action, and, when requested, by supporting national and private institutions and organizations dealing with population questions. (UN, 1975: Recommendation 106)

The WPPA thus clearly assigned a secondary role to NGOs, compared with that of governments in the implementation of the 'goals and policies' of the WPPA.

In the early 1970s, many governments in Africa and Asia viewed NGOs with a certain amount of scepticism and suspicion. NGOs that were affiliated to international organizations or received contributions from abroad were suspected of reflecting foreign interests or concerns, while national or local NGOs that were active on policy issues were regarded as being either disruptive or confrontational. These views were reflected in the stance many governments took at the Bucharest Conference. These began to change as an increasing number of governments in these regions became more responsive to public debate, pressure and criticism.

In the post-Bucharest period, three developments regarding NGOs were particularly noticeable. First, the number of NGOs devoted to development, the environment and population increased tremendously. Many of them were established with foreign technical and financial assistance; others came into existence to respond to national or local situations or issues. Second, in many countries NGOs began receiving more funding from both governmental and non-governmental sources. Third, NGOs received increasing recognition and support from the international community, in particular the UN. In Bucharest, official accreditation at the main Conference was limited to the organizations in consultative status with ECOSOC. In Mexico, a broader interpretation of the rules permitted accreditation not only of the organizations listed with ECOSOC, but also of those that were recognized by a UN agency or organization. This enabled UNFPA, which maintained its own list of NGOs, to recommend the accreditation of several NGOs that were placed on its own list, but not that of ECOSOC.

NGOs AND THE MEXICO CONFERENCE

Prior to the Mexico Conference, NGOs involved in population and development activities organized a Working Group within the CONGO to contribute to the Mexico process. They held a large NGO Conference in Geneva in October 1983 to formulate their recommendations for Mexico, and were represented at the two meetings of the Mexico Preparatory Committee. Though no separate NGO tribune or forum took place in Mexico, NGOs were well represented at the Conference: 154 NGOs with 367 representatives were accredited by the Conference, and 16 of them had the opportunity to address the Conference. Moreover, 41 papers prepared by NGOs were distributed as background documents (Salas, 1984). NGOs were given daily briefings by the Conference Secretariat on the progress of the Conference and held frequent meetings of their own to discuss various issues and strategies.

The Mexico recommendations reflect the changes in governmental attitudes and perceptions towards NGOs. Mexico invited national NGOs

> *to continue, in accordance with national policies and laws, their pioneering work in opening up new paths and to respond quickly and flexibly to requests from Governments, intergovernmental and international non-governmental organizations, as appropriate, for the further implementation of the World Population Plan of Action.* (UN, 1984: Recommendation 84)

Governments were also urged 'to encourage the innovative activities of non-governmental organizations and to draw upon their expertise, experience and resources in implementing national programmes' (UN, 1984: Recommendation 84). The Mexico Conference thus gave recognition to the pioneering work of NGOs, their formulation and implementation of innovative activities and the importance of utilizing their expertise, experience and resources.

Recommendation 12 urged that in order to ensure that population and development programmes are responsive to local values and needs and that those directly affected are involved in the decision making process at all levels, the full participation of the community and concerned NGOs, in particular women's organizations, should be encouraged. Taking note of NGOs' financial needs, Recommendation 84 invited donors to increase their financial support.

Writing in *Populi* soon after the Mexico Conference, Dr Sai applauded the recognition accorded by Mexico to the NGOs:

> *it was interesting to take note of the recognition given in Mexico to the invaluable contributions made by non-governmental organizations. The original Plan of Action barely acknowledged the existence of NGOs while suggesting that they should take their lead from governments. Mexico put this matter straight by giving clear recognition to the pioneering and innovative activities through which NGOs have shaped solutions to population problems.* (Sai, 1984: 25)

In the period following the Mexico Conference, UNFPA continued to strengthen and enlarge its relations with a wide variety of NGOs. It sponsored two annual consultations with NGOS – one in New York and the other in Geneva. It provided support for the organization of several parliamentarians' conferences, and for meetings of youth and women's groups, at international and regional levels. The International Forum on Population in the Twenty-First Century (Amsterdam, 1989), which was organized by UNFPA to focus on operational experiences in the population field five years after Mexico, was attended by representatives of population, development and environmental NGOs, youth and women's groups, parliamentary organizations and research and academic institutions, and they all participated actively in the Forum's deliberations. The ICPD Secretariat, in developing its contacts and consultations with NGOs, was able to draw upon UNFPA's considerable and wide-ranging experience with NGOs.

NGOs AND THE CAIRO CONFERENCE

One of the most important questions the ICPD Secretariat had to grapple with, right at the beginning, concerned the kind of role NGOs would play in the ICPD process. Given the history of increasing collaboration between growing numbers of population- and development-related NGOs, UNFPA and the UN over the previous 20 years, there was no doubt in our mind that NGOs would want to play an active and important role and that we should seek to facilitate it. Some of us had also attended UNCED-related meetings, and had seen at first hand what a difference NGOs could make to the deliberations on important issues.

However, on the question of whether there should be a separate NGO tribune or forum at the Conference, the ICPD Secretariat's views evolved over 1990–1992. The size and character of the Conference had to be worked out before anything else. Initially, it was going to be a relatively modest event, probably devoted to updating the Bucharest and Mexico recommendations. The move towards enlarging the Conference, which was supported by numerous delegations and the submission of a new plan or programme of action to the Conference, which was proposed by the Secretary General of the Conference, also enlarged our perception of the role NGOs would play in the ICPD process. Then there was the question of costs. When the UN Secretary General issued his first communication on the Conference in mid-1990, the Secretariat was not quite sure how much money could be raised for the Conference. The US had not contributed to UNFPA since 1986 and it was not clear whether it would offer any substantial support to the Conference or any of its associated activities. As it turned out, the US gave an initial grant of US$500,000 for the Conference through the UN in 1991, followed by another US$500,000 in 1993. The Secretariat received promises of additional support from several other major donors, who also informed us that they would be willing to support NGO activities in the context of Cairo. Second, Dr Sadik wanted to ascertain the views of a variety of NGOs on whether there should be a parallel NGO meeting or whether the Secretariat should concentrate on helping NGO activities prior to the Conference so that they could contribute effectively to the formulation of the draft recommendations. This canvassing of views led her and members of the Secretariat to the conclusion in 1992 that there was a great deal of interest in and support for active NGO involvement in the preparatory process and in a parallel NGO tribune, on the part of the NGO community and also many governments and private foundations.

In 1992, the Conference Secretariat received funds from the Canadian International Development Agency (CIDA) to hire a full-time NGO Liaison Officer. In addition, a Junior Professional Officer was assigned to work with NGOs. This two-person unit was given the task of receiving and processing NGO requests for accreditation, with the help of several other staff members. The thoroughness with which it dealt with more than 1300 requests for accreditation can be judged by the fact that none of the recommendations by the Secretariat was turned down by the Preparatory Committee or by the Conference.

NGO ACCREDITATION

The Conference Secretariat found the process developed for NGO accreditation to the UNCED particularly relevant. Hundreds of environmental and development NGOs were interested in the preparatory process for the UNCED and many had no official status with the UN. The Preparatory Committee for the UNCED, at the urging of NGOs, established its own criteria for accrediting NGOs to the Preparatory Committee and the Rio Conference and decided to admit on a provisional basis a very large number of such NGOs that were not on the UN (ECOSOC) list. This set a precedent for the ICPD and several other major UN conferences. On 12 February 1993, ECOSOC decided upon a procedure that was similar to that used for the UNCED for accrediting NGOs (ECOSOC Resolution 1993/4).

ECOSOC recognized 'the importance of non-governmental part-icipation in the preparatory process and the Conference itself' and encouraged 'all support to enable representatives of non-governmental organizations from developing countries to participate fully'. This encouragement was treated by the Conference Secretariat as a mandate to raise funds also for the participation of NGOs from developing countries in the ICPD process. The Secretariat was able to get support from several bilateral agencies and foundations to enable NGOs from developing countries to be represented at PrepCom II, PrepCom III and the Conference itself.

The ECOSOC resolution 1993/4 laid down a detailed procedure for the participation of NGOs in the ICPD process. In addition to NGOs in consultative status with ECOSOC, other NGOs that wished to be accredited could apply to the Conference Secretariat. All such organiz-ations were expected to provide information on the organization's competence and relevance to the work of the Preparatory Committee, indicating the particular areas of the Conference preparations to which such competence and relevance pertained, and to provide adequate documentation on

(a) The purpose of the organization; (b) Information on its programmes and activities in areas relevant to the Conference and its preparatory process and in which country(ies) they are carried out; (c) Confirmation of its activities at the national and/or international level; (d) Copies of its annual reports with financial statements, and a list of members of the governing body and their country of nationality; and (e) A description of its membership, indicating the total number of members and their geographical distribution.

NGOs which are on the ECOSOC list have always been given an opportunity to address the ECOSOC or its subsidiary bodies. But this resolution opened the possibility also for other NGOs to briefly address the Preparatory Committee in plenary sessions as well its subsidiary bodies. 'If the number of requests is too large, the Preparatory Committee shall request the non-governmental organizations to form themselves into constituencies, each constituency to speak through one spokes-person.' Responding to the concern expressed by some delegates that NGOs might seek to get involved in the actual negotiating process, the Resolution said, '[i]n recognition of the intergovernmental nature of the International Conference on Population and Development, non-governmental organizations shall have no negotiating role in the work of the Conference and its preparatory process'. Pursuant to this decision, the Preparatory Committee accredited 396 NGOs at its second Session and another 538 at its third Session. The Conference itself admitted several more NGOs, bringing the total number of NGOs accredited to Cairo to 1254 representing 138 countries and territories (see Table 5.1).[1]

NGOs IN THE ICPD PROCESS

The NGO involvement in the ICPD process, which was limited in the case of the first Session of the Preparatory Committee to several population organizations on the ECOSOC list, grew substantially after the UNCED in June 1992. Many of the environment, development and women's NGOs had been so involved in the UNCED that they had little time for any other major activity. Once the UNCED was over, they turned their attention and energy towards the Cairo process. During 1992–1993, many NGOs participated in the regional conferences that were held in preparation for the ICPD.

To start with, there were a relatively small number at the Bali Conference for Asia and the Pacific, but many more participated in the subsequent regional conferences. IPPF and many other NGOs formulated their own contribution to the ICPD at their regular assemblies or conferences during 1992–1993.

The Proposed Conceptual Framework of the Draft Recommendations of the Conference (UN, 1993c) proposed a separate chapter devoted to the NGO sector: chapter XII, entitled 'Supporting a Workable Partnership'. The document pointed out that '[t]here is growing acceptance in many countries of the positive contribution which non-governmental groups can make to the development and implementation of population-related activities'. It therefore proposed 'that the contribution of community groups, non-governmental organizations, the private sector and other relevant participants be acknowledged' (Para. 44).

PrepCom II participants responded well to this proposal. A large number of delegations saw the need for a real partnership between governments, NGOs and the private sector, and felt that the Cairo Document should address the issue of adequate and reliable funding for the activities of NGOs. Though the private sector did not receive as much attention, there was no opposition to the view expressed by some delegations that the importance of the cost-effective services provided by the private sector to the family planning and reproductive health sector should be taken into account in devising future strategies. According to the Report of the Preparatory Committee, '[n]on-governmental organizations were seen not as substitutes for government action but as partners acting as catalysts for change, setting quality standards for population programmes and developing innovative approaches' (UN, 1993j: Para. 56).

NGOs played an extremely important role at PrepCom II. They organized themselves into thematic and regional caucuses, and

Table 5.1   NGOs Accredited to the ICPD by Region and Country

Sub-Saharan Africa (206)		Libya	1
Benin	1	Morocco	23
Botswana	2	Palestinian NGOs	8
Burkina Faso	12	Saudi Arabia	2
Burundi	1	Syria	2
Cameroon	12	Tunisia	5
Central African Republic	2	Turkey	4
Chad	1	Yemen	1
Congo	1		
Cote d'Ivoire	4	*Europe* (188)	
Equatorial Guinea	1	Albania	1
Ethiopia	12	Austria	5
Gambia, The	1	Belgium	16
Ghana	7	Bulgaria	2
Guinea (Conakry)	4	Croatia	1
Kenya	24	Cyprus	1
Lesotho	4	Czech Republic	3
Liberia	2	Denmark	5
Malawi	1	Estonia	1
Mali	3	Finland	1
Mauritius	5	France	13
Mozambique	6	Georgia	1
Namibia	2	Germany	14
Nigeria	22	Greece	3
Rwanda	5	Hungary	3
Senegal	10	Italy	8
Sierra Leone	5	Kazakhstan	1
South Africa	9	Latvia	1
Sudan	4	Lithuania	1
Tanzania	2	Moldova	1
Togo	5	Netherlands	14
Uganda	12	Norway	3
Zaire	8	Poland	2
Zambia	7	Romania	2
Zimbabwe	9	Russian Federation	3
		Slovak Republic	1
North Africa, Middle East (135)		Slovenia	1
Algeria	3	Spain	5
Bahrain	2	Sweden	6
Egypt	77	Switzerland	26
Iraq	1	Ukraine	3
Jordan	3	UK	39
Lebanon	3	Uzbekistan	1

Table 5.1   NGOs Accredited to the ICPD by Region and Country
(*continued*)

North America (286)		Jamaica	6
Canada	26	Haiti	2
USA	260	Netherlands Antilles	1
		Saint Lucia	1
Latin America (178)		Saint Vincent	1
Argentina	6	Trinidad and Tobago	5
Belize	1		
Bolivia	20	*Asia/Pacific* (238)	
Brazil	25	Australia	8
Chile	5	Bangladesh	26
Colombia	8	China	16
Costa Rica	8	Cook Islands	2
Cuba	1	Fiji	3
Dominican Republic	3	India	71
Ecuador	8	Indonesia	11
El Salvador	7	Japan	17
Guatemala	7	Korea	2
Guyana	3	Malaysia	4
Honduras	3	Maldives	2
Mexico	17	Mongolia	1
Nicaragua	6	Nepal	8
Panama	2	New Zealand	4
Paraguay	5	Pakistan	12
Peru	27	Papua New Guinea	1
Suriname	3	Philippines	25
Uruguay	4	Sri Lanka	12
Venezuela	10	Solomon Islands	3
		Thailand	3
Caribbean (22)		Tonga	2
Antigua	1	Viet Nam	2
Bahamas	1	Western Samoa	3
Barbados	3		
Granada	1	Total	1,254

formulated their positions on PrepCom issues on a day-to-day basis. One of the most effective of these caucuses was the Women's Caucus organized by WEDO, under the energetic leadership of Bella Abzug. WEDO, which grew out of an organization called Women's Foreign Policy Council/Women USA Fund Inc., had played a leading role in organizing the World Women's Congress for a Healthy Planet (Miami,

8–12 November 1991) to formulate recommendations on women's concerns and issues for Agenda 21. Subsequently it had also helped to organize a Women's Caucus at UNCED Preparatory Committee meetings which was extremely effective in promoting many women's concerns in the UNCED preparatory process.

The Women's Agenda 21, adopted at the Miami Congress, included a clear statement on women's reproductive health issues.

We condemn any attempt to deprive women of reproductive freedom or the knowledge to exercise that freedom.

We demand women-centred, women-managed comprehensive reproductive health care and family planning, including the right to prenatal care, safe and legal voluntary contraception and abortion, sex education and abortion. (WEDO, 1992: 20)

The UNCED Women's Caucus was able to get a number of major proposals included in Agenda 21, but, as pointed out earlier, the UNCED process did not particularly focus on population or reproductive health issues. However, at PrepCom II, Ms Abzug used the experience gained in the UNCED process to organize an expanded caucus, including environmental, population and development activists as well as those devoted to feminist causes.

The Women's Caucus at PrepCom II had an estimated membership of 132 women from 41 countries. They were all able to agree upon a common platform, even though it did not satisfy some of the more radical members. This expanded group produced a document entitled 'Suggested Revisions to the Conceptual Framework for the Draft Recommendation of the ICPD, Offered by Women's Groups from All Regions' (WEDO, 1993a). This document was given to all the NGOs as well as all the official delegations and many of its suggestions were picked up by them. The Women's Caucus emerged as one of the most successful lobbying groups at PrepCom II.

NGOs also organized regional caucuses at PrepCom II, and several organizations such as IPPF, CEDPA and the Commonwealth Medical Association brought together their own members and affiliates for regular briefings and discussions. NGOs received daily briefings from the Conference Secretariat, and were given the opportunity to place their position papers and proposals in various Conference rooms.

After PrepCom II, when the Conference Secretariat began to prepare the Draft Final Document, NGOs, along with governments, were invited to offer suggestions and proposals, and many of them responded with extensive drafts. WEDO, after consulting with its members, prepared a revised set of proposals and submitted it to the Secretariat in November 1993. These along with the proposals offered by other NGOs were extremely useful to the Secretariat in preparing the final draft of Chapter

XV, which was now entitled 'Partnership with the Non-Governmental Sector'.

NGOs also organized, in many countries, national and local level consultations on ICPD-related themes. For example, NGOs in India, with the help of the local office of the Ford Foundation and UNFPA, organized 18 consultative meetings in various regions of India between October 1993 and February 1994 (Singh, 1994). The conclusions and findings of these meetings were widely distributed among NGO activists at the local level. Several of the NGO representatives who participated in these meetings were able to obtain travel support to attend PrepCom III.

PrepCom III had an even larger contingent of NGOs than PrepCom II, with the attendance of more than 1000 NGO representatives. With funds provided by several bilateral agencies and foundations, the Conference Secretariat was able to bring NGO participants from a large number of developing countries; in other cases their attendance was made possible by grants provided by national governments, international organizations or local offices of donor agencies.

Many individual NGOs as well as NGOs representing specific constituencies spoke at the Plenary Session. Breaking with past tradition, NGOs representing specific constituencies were invited, at the discretion of the Chairman, to present their views at Working Group meetings and were, of course, free to circulate among government delegations their proposals for changes and additions. Though they were not expected to be directly involved in the negotiating sessions, they were in a position to lobby the delegates in the corridors and, as many NGO representatives were also on country delegations, they were able to communicate to governmental representatives NGO views and concerns on the evolving issues.

The Women's Caucus was, again, among the most active lobbying groups. Its meetings were attended by more than 300 women and men from 44 countries. The Caucus organized itself into five task forces, which prepared and circulated priority amendments for each chapter. The Caucus was helped immensely in its task by the fact that many of its members (including Ms Abzug) were also on their respective national delegations and were able to communicate the views of the Women's Caucus to their delegations and vice versa. At a smaller level, a group of youth organizations working together was able to get specific language concerning several youth concerns inserted into the document that came out of PrepCom III.

Following PrepCom III, WEDO prepared a further set of proposals entitled 'Recommendations on Bracketed Text in the Draft Programme of Action of the ICPD' (WEDO, 1994). These were offered in advance to a number of delegations and distributed at the Conference to all the delegations 'on behalf of 280 NGOs from 62 countries'. During the Cairo Conference, the Women's Caucus met daily at the NGO Forum from 9 to 10 am to review developments at the Conference and to plan strategies. Several individual NGOs that had a large number of representatives at the NGO Forum and the NGO Forum itself also held regular briefings for their constituents.

In total, 37 NGO representatives spoke at the Conference. They were also able to observe the proceedings of the Main Committee and to find opportunities to meet with official delegations. However, it would be true to say that their influence was probably at its highest during PrepCom III, where many significant proposals made by them were incorporated in the Draft Final Document. At the Conference itself, NGO representatives, including those who formed part of the official delegations, sought to reinforce support for their views on several of the bracketed phrases by interacting actively with the delegates.

The NGO Forum which met from 4 to 12 September 1994 was organized by a Planning Committee established by the CONGO and involved more than 260 NGOs. The Planning Committee was able to raise funds from a variety of sources for the NGO Forum, and appointed a small staff to look after the organization of the Forum. The Committee, in consultation with the Conference Secretariat, also negotiated the agreement for the site (Cairo's Indoor Sports Stadium Complex) and other necessary facilities with the Government of Egypt.

NGO EVENTS

The NGO Forum attracted 4200 participants, including representatives of more than 1500 NGOs from 133 countries. Developing countries were well represented, thanks to travel assistance provided by governments, bilateral agencies, foundations and the Conference Secretariat. On average, 90 sessions were organized each day, including plenary meetings, keynote lectures, workshops, thematic and organizational meetings, panel discussions, training sessions, briefings and press conferences, NGO exhibits and an impressive Multimedia Centre (UN, 1995a).

Following the pattern it had set for its own activities at Bucharest, IUSSP organized a Distinguished Lecture Series at the NGO Forum. Earlier, in preparation for the Conference, it had organized a one-day special session at its triennial Conference in Montreal (August 1993) to analyse the outcome of the expert group meetings in preparation for the ICPD, as well as national workshops on ICPD-related themes in Belgium and Germany in cooperation with the governments concerned. Serving as the principal international organization of demographers and other population specialists, IUSSP has always emphasized its scientific and technical role in the series of international population conferences.

Two other major NGO events took place in conjunction with the Cairo Conference. The International NGO Youth Consultation on Population and Development, organized by nine youth and youth-related international NGOs, was held at the Cairo International Scout Centre from 31 August to 4 September 1994. Its programme provided an opportunity for more than 100 youth representatives from all major regions of the world to discuss several Conference-related topics, such as youth and reproductive health, teenage pregnancy, safe sexual behaviour, environmental protection, human rights and sustainable development.

The Cairo Youth Consultation was similar to that organized by a group of youth NGOs prior to the Bucharest Conference. But this time around the discussions were held without any tension among the youth representatives. The end of the Cold War had removed several contentious issues from the list of items for discussion and since Bucharest many youth organizations, particularly at the local level, had acquired considerable experience in running youth and population programmes. Participants in the Youth Conference were able to agree easily on the Cairo Youth Declaration on Population and Development, for presentation to the Cairo Conference. The Declaration asked governments to commit themselves to 'implementing equal and genuine partnership with youth and their NGOs from the beginning; developing trust between partners; respecting autonomy of developing countries in so far as developed countries are concerned; coordinating and networking between projects; [and] promoting sustainable projects'. At the same time, it urged the UN system to strengthen its support for youth NGOs (Family Life Education Sub-Committee, CONGO, 1994: 10–11).

The other NGO event was the International Conference of Parliamentarians on Population and Development, which took place in Cairo on 3–4 September 1994, with the participation of 300 parliamentarians from 107 countries. The Parliamentarians Conference, which was hosted by the Government of Egypt, was organized by a coalition of parliamentary groups: the Asian Forum of Parliamentarians on Population and Development, the Global Committee of Parliamentarians on Population and Development, the Inter-American Parliamentary Group on Population and Development, the International Medical Parliamentarians Organization, and Parliamentarians for Global Action. The Cairo Declaration on Population and Development, which was adopted by this meeting, underscored the mainstream views on various topics that had emerged at PrepCom III. The Declaration was presented to the Cairo Conference by the Chairman of its Steering Committee, Shin Sakurai, a member of parliament from Japan. Also, in the context of the ICPD, the Inter-Parliamentary Union (IPU) organized a Parliamentarians Day at the People's Assembly in Cairo on 7 September. At the conclusion of this event, IPU submitted a statement to the ICPD, emphasizing its interest in population and development issues.

Walter Mertens, in a monograph he wrote for the IUSSP, offers an interesting commentary on the role NGOs played in the ICPD process:

it should be admitted that the increasing importance of NGOs also presents certain problems which are not always sufficiently recognized. Many NGOs normally arise from concerns with particular issues about which they have strong feelings. Three dangers follow from this situation. One is lack of focus on the main theme of the Conference. The second is that certain NGOs, in the eagerness to press their programs, frequently promote points of view which are not sufficiently corroborated by detached scientific analysis. The third is a lack of democratic representation because only the most vocal opinions are present. Both benefits and dangers were very much visible at ICPD. (Mertens, 1995: 16)

Most NGOs that were involved in the Cairo process were indeed much more concerned with specific issues or themes and much less with the overall theme of the Conference. But what was remarkable about the ICPD process was the emergence of ad hoc coalitions and networks of NGOs that cut across their more immediate concerns and worked together to promote selected proposals very effectively, despite deep differences among them on many other issues. The Women's Caucus was one of these coalitions, including in its ranks members with widely different viewpoints, but coalescing to agree on a common strategy for the ICPD. The ICPD also had a number of NGOs with extremist or absolutist views and they formed their own coalitions. Many of them addressed the Preparatory Committee and Conference sessions and had the opportunity to distribute their literature among the delegates and to lobby them. As it happened, they were unable to persuade the Conference to accept their views.

The decision making process at UN conferences has now become an increasingly complex and difficult process, with many actors. In the case of the ICPD, however, two things were very clear. First, NGOs were very much part of the decision making process. Second, they were among those responsible for the acceptance of a programme of action that broke new ground on many policy and programme issues.

Chapter XV of the Programme of Action, which was adopted by the Conference without any major changes in the text submitted by PrepCom III, goes much further than Bucharest and Mexico in emphasizing the crucial role of NGOs in population and development activities. The Programme of Action recognizes unequivocally that 'non-governmental organizations should have a key role in national and international development processes' (UN, 1995a: Para. 15.8). It stresses the import-ance of 'dialogue' with NGOs, 'full respect for their autonomy' and the need for governments and intergovernmental organizations to integrate NGOs in their decision making.

Respect for the autonomy of NGOs is emphasized in several other recommendations (eg Paras. 15.10 and 15.11). While arguing for auto-nomy, NGOs also wanted greater financial and technical resources for their activities, and the Conference endorsed their needs in this regard

(Para. 15.10). The Conference asked governments, intergovernmental organizations and international financial institutions to share adequate information and documentation with NGOs to ensure 'transparency and accountability and effective division of labour' (Para. 15.10). On their part, NGOs were also asked to ensure 'transparency of their activities' (Para. 15.12). Supporting the practice of including NGO representatives in governmental delegations (many delegations at PrepCom II, PrepCom III, and the Cairo Conference included NGO representatives at government cost or, in other cases, NGO representatives who had been able to find travel support from other sources), the Conference suggested that '[g]overnments, where appropriate, should include representation of non-governmental organizations on country delegations to regional and international forums where issues on population and development are discussed' (Para. 15.12).

COOPERATION WITH THE PRIVATE SECTOR

Cairo also made recommendations on possible areas of cooperation with the private sector (health service providers, pharmaceutical and contraceptive manufacturers, marketing groups and so on). The previous two conferences had not touched this topic. Until the 1980s, experiences in the area of direct collaboration with private sector organizations were limited to the US and, to a lesser extent, Canada, the UK, Germany and a few other countries. There was a brief discussion at the Amsterdam Forum of the role of the private sector and the GA Resolution on the outcome of the Forum refers to the need to study cost recovery. At the beginning of the 1990s, UNFPA began to study the role of the private sector in meeting contraceptive requirements and the UNFPA's Procurement Unit became a major actor in the area of procuring contraceptives for developing countries. These developments had a direct bearing on the interest shown by Cairo in the role of the private sector.

Paras. 15.16–15.20 outline Cairo's approach to the private sector. Cairo urges governments and non-governmental and international organizations to

intensify their cooperation with the private, for-profit sector in matters pertaining to population and sustainable development in order to strengthen the contribution of that sector in the implementation of population and development programmes, including the production and delivery of quality contraceptive commodities and services with appropriate information and education, in a socially responsible, culturally sensitive, acceptable and cost-effective manner. (Para. 15.16)

Cairo also encourages the exchange of information and research findings between non-profit and profit-oriented organizations (Para. 15.17) and the provision of financial and other types of assistance by the profit-oriented sector to NGOs (Para. 15.19).

In order to promote greater involvement of the private sector in family planning and reproductive health programmes, Cairo strongly encourages governments

> *to set standards for service delivery and review legal, regulatory and import policies to identify and eliminate those policies that unnecessarily prevent or restrict the greater involvement of the private sector in efficient production of commodities for reproductive health, including family planning, and in service delivery. Governments, taking into account cultural and social differences, should strongly encourage the private sector to meet its responsibilities regarding consumer information dissemination.* (Para. 15.18)

The last paragraph in this section is on the provision of services by the private sector.

> *Private-sector employees should continue to devise and implement special programmes that help meet their employees' needs for information, education and reproductive health services, and accommodate their employees' needs to combine work and family responsibilities. Organized health-care providers and health insurers should also continue to include family planning and reproductive health services in the package of health benefits they provide.* (Para. 15.20)

The unprecedented involvement of NGOs in the ICPD process has gained them the recognition they fully deserve, and for the first time they are being regarded as partners in population and development activities. At the international level, the NGOs' role as representatives of civil society will continue to become more important. Most of the networks and coalitions of NGOs that emerged during the ICPD process show every sign of continuing and strengthening their role in monitoring the implementation of the ICPD Programme of Action and holding governments and the international community accountable for the promises they made at Cairo.

At the national level, policy-related and practical issues need to be sorted out in many countries, particularly as they relate to the legal autonomy of the NGOs and the fulfilment on their part of financial, accounting and auditing requirements. As Cairo pointed out, NGOs themselves will have to become more transparent in their activities, in order to ensure greater community participation and public support. As for the private sector, its role in the provision of information and services is bound to increase in the future. Continuing dialogue between the private sector, governments and international organizations will help to ensure that this sector responds to demonstrated needs and provides quality services.

6   MOBILIZING RESOURCES FOR POPULATION PROGRAMMES

Cairo was unusual among the major UN conferences in that it provided fairly specific estimates of the funds that would be needed from national and external resources to implement the 20-year programme it proposed in the areas of reproductive health and related population data and analysis activities. These estimates, which suggest that up to two-thirds of the costs should be met by the countries themselves while the other third should be provided by external resources, were agreed to by both developed and developing countries.

Cairo did not attempt to cost the funding targets for reaching the goals in other areas of social development that its Programme of Action had affirmed. What it did do was to note that additional resources would be needed for other social development goals and it asked governments, NGOs and the international community to strive to mobilize the resources needed to meet the commitments made by governments and the international community at previous UN conferences.

On the broader theme of development cooperation, Cairo asked the international community to

> strive for the fulfillment of the agreed target of 0.7 percent of the gross national product for overall official development assistance and endeavor to increase the share of funding for population and development programmes commensurate with the scope and scale of activities required to achieve the objectives and goals of the present Programme of Action. (UN, 1995a: Para. 14.11)

It was much more specific in stating the requirements for the population sector. It spelled out the amounts needed from donor countries for population activities (in 1993 dollars): US$5.7 billion in 2000, US$6.1 billion in 2005, US$6.8 billion in 2010, and US$7.2 billion in 2015.

HISTORICAL PERSPECTIVE

The first global conference on population – the WPC (Bucharest, 1974) – was held at a time of increasing support for population activities, but the Conference did not discuss any specific resource estimates for population assistance. With the establishment of the large-scale population programme of the USAID in 1968 and the beginning of UNFPA's operations in 1969, the scope and volume of international population assistance had grown rapidly in the early 1970s (see Table 6.1).

The total amount went up from US$58 million in 1968 to US$257 million in 1974. An increasing number of developing countries had begun to formulate and implement family planning and other population programmes, and the major donor countries (Australia, Canada, Denmark, Finland, Germany, Japan, the Netherlands, Norway, Sweden, the UK and the US) were willing to commit increasing amounts for such programmes.

It was also becoming clear that UNFPA and the bilateral donors would need to provide more funds to meet the increasing demand for assistance from developing countries. But there was no way that this increasing demand could have been translated at that time into precise estimates. Rafael Salas, Executive Director of UNFPA at that time, used to talk about the need to double UNFPA resources. But this was predicated on increasing the capacity of developing countries to absorb more funds for population activities.

The WPPA adopted at Bucharest issued a general appeal that urged donor countries 'to increase their assistance to developing countries in accordance with the goals of the Second United Nations Development Decade', recognizing at the same time that 'in view of the magnitude of the problems and the consequent national requirement for funds, considerable expansion of international assistance in the population field is required for the proper implementation of this Plan of Action' (UN, 1975: Recommendation 104).

Another recommendation of the Bucharest Conference 'suggested that the expanding, but still insufficient, international assistance in population and development matters requires increased cooperation'; and in this context urged UNFPA, in cooperation with all organizations responsible for international population assistance, 'to produce a guide for international assistance in population matters which would be made available to recipient countries and institutions and be revised periodically' (UN, 1975: Recommendation 105). In response, UNFPA issued the first *Guide to Sources of International Population Assistance* in 1976. The Guide, which has been issued every three years since then, provides factual information on bilateral and multilateral agencies as well as on foundations and NGOs that support population programmes.

Table 6.1 International Population Assistance (Current US Dollars, Millions)

Year	Population assistance	Year	Population assistance	Year	Population assistance	Year	Population assistance
1961	6	1968	58	1975	281	1982	429	1989	801
1962	5	1969	86	1976	304	1983	432	1990	972
1963	11	1970	125	1977	349	1984	523	1991	1306
1964	16	1971	169	1978	394	1985	588	1992	1033
1965	18	1972	186	1979	455	1986	678	1993	1310
1966	34	1973	211	1980	476	1987	629	1994	1637
1967	30	1974	254	1981	491	1988	695	1995	2034

Sources: Figures for 1961–1979 are from Gille (1982); figures for 1980–1985 are from UNFPA (1996); and the figure for 1995 is from UNFPA (1997a).

Starting in 1973–1974, UNFPA also began to issue an annual *Inventory of Population Projects in Developing Countries*. This publication put together data and information provided by donor governments, UNFPA and other intergovernmental organizations and NGOs on individual projects supported by them in developing countries and the amounts allocated to these, but there was no attempt to provide any assessment of the need or demand for population assistance.

Ten years after Bucharest, the International Conference on Population issued another general appeal for increased funding for population in the context of the International Development Strategy for the Third United Nations Development Decade, which was similar to that of the Bucharest Conference. However, taking note of the view expressed by many developing countries that any increase in population assistance should not come at the expense of development assistance in other areas, the Mexico Conference also asked that 'increased contributions for population and population-related programmes ... should not be detrimental to the levels of economic development assistance in other areas' (UN, 1984: Recommendation 82).

A few years after the Mexico Conference, UNFPA issued its first comprehensive report on international population assistance, *Global Population Assistance Report, 1982–1985* (UNFPA, 1988). UNFPA had been urged by several donors, foundations and NGOs to prepare such a report, because the Organization for Economic Cooperation and Development (OECD) which used to collect and analyse such data had decided to discontinue the exercise. This first UNFPA report, which was prepared with the help of Dorothy Nortman, was several years in the making, as the methodology for the collection and analysis of data needed to be revised and updated. The report finally came out in 1988. Starting in 1989, UNFPA began issuing the report on an annual basis, and it has become a popular document among programme managers and researchers and among participants in population-related meetings and conferences.

UNFPA REVIEW AND ASSESSMENT

The first serious attempt at estimating the specific amounts needed for population activities was made in the context of a comprehensive review and assessment of its operational experience undertaken by UNFPA during 1987–1989. For this purpose, UNFPA used the data generated by the World Fertility Survey, subsequent Demographic and Health Surveys and three draft studies that offered estimates of requirements in the year 2000.[1] Two of these studies did not cover China. By including China and making some other adjustments to include the contributions of private users, UNFPA came up with estimates for three areas: family planning, data and research, and MCH.

CPR was the major determinant for assessing future needs in the population sector. As a UNFPA report submitted to its Governing Council in June 1989 suggested:

> [p]erhaps the simplest technique for forecasting financial requirements for family planning services is to calculate future costs in terms of the average annual cost per contraceptive user and of projected number of users by the year 2000. Most experts believe that the per capita cost varies widely across countries and that best estimates range between $10 and $20. Other methods indirectly estimating the per capita user cost also confirm the wide variation in that figure. For example, a simple analysis of dividing annual expenditure for family planning by the number of estimated users . . . indicates that, in a majority of cases, the per capita cost varies between $8 and $11. A study undertaken by the World Bank in 1985 estimates the per capita cost to range between $10 and $15. Also, a simple ratio of estimated total annual expenditure for family planning in all developing countries in 1987 ($3 billion) and total number of projected users (326 million) also yield some per capita user cost of around $10. All these estimates are affected by a host of factors, including mode of service delivery, national per capita income, exchange rates, inflation rates, duration of programme effort, programme efficiency, attribution of direct costs to family planning services and so forth.
>
> On the other hand, a recent study has attempted to estimate the per capita cost of users by disaggregating the cost of commodities required and the cost of service delivery for the total number of projected users in the year 2000. The average cost per user in the year 2000 by this method is estimated at $15. Thus, a conservative estimate of per user cost seems to range between $10 and $15. On the basis of these estimates, and adopting a crude average of $10–$15, we can estimate global costs to accommodate 500 million users by the year 2000. These costs range from $5.0 billion to $7.5 billion at 1987 prices and exchange rates. (UN, 1989: 22–23)

The UNFPA report also suggested a way of calculating the costs of data collection and analysis by using per capita costs for census and related activities in the year 2000, based on an average cost of US$1.00–US$1.20. For other types of population activities, estimates were prepared by taking the relative ratio of past combined expenditures for family planning and censuses to expenditures for all other population activities.

AMSTERDAM FORUM

A combination of these methodologies was used by UNFPA to prepare the estimates for the International Forum on Population in the Twenty-First Century held in Amsterdam in 1989 (and basically for preparing all subsequent estimates).[2] The working document prepared by UNFPA for the Forum suggested that these estimates should be considered under three broad categories: (1) family planning – a minimum of US$5.6 billion to reach the UN medium variant population projection (though the document cautioned that the costs for reaching this goal could run as high as US$11 billion);[3] (2) other population activities including data, research, information and communication and policy development and analysis – annual costs in the year 2000 in the range of US$3.1 billion to US$4.6 billion; and (3) safe motherhood, grouping together activities aimed at lowering infant and maternal mortality and improving the health of the family – the annual costs would range between US$4.1 billion and US$7.6 billion in the year 2000 (UNFPA, 1989c).

Joseph E Wheeler, then Chairman of the OECD Development Assistance Committee, who was invited to address the Forum from the viewpoint of resources, concurred with the proposals outlined in the document. In his view 'the estimated annual costs were important not so much in terms of whether or not they were accurate but rather as an indication of the movement in the right direction from the amount available for those items today' (UNFPA, 1989a: 50).

When it came to preparing the Amsterdam Declaration, the Drafting Committee, chaired by Haryono Suyono (then head of the Family Planning Coordination Board of Indonesia), chose to focus strategically on two of the three estimates – 'family planning' and 'other population activities' – regarding these as the core population activities. In its view, the estimates for 'safe motherhood', while important in their own context, did not form part of the core activities. The total estimates were, therefore, brought down, excluding those for safe motherhood, and rounded at US$9 billion. US$9 billion was the figure included in the Amsterdam Declaration on a Better Life for Future Generations proposed by the Drafting Committee and adopted, with minor changes, by the Forum participants.

The Declaration noted that the total annual expenditures on family planning and other population activities in the developing countries in 1987 amounted to approximately US$4.5 billion; taking into account the increasing demand for such activities, the annual costs for population programmes in the year 2000 would come to around US$9 billion. The Declaration called upon all countries 'to make every effort to provide the financial resources necessary to reach the medium variant population projection by the year 2000, *viz.* a total of almost US$9 billion a year for core population activities' (UNFPA, 1989a: 9). Essentially what was being proposed was the doubling of the allocations for family planning and other population activities in little more than a decade.

A few months after the Forum, UNFPA prepared a report examining the implications of the Amsterdam Forum, and submitted it to its Governing Council in June 1990. The report underscored the conclusion reached by the Forum that the minimum total amount needed in the year 2000 to support population activities would be in the order of US$9 billion from all sources. 'This estimate is based upon an assessment of the annual cost – from all sources – for providing family planning services in the developing countries to the 535 million couples that would have to be practising contraception in the year 2000, as well as for undertaking other support population activities' (UN, 1990: 16). The report noted that this would require a doubling of resources needed for population programmes from US$4.5 billion to the projected US$9 billion in the year 2000, and suggested the following formula for sharing the target: 50 per cent from domestic sources, another 45 per cent from international donors and the remainder from the World Bank and NGOs.

When the Amsterdam Forum was first brought to the attention of the GA at its 44th session, the GA noted with appreciation the Amsterdam Declaration but did not comment on the US$9 billion target. It did request the Executive Director of UNFPA to 'examine, in particular, the implications for the population programmes of the Declaration and to develop further the analysis of resource requirements for international population assistance' (GA Resolution 44/210). At its next session in 1990, the GA was much more forthcoming. In a resolution on population and development, it specifically took note of the US$9 billion figure, when it urged

> *all Governments, each according to its capacity, concerned international and regional organizations, including the World Bank, and non-governmental organizations to make every effort to mobilize the resources required for population activities, which are estimated at $9 billion, taking into account the potential for user contribution, where feasible and advisable.* (GA Resolution 45/216)

The reference to user contributions was brought in at the insistence of the Netherlands delegate, who felt that family planning and related activities should become progressively self-financing.

For the next two or three years, UNFPA and several other population organizations used the US$9 billion target in their resource development campaigns. In a complementary fashion, the proposal to double the allocation to population sectors within official development assistance (ODA) from around 2 per cent to 4 per cent by the year 2000 was also highlighted in these campaigns, noting in particular the case of Norway, which was already allocating 4 per cent of its ODA to the population sector.

ICPD PREPARATORY ACTIVITIES

In organizing various expert group meetings for the Cairo Conference, the ICPD Secretariat chose the Amsterdam target figure as the benchmark for resource requirements. A paper presented by Mr Sinding at the Expert Group Meeting on Population Policies and Programmes (Cairo, 12–16 April 1992) noted that in 1990, the total volume of international population assistance (including World Bank loans) amounted to around

US$971 million. The demand for population assistance was growing rapidly because of increasing governmental commitment to family planning and MCH programmes, and rising demand for services. How to keep pace with this rising demand constituted a major challenge for both the developing countries and the donors.

Another report, *Global Population Assistance 1982–1990* (UNFPA, 1992b), pointed out that while population assistance in current dollars had grown in the 1960s at an average annual rate of 45 per cent (starting from a very small base), it had declined to around 10 per cent in the 1970s and about 7 per cent in the 1980s.

In this context, the participants in the Cairo Expert Group Meeting welcomed the Amsterdam Forum's call for a doubling of support to the population sector by the year 2000, but they also noted that 'the funding environment had changed. The AIDS crisis had continued to present ever-growing needs, while Eastern Europe and the environment represented "new", competing needs. In addition, the economic situation of donor countries themselves had not improved' (UN, 1992d: Para. 66).

Recommendation 13 of the Expert Group suggested the doubling of international assistance by the year 2000, in line with the Amsterdam Declaration:

> [i]n order to meet the existing need and rapidly growing demand for family planning services and to respond to the growing requests for assistance in the population field from Governments and non-governmental organizations, multilateral and bilateral donors should strive to at least double their 1990 contributions to population programmes by the year 2000, as was endorsed in the Amsterdam Declaration on a Better Life for Future Generations.

Recommendation 14 emphasized the need to generate greater domestic resources and the importance of providing the highest quality of services to all groups:

> [d]eveloping countries should make all possible efforts to generate domestic resources to support service-delivery programmes and the provision of contraceptives, including the selective use of user fees and other forms of cost-recovery, cost-sharing, social marketing, and gaining access to local sources of philanthropy, inter alia. In doing so, they should take all necessary measures to ensure the availability of the highest possible quality of services to all groups and to take special care to protect the interests and meet the needs of those least able to pay.

The Expert Group Meeting on Family Planning, Health and Family Well-Being (Bangalore, 26–30 October 1992) was another technical meeting that commented on the need for additional resources. It strongly reiterated the appeal to governments and international and non-governmental organizations to provide additional resources for family planning (UN, 1993b: Recommendation 27). It also pointed out that *in order to better address the quantity of resources required, further work is needed to estimate all the component costs of family planning programmes. At the same time, more attention must be paid to cost-effectiveness, efficiency, cost recovery, cost-subsidization, community-resource mobilization, local production of contraceptives, where appropriate, and other mechanisms to ensure the optimum use of existing resources.* (Recommendation 28)

Many of these themes would be underscored by both government and NGO representatives at regional meetings as well as at the Preparatory Committee meetings in 1993–1994. Recommendations on all of these themes are included in the Programme of Action.

All five of the regional conferences organized by the regional commissions, in cooperation with UNFPA, urged increasing support from donor governments and the international community for population and development activities. Four of the five (Bali, Dakar, Geneva and Amman) also referred to the specific recommendation in the Amsterdam Declaration urging donors to increase their assistance in the field of population to US$9 billion in total by the year 2000 (UN, 1994a). Two of the conferences (Bali and Dakar) further urged donors to allocate at least 4 per cent of ODA to population, as recommended by the Amsterdam Forum. Dakar and Geneva urged that in providing population assistance, higher priority should be given to Africa.

The Geneva Conference, as was to be expected from an event attended by most of the donors in the population field, formulated the largest number of recommendations (18 in total) on 'international cooperation in the field of population', grouping them under six sub-headings: cooperation within the region, cooperation with developing countries, the commitment, basic principles of cooperation, objectives of cooperation, and action (UN, 1993f). Taking note of the problems within its own region, the Conference recommended that governments should, as a matter of urgency, assist the countries in transition, particularly in the field of reproductive health, including family planning, in the implementation of reforms in the health systems, in the field of migration and in developing and implementing integrated activities on health–population–environment issues. At the global level, the Conference noted that there is already a large and growing demand for family planning services. While endorsing intensified efforts to ensure the availability of family planning services to all those who wish to make use of them, the Conference called upon donors to consider a significant increase in their development assistance allocated for population activities. The negotiating positions on resource mobilization taken by members of the EU at PrepCom III and at the Conference were largely based on these recommendations.

FUNDING ESTIMATES

While these preparatory activities were taking place in 1992–1993, the ICPD Secretariat also became engaged in the task of updating and revising the estimates for funding needed for population activities. It came to the conclusion that this would require information at three levels: domestic spending, international assistance, and estimates of the unmet needs converted into dollars and cents. A system for gathering data on international population assistance had already been established by UNFPA by the early 1980s, even though the comparability of data provided by donors essentially depended on their own interpretation of what constituted population activities. The gathering of data on domestic spending proved much more difficult, as in many countries data for family planning and other reproductive health programmes formed part of the general data on health expenditures and in other countries there was a lack of adequate or reliable data. When it came to estimating the cost of meeting unmet needs, the methodology developed for estimating family planning costs was in place. The seminal work done by Parker Mauldin on assessing contraceptive requirements and the demand for contraceptive commodities in developing countries in the 1990s was extremely helpful in this regard.[4] It was much more difficult to work out estimates for other reproductive health services.

The Proposed Conceptual Framework of the Draft Recommendations of the Conference (UN, 1993c), which was presented by the Secretariat to PrepCom II, did not go into any of these issues. In chapter XI.B of the proposed outline of the recommendations, entitled 'International Cooperation', it simply pointed out that

> *the existing spectrum of intergovernmental cooperation relating to population issues requires recommendations for its further development. Attention should be given to cooperation between the developing countries as well as to assistance by the developed countries to their developing country partners. It is proposed that this section also address the interrelationship between assistance directed to population-related activities and international cooperation connected to the broader areas of socioeconomic development and sustainability. (Para. 43)*

The Secretariat was thus signalling the need for the Conference to deal with three major themes under international cooperation: (1) cooperation among developing countries themselves (South–South cooperation); (2) population assistance to be provided by donors; and (3) the interrelationship between population assistance and overall ODA.

During the PrepCom II discussions, the need for updating and revising the estimates of resource requirements was noted and emphasized by many delegations. The Chairman's Summary of these discussions suggested that

The Amsterdam Declaration on a Better Life for Future Generations, the only international forum to have addressed the issue of resource mobilization for population activities, should be redefined in this respect, so as to provide the Cairo Conference with more precise estimates of the resources required over the next decade. (UN, 1993j: Para. 59)

The Summary also noted that 'delegations suggested a broadening of the scope of resource mobilization beyond family planning to encompass sexual and reproductive health care' (UN, 1993j: Para. 54).

Following PrepCom II, UNFPA undertook a survey of selected developing countries, in cooperation with its field offices, to determine the range and scope of their allocations for population activities. About 20 countries responded and the estimated total of domestic expenditure provided to PrepCom III and the Cairo Conference was worked out on the basis of these responses. Within the Secretariat, we were conscious of the inadequacy of the data collected and agreed that similar enquiries and surveys would have to be conducted on a regular basis and that the UN would have to assist the countries in developing or refining the systems for collecting and analysing the relevant data.

Updated information on the volume of international population assistance was obtained from the annual enquiries conducted in the context of the UNFPA report, *Global Population Assistance*. The report was prepared by the University of Michigan between 1988 and 1991. Starting in 1992, UNFPA decided to prepare the report using its own staff resources.

The third area of enquiry was sought to assess the parameters of the demand or need for information and services with a view to developing more precise resource estimates. The discussions at PrepCom II, and the subsequent consultations with both experts and programme managers brought up four major changes in the estimation process. First, the Secretariat sought to define resource requirements in the context of the 'unmet need' of couples and individuals for services. This marked a significant departure from the Amsterdam Declaration, even though the methodology for developing cost estimates remained essentially the same (projected numbers of users of family planning, multiplied by the estimated cost per user). The Amsterdam goals were articulated in the context of attaining the fertility levels projected in the UN medium variant population projections. In contrast, the new estimates were based on existing levels of assessed 'unmet need'.[5] This approach emphasizes the need to provide the widest possible choices and options to individuals and couples in the area of reproductive health,[6] with a view to providing universal access to reproductive health care. These two approaches are not really that far apart. Recent research indicates that making family planning services available to all those women who wish to space or limit births would reduce fertility levels to between the medium variant and the low variant projections of the UN. Second, the Secretariat responded to the request to develop resource estimates in the broader context of reproductive health, and to take into account such newly emerging themes as HIV/AIDS prevention and the needs and requirements of the 'economies in transition' (Eastern and Central Europe and Central Asia). Third, the Secretariat disaggregated the global estimates by region. This proved politically very important, as delegates and NGO representatives from different geographical regions were able to see more clearly what the global figures meant for their own specific regions. Fourth, an attempt was made for the first time to include in the global estimates numbers of unmarried individuals and couples. The enquiries undertaken under the World Fertility Survey and the Demographic and Health Survey projects largely focused only on married couples; obtaining an accurate understanding of contraceptive use among the unmarried was considered rather problematic because of sociocultural traditions and taboos in many developing countries. Mr Mauldin included in his studies estimates of contraceptive use among the unmarried for sub-Saharan Africa and Latin America, but not for Asia. In its work, the Secretariat included a conservative estimate of contraceptive use among the unmarried in Asia, and added estimates for short-term assistance to the countries with economies in transition.

Several NGOs also wanted the Secretariat to develop resource estimates for other areas of social development such as education for girls. For this purpose, the Secretariat sought the help of other UN agencies: WHO and UNICEF for updating the costs for MCH/safe motherhood activities, and UNESCO for updating the costs for Education for All, with particular reference to girls' education. These updates were provided to the delegates at PrepCom III for their information.

Our own work focused on developing the resource estimates within the 20-year framework of goals and objectives proposed by Dr Sadik, Secretary General of the Conference, and agreed to in principle at PrepCom II for family planning and reproductive health services and related data, research and analysis activities. The Secretariat convened a meeting in New York on 8 November 1993, which was attended not only by technical staff from the UN Population Division and UNFPA, but also by experts with considerable experience in estimating resource requirements for population programmes. The organizations they came from included the World Bank, USAID, the Rockefeller Foundation, Population Action International (PAI) (formerly the Population Crisis Committee), Family Health International, the University of North Carolina, Futures Group International and the Population Council.

A background paper presented to this meeting provided a review of the prior estimates made available to the Amsterdam Forum and updated estimates of the resources needed to realize the unmet need of couples and individuals.[7] While basically agreeing with the estimates, the Consultation suggested that the components of an integrated reproductive health and population programme should be grouped under four categories: (1) a basic family planning component; (2) other components of reproductive health; (3) the prevention of STDs, including HIV/AIDS; and (4) data, research and policy analysis. This would become the four-part framework for the presentation of resource estimates.

A second consultative meeting held in New York on 21 December 1993 reviewed the revised four-part estimates. Besides those who had participated in the first consultation, additional experts from Tulane University, the University of Michigan and IPPF also participated in this meeting. The meeting agreed that the four-part formula provided a good basis for going forward:

> *[t]he consensus of the meeting was that a credible methodology had been employed and reasonable estimates produced which could serve as a basis for mobilizing the needed resources, that continued improvement was required in the monitoring of the levels and sources of population programme funding, and that further development of methods for projecting and evaluating the effectiveness of contributions of different supporters of population programmes was required.*
> (UNFPA, 1994b: 2)

A third informal consultation was organized at the UN on 10 March 1994. In addition, the Secretariat was also represented at three other consultations on related topics, organized by USAID, the US Office of Management and Budget (OMB) and Harvard University.[8] During PrepCom III, as ICPD Executive Coordinator I held several informal meetings with interested delegations to explain to them in some detail the basis on which the estimates were arrived at. We were thus involved in six consultations with experts and researchers on various aspects of the proposed resource estimates, and met several times with delegations to provide detailed information and exchange views on these estimates. The estimates that were included in the Draft Final Document took fully into account what transpired at all of these consultations and briefings.

The Draft Final Document of the Conference (UN, 1994d) presented to PrepCom III talked of mobilizing resources primarily at the national level, which would be assisted by the international community upon the request of the national authorities (Paras. 13.9–13.10):

> *[t]he envisaged reduction of unmet needs for family planning information and services in the period up to 2015 implies that the number of couples using contraception in the developing countries and countries in economic transition would rise from some 550 million in 1995 to nearly 640 million in the year 2000 and 880 million in 2015. The contraceptive prevalence rate as derived from these figures would increase from about 58 percent in 1995 to 69 percent in 2015.*
> (Para. 13.13)

The Draft Final Document proposed the four-part package of family planning and population programmes endorsed by the experts: (1) family planning and related activities; (2) reproductive health services that could be delivered within the framework of primary health care; (3) the prevention of STDs, including HIV/AIDS; and (4) population data and policy formulation and analysis. The total costs for this package were estimated (in 1993 dollars) as US$13.2 billion in the year 2000, US$14.4 billion in the year 2005, US$16.1 billion in the year 2010 and US$17.0 billion in the year 2015.

PREPCOM III

These proposals aroused a great deal of interest and discussion at PrepCom III. The Secretariat was asked to provide further information on how the final estimates were arrived at and to explain clearly various terms used in the section on resource mobilization.

The developing countries were generally supportive of the proposals made by the Secretariat, as were the US and some other donors. However, several members of the EU continued to seek further information and clarifications before taking a decision on the proposals.

The countries with economies in transition emerged as another group of important players in the field. Several of their delegates who spoke during the debate were mainly interested in ensuring that their needs, though of a temporary nature, were specifically mentioned along with those of the developing countries. The G77 felt, on the other hand, that Eastern and Central European countries did not face the same problems of acute poverty and lack of resources as did most of the developing countries and should not therefore seek to share with developing countries the amounts normally available for population assistance. References to countries with economies in transition in Paras. 14.14 and 14.15 were therefore bracketed in the Draft Programme.

Population NGOs were generally supportive of the efforts towards mobilizing a much larger volume of resources for population activities from the international community. These included IPPF, IUSSP, the Population Council, PAI, formerly the Population Crisis Committee, and the Population Institute. PAI had produced its own set of estimates in the early 1990s, which were somewhat at variance with those produced by the ICPD Secretariat, but these had been reconciled by the time we got to PrepCom III.

The Women's Caucus emphasized a broad approach in developing strategies for resource allocation and resource mobilization 'within the context of capacity building and the release of human potential, particularly of women' (WEDO, 1993b). In its suggestions on the Draft Final Document, the Caucus gave its full support to 'quantitative resource goals' as 'an important guideline for governments as they seek to achieve the objectives of the Programme of Action' (WEDO, 1994). This support was very helpful in convincing many delegations of the validity of the approach put forward by the Secretariat.

At the end of PrepCom III, the global estimates as well as the estimates for the four components remained within brackets. However, our own impression was that we were very near a consensus on these estimates. In the Draft Programme of Action, the total estimates for family planning (US$10.2 billion in the year 2000, US$11.5 billion in the year 2005, US$12.6 billion in the year 2010 and US$13.8 billion in the year 2015) and the prevention of STDs including HIV/AIDS (which were estimated by the WHO Global Programme on AIDS to cost US$1.3 billion in the year 2000, US$1.4 billion in the year 2005, approximately US$1.5 billion in the year 2010 and US$1.5 billion in the year 2015) remained unchanged from the draft submitted to PrepCom III. On the other hand, the total amounts proposed for reproductive health services were increased substantially to accommodate more comprehensive cost estimates for safe motherhood and related initiatives (US$5 billion in the year 2000, US$5.4 billion in the year 2005, US$5.7 billion in the year 2010 and US$6.1 billion in the year 2015). About 65 per cent of these costs are for the delivery systems. The revision of the cost estimates for reproductive health services seemed to satisfy, to a large extent, those EU delegations and NGOs that had earlier criticized what they regarded as the underestimation of the costs of the reproductive health component *vis-à-vis* the family planning component. The estimated cost for data, research and policy was worked out at US$500 million in the year 2000 (coinciding with the decennial census exercises), US$200 million in the year 2005, US$700 million in the year 2010 (to coincide again with censuses) and US$300 million in the year 2015.

The overall estimates in the Draft Programme of Action, which came out of PrepCom III, were in the order of US$17.0 billion in the year 2000, US$18.5 billion in the year 2005, US$20.5 billion in the year 2010 and US$21.7 billion in the year 2015. Two-thirds of the costs would be met by the developing countries and the countries with economies in transition, while the other third would be provided by the international community. These estimates were discussed further in a global consultation organized by the Secretariat at the UN on 15 July 1994 under the chairmanship of Ambassador Biegman of the Netherlands.

Looking back, I would like to note that the US, as the largest donor in the area of population assistance, played a key role in convincing several other donors that there was no alternative to the methodology used for calculating these estimates, and that globally these could indeed be used as benchmarks to measure progress towards resource mobilization. On behalf of the Clinton administration, Senator Wirth, the US Under Secretary of State in charge of global issues, travelled to a number of donor countries in order to convince them of the importance of substantially increasing the volume of population assistance. He was able to convince Japan to join the US in pledging much greater support for such global issues as population, HIV/AIDS, the environment, and the empowerment of women. Germany was another donor that committed itself to substantially increasing its assistance in these areas to developing countries.

Elizabeth Maguire, the Director of the USAID's Office of Population, and Mr Sinding, the Director of Population Sciences, the Rockefeller Foundation, who were both in the US delegation, worked closely with other donors as well as members of the Secretariat in clearing up questions on cost estimates. Michael Bohnet, Deputy Director General of German Development Cooperation, played a crucial role within the EU group, especially when Germany served as the chair of the group in the second half of 1994. Also, Ambassador Biegman and his colleagues in the Netherlands delegation were both publicly and privately very supportive of the efforts to raise the volume of international population assistance.

Before we got to Cairo, the US announced its intention to seek from Congress an increase in its contribution to population assistance from around US$500 million in 1994 to US$1 billion in the year 2000. Japan announced a global package of US$3 billion to be provided in support of global issues during 1995–2000. Germany indicated its intention to increase its support for population activities by spending US$2 billion over the same period. A great deal of momentum was thus provided to the efforts aimed at firming up the resource mobilization goals.

NEGOTIATIONS IN CAIRO

Most of the ministers, senior officials and NGO representatives who addressed the plenary sessions of the Cairo Conference spoke of the importance and urgency of the need to mobilize additional resources, domestic and international, for population activities. The US, Japan and Germany officially confirmed their intention to increase their support to the population sector. The UK announced that it would spend approximately US$160 million over the next two years, thus increasing its support to population activities by more than 60 per cent. The World Bank announced plans to increase its spending on family planning and reproductive health by more than 50 per cent; and the EU indicated that it would try to reach approximately US$400 million on population by the year 2000.

When talking of the need for international assistance, many of the developing countries made a point of outlining their own contribution to population activities and the adverse impact of structural adjustment on social development programmes. The Cairo Programme of Action emphasizes the importance of domestic resource mobilization, on the one hand, and the need to complement efforts in this area with 'a significantly greater provision of financial and technical resources by the international community':

> [d]omestic resources provide the largest portion of funds for attaining development objectives. Domestic resource mobilization is, thus, one of the highest priority areas for focused attention to ensure the timely actions required to meet the objectives of the present Programme of Action. Both the public and the private sectors can potentially contribute to the resources required. Many of the countries seeking to pursue the additional goals and objectives of the Programme of Action, especially the least developed countries and other poor countries that are undergoing painful structural adjustments, are continuing to experience recessionary trends in their economies. Their domestic resource mobilization efforts to expand and improve their population and development programmes will need to be complemented by a significantly greater provision of financial and technical resources by the international community, as indicated in chapter XIV. In the mobilization of new and additional domestic resources and resources from donors, special attention needs to be given to adequate measures to address the basic needs of the most vulnerable groups of the population, particularly in the rural areas, and to ensure their access to social services. (UN, 1995a: Para. 13.12)

The emphasis on domestic resource mobilization was, in my view, one of the high points of the debate on resources. Population was an area in which many developing countries were investing increasingly large amounts of their own resources. There were other developing countries that had started their family planning/population programmes with external support in the early 1970s but, by the beginning of the 1990s, had taken over most of the financing needed. They did not therefore need to be convinced of the necessity or the importance of domestic resource mobilization. The G77 agreed, without too much fuss, to the idea of developing countries themselves mobilizing two-thirds of the resources needed. But they also made it clear that they wanted a firm commitment from the international community on the balance of the resources needed.

The need for increased investment in population is emphasized strongly in Para. 14.8:

> [t]here is a strong consensus on the need to mobilize significant additional financial resources from both the international community and within developing countries and countries with economies in transition for national population programmes in support of sustainable development. The Amsterdam Declaration on a Better Life for Future Generations, adopted at the International Forum on Population in the Twenty-first Century, held at Amsterdam in 1989, called on Governments to double the total global expenditures in population programmes and on donors to increase substantially their contribution, in order to meet the

needs of millions of people in developing countries in the fields of family planning and other population activities by the year 2000. However, since then, international resources for population activities have come under severe pressure, owing to the prolonged economic recession in traditional donor countries. Also, developing countries face increasing difficulties in allocating sufficient funds for their population and related programmes. Additional resources are urgently required to better identify and satisfy unmet needs in issues related to population and development, such as reproductive health care, including family-planning and sexual health information and services, as well as to respond to future increases in demand, to keep pace with the growing demands that need to be served, and to improve the scope and quality of programmes.

The figures proposed for resource mobilization required several hours of discussion in the Main Committee. I was asked to provide, on behalf of the Secretariat, numerous clarifications and explanations. The developing countries expressed full support for the proposed figures and the US did a lot of lobbying among the donors in support of these figures. But there were still some delegates who wanted further studies undertaken. To satisfy them, the following text was added to Para. 13.15 in explanation of the estimates provided:

[t]hese are cost-estimates prepared by experts, based on experience to date, of the four components referred to above. These estimates should be reviewed and updated on the basis of the comprehensive approach reflected in paragraph 13.14 of the present Programme of Action, particularly with respect to the costs of implementing reproductive health service delivery.

Another set of negotiations took place at Cairo, between the G77 and the group of countries with economies in transition. With some reluctance, the G77 agreed to include references to the temporary resource requirements of the countries with economies in transition. The Programme of Action now says that 'countries with economies in transition should receive temporary assistance for population and development activities in the light of the difficult economic and social problems these countries face at present' (Para. 14.15).

In the end, the funding estimates were agreed to by all the interested groups. At the same time, the Programme of Action, at the suggestion of developing countries, also outlined five major criteria for the allocation of external financial resources for population activities in developing countries.

(a) Coherent national programmes, plans and strategies on population and development; (b) Recognized priority to the least developed countries; (c) The need to complement national financial efforts on population; (d) The need to avoid obstacles to, or reversal of, progress achieved thus far; (e) Problems of significant social sectors and areas that are not reflected in national average indicators. (Para. 14.14)

SOUTH–SOUTH COOPERATION

The Programme of Action also gave strong support to the concept of South–South cooperation as a way to strengthen the impact and effectiveness of population programmes. Para. 14.9 says:

> [t]o assist the implementation of population and reproductive health care, including family-planning and sexual health programmes, financial and technical assistance from bilateral and multilateral agencies have been provided to the national and subnational agencies involved. As some of these began to be successful, it became desirable for countries to learn from one another's experiences, through a number of different modalities (e.g., long- and short-term training programmes, observation study tours and consultant services).

Para. 14.10 proposes increasing international financial assistance to direct South–South cooperation and facilitating financing procedures for direct South–South cooperation. Para. 14.16 suggests that

> more attention should be given to South–South cooperation as well as to new ways of mobilizing private contributions, particularly in partnership with non-governmental organizations. The international community should urge donor agencies to improve and modify their funding procedures in order to facilitate and give higher priority to supporting direct South–South collaborative arrangements.

The Programme of Action thus proposes three specific channels for South–South cooperation: (1) technical and financial cooperation among developing countries themselves; (2) the mobilization of support among population donors for South–South activities; and (3) partnership between governments, foundations and NGOs in formulating and implementing South–South projects.

A new initiative to promote and strengthen South–South cooperation among developing countries (Partners in Population and Development) was announced by a group of ten developing countries (Bangladesh, Colombia, Egypt, Indonesia, Kenya, Mexico, Morocco, Thailand, Tunisia and Zimbabwe) while the ICPD was in session. Three additional countries (China, India and Pakistan) have joined the Partners since Cairo: and its secretariat in Dhaka (Bangladesh) is now actively engaged in the task of helping its members raise funds from bilateral and multilateral sources for training, information and advisory services. Many of the Partner countries are also allocating increasing funds from their own budgets for fellowships at their training institutions and technical advisory services for other developing countries.

20/20 CONCEPT

Another topic of discussion at Cairo was the 20/20 concept under which developed countries would allocate 20 per cent of ODA to social development activities, while developing countries would agree to allocate 20 per cent or more of their national budgets to the social development sector. The concept was first brought up in UNDP (1991) and elaborated further in UNICEF (1993).

The 20/20 initiative was first discussed at PrepCom III but as no clear agreement could be reached on what kind of endorsement should be given to the concept, the Draft Programme of Action made two alternative proposals in this regard:

> *Governments, non-governmental organizations, the private sector and local communities, assisted upon request by the international community, should strive to mobilize the resources to meet reinforcing social development goals, and in particular to satisfy the commitments Governments have undertaken previously with regard to Education for All (the Jomtien Declaration), the multisectoral goals of the World Summit for Children, Agenda 21 and other relevant international agreements, and to further mobilize the resources to meet the goals in this Programme of Action. In this regard, Governments are urged to devote [at least 20 percent] or [an increased proportion] of public sector expenditures to the social sectors, as well as [20 percent] or [an increased proportion] of official development assistance, stressing, in particular, poverty eradication within the context of sustainable development.* (UN, 1994e: Para. 13.23)

The governments would thus be urged to either devote 'an increased proportion' of national budgets or ODA, as appropriate, in the context of this proposal or earmark 20 per cent. In a note produced for distribution at Cairo, the UN Development Programme (UNDP), UNICEF and UNFPA provided a detailed analysis of this concept, with the hope that this would help generate greater support at Cairo. The note provided a comparison of annual cost estimates prepared by various organizations, including the specific estimates prepared for the ICPD in the areas of family planning and other aspects of reproductive health. According to the authors of the note, 'attaining universal access to basic social services would require over the rest of the decade additional spending in the amount of some US$30–40 billion per annum. Beyond that period, further additional funding will be required' (UNDP, 1994: 2).

In their statements to the Conference, both James Grant, Executive Director of UNICEF, and Gus Speth, Administrator of UNDP, strongly endorsed the 20/20 concept and expressed the hope that the Conference would incorporate it in the Programme of Action. The proposal received a mixed response. Two of the donors, Norway and the Netherlands, were very enthusiastic about it. The EU members as a group, however, did not share this enthusiasm. Germany, on behalf of the EU, supported mentioning 'an increased proportion' rather than the '20 percent'.

Members of the G77 did not reject the proposal, but wanted it to be discussed further at the Social Development Summit in Copenhagen. Those who did not want a fixed percentage mentioned carried the day. The final text of Para. 13.23 urges governments to devote 'an increased proportion' of public sector expenditures to the social sector, as well as 'an increased proportion of official development assistance, stressing, in particular, poverty eradication in the context of sustainable development'.

The reference to the Social Development Summit comes later, in Para. 14.11: 'The international community takes note of the initiative to mobilize resources to give all people access to basic social services, known as the 20/20 initiative, which will be studied further in the context of the World Summit for Social Development'. Supporters of the 20/20 initiative were unhappy at this outcome, but given the lack of enthusiasm among a large group of countries, which included both members of the G77 and donor countries, this was perhaps the only outcome one could have hoped to obtain at Cairo.[9]

The Social Development Summit Meeting in Copenhagen in March 1995 did endorse the initiative for the interested countries. Norway and the Netherlands have continued to work with a group of developing countries to promote its implementation. Also, the UN Task Force on Basic Social Services for All, which groups together major UN funds and programmes with Dr Sadik as its Chair, is a strong proponent of the 20/20 initiative, arguing that 'access to basic social services for all the world's people could be ensured by an additional US$30–40 billion a year'.

ADDITIONAL RESOURCES FOR DEVELOPMENT

On the broader front, the Conference called on the international community to fulfil the agreed target of 0.7 per cent of gross national product (GNP) for ODA (Recommendation 14.11), and suggested that 'innovative financing, including new ways of generating public and private financing resources and various forms of debt relief should be explored' (Recommendation 14.17).

The Programme of Action, as indicated earlier, does not set resource mobilization targets for other development sectors, but does note that additional resources will be needed for health care, education, the status and empowerment of women, the environment and poverty alleviation:

13.17. Additional resources will be needed to support programmes addressing population and development goals, particularly programmes seeking to attain the specific social- and economic-sector goals contained in the present Programme of Action.

The health sector will require additional resources to strengthen the primary health-care delivery system, child survival programmes, emergency obstetrical care and broad-based programmes for the control of sexually transmitted diseases, including HIV/AIDS, as well as the humane treatment and care of those infected with sexually transmitted diseases/HIV/AIDS, among others. The education sector will also require substantial and additional investments in order to provide universal basic education and to eliminate disparities in educational access owing to gender, geographical location, social or economic status etc.

13.18. Additional resources will be needed for action programmes directed to improving the status and empowerment of women and their full participation in the development process (beyond ensuring their basic education). The full involvement of women in the design, implementation, management and monitoring of all development programmes will be an important component of such activities.

13.19. Additional resources will be needed for action programmes to accelerate development programmes; generate employment; address environmental concerns, including unsustainable patterns of production and consumption; provide social services; achieve balanced distributions of population; and address poverty eradication through sustained economic growth in the context of sustainable development. Important relevant programmes include those addressed in Agenda 21.

Besides Agenda 21, two other international agreements are specifically mentioned in paragraph 13.23: the Jomtien Declaration on Education for All, and the World Summit for Children. But the cost estimates for implementing these agreements are not included.

The Programme of Action, while reiterating the need for increased resources for population in the near future, also pointed out that 'the benefits of these investments can be measured in future savings in sectoral requirements; sustainable patterns of production and consumption and sustained economic growth in the context of sustainable development; and overall improvements in the quality of life' (Para. 13.20).

In summary, three extremely significant agreements were hammered out at Cairo on resource mobilization. First, the developing countries willingly endorsed the importance of domestic resource mobilization and agreed to the challenge that up to two-thirds of the resources required would be provided by the countries themselves. It was of course understood that 'the least developed countries and other low income countries will require a greater share of external resources on a concessional grant basis' (Para. 13.16). Second, the financial requirements for various sectors were spelled out clearly. Third, the concept of South–South cooperation as a means of increasing the transfer of knowledge, expertise and resources among developing countries themselves received strong support in the Programme of Action.

7   IMPLEMENTING CAIRO

Cairo began with uncertainties and tensions; it ended in a blaze of glory, with a series of remarkable accomplishments. The appeal by some fundamentalist groups to individual countries to boycott the Conference failed almost completely: 179 countries sent official delegations to the Conference and another six came as observers. Security considerations did keep away some individuals and groups from Cairo, but there were no untoward incidents during the Conference and, thanks to the vigilance of thousands of Egyptian army and security personnel and a relatively small but highly efficient corps of UN security officers, some 15,000 people who were in Cairo for two weeks in September 1994 felt well guarded and secure. There were no problems with the arrangements and facilities at the vast International Conference Centre and the Egyptian government and people proved extremely generous and considerate hosts to the visitors. The NGOs played a highly effective role at the Conference and were happy to see adequate recognition accorded to them. The media coverage received by the Conference was exceptional, and no other global conference has ever received the kind of intense media scrutiny and analysis as Cairo did. And above all, Cairo succeeded, against dire predictions of gloom and doom, in adopting a new global consensus on population embodied in the ICPD Programme of Action.

Two and a half years after the Cairo Conference, I asked several of the key participants, in personal interviews, what, in retrospect, was their view of the Conference. Senator Wirth, US Under Secretary of State, thought the ICPD was unquestionably the most successful of all post-Rio conferences, and cited three reasons for its success. First, it had a clear agenda. Second, it was a very well run conference. Third, the Programme of Action that came out was very specific.[1] Mr Biegman, the Ambassador of the Netherlands at the UN, commented that the concept of 'unmet need' that was introduced into the discussions on reproductive health, reproductive rights and the empowerment of women was probably the most significant factor in the successful completion of the negotiations on these themes.[2] For Haryono Suyono, Minister of Population in Indonesia, the broad agreement on resource requirements and the strong support given to South–South cooperation were two of the most important achievements of Cairo.[3]

I also asked several key NGO representatives about their impressions of Cairo. Ms Abzug of WEDO spoke of the critical role the Women's Caucus had played in enabling female delegates and observers to understand and utilize the negotiating process and in defining the ICPD position on reproductive rights and women's empowerment.[4] Cairo and Beijing were totally interconnected, according to Ms Abzug, and the members of the ICPD Women's Caucus who were at Beijing worked hard to make sure that the gains of Cairo were not lost at Beijing. The ICPD-related Caucus at Beijing was, as a matter of fact, called the Linkage Caucus. Ms Joan Dunlop and Ms Adrienne Germain of IWHC thought that Cairo represented a watershed and that the Programme of Action demonstrated new approaches to population and development that place women's health, their empowerment and rights at their centre.[5]

Ingar Brueggemann and Mark Laskin of IPPF, Werner Fornos of the Population Institute and many other NGO representatives I have spoken to in the course of writing this book applaud the goals and objectives of the Programme of Action and point out the need to give particular attention to resource mobilization as the key to achieving these goals and objectives.[6] Taken together, these views provide a wide-ranging perspective on the achievements of Cairo as well as the potential of its Programme of Action.

In the long run, Cairo's success will be measured by its impact on the policies and programmes of governments, NGOs and the international community. The ICPD Programme of Action includes 243 recommendations, all requiring implementation and follow-up. Most of them are addressed to governments, but they are also addressed to NGOs and members of the international community as appropriate. While it is too early to make a definitive assessment of the implementation of the Programme of Action, it is possible to point out some emerging trends by looking at what actions are being taken, at various levels, to implement the Cairo Programme. A brief account follows under the following sections: (1) follow-up by the UN; (2) governance of UNFPA; (3) institutional arrangements; (4) agency follow-up and inter-agency collaboration; (5) follow-up by UNFPA and other UN organizations; (6) reorientation of policies and emerging issues; (7) the integration of FP and reproductive health services; (8) the empowerment of women; (9) the increasing role of the NGO sector; and (10) the mobilization of resources. The first five offer a synoptic view of the institutional response, within the UN system, to the ICPD; the other five present illustrative examples of activities and programmes being undertaken at national, regional and international levels to implement the ICPD Programme of Action.

FOLLOW-UP BY THE UN

Immediately after the ICPD, members of the ICPD Secretariat started preparing for the 49th Session of the UN GA, which was to receive and consider the report of the ICPD. It was their sincere hope that there would be no reopening of any of the debates which had been settled in Cairo. But the GA was expected to debate institutional follow-up to the ICPD, in the context of recommendations included in chapter XIV ('International Cooperation') and chapter XVI ('Follow-Up to the Conference'). The GA would focus, in particular, on (1) the respective roles of the Population Commission, the UNDP/UNFPA Executive Board, ECOSOC and the GA, (2) future arrangements for substantive follow-up within the UN Secretariat, and (3) strengthening UNFPA.

At the GA there was no debate or dispute on the principal role of the GA in policy formulation and the role of ECOSOC in overall guidance and coordination. There was also considerable agreement, from the beginning, on the need to revitalize the Population Commission by enlarging both its composition and its mandate. However, the formulation of specific proposals for this purpose needed several weeks of negotiations among various political and regional groups. The GA finally reached two agreements: to rename the Commission as the Commission on Population and Development and to ask the Commission to meet annually beginning in 1996. The Commission's terms of reference, its mandate and its composition, were left for further consideration by the Commission itself at its substantive session in 1995.

The GA resolution describes the three-tiered intergovernmental structure for follow-up to the ICPD as follows:

> *the General Assembly, through its role in policy formulation, the Economic and Social Council, through its role in overall guidance and coordination, in accordance with Assembly resolution 48/162, and a revitalized Population Commission shall constitute a three-tiered intergovernmental mechanism that will play the primary role in the follow-up to the implementation of the Programme of Action, keeping in mind the need to develop a common framework for a coherent follow-up to United Nations summits and conference, and to this end:*

> *(a) The General Assembly, being the highest intergovernmental mechanism for the formulation and appraisal of policy on matters relating to the follow-up to the International Conference on Population and Development, will organize a regular review of the implementation of the Programme of Action;*

(b) The Economic and Social Council, in assisting the General Assembly, will promote an integrated approach, provide system-wide coordination and guidance in the monitoring of the implementation of the Programme of Action and make recommendations thereon;

(c) The revitalized Population Commission, as a functional Commission assisting the Economic and Social Council, will monitor, review and assess the implementation of the Programme of Action at the national, regional and international levels and advise the Council thereon. (GA Resolution 49/128, 12 December 1994)

Soon after the adoption of GA resolution 49/128, the ICPD Secretariat was wound up (on 31 December 1994). Those of its members who had been seconded on a temporary basis returned to their parent organizations. Three of them were absorbed by UNFPA in regular posts, and others moved on to new careers or opportunities. UNFPA set up an internal task force on ICPD follow-up and continued to collaborate with the Population Division on the technical preparations for the ICPD-related items in the agenda of the future meetings of the three UN bodies mentioned in GA Resolution 49/128.

The 28th Session of the Commission, which took place from 21 February to 2 March 1995, discussed, in the light of GA Resolution 49/128, its own terms of reference and mandate and proposed several revisions. It defined its main task, as a subsidiary body of ECOSOC, to monitor, review and assess the implementation of the ICPD Programme of Action at national, regional and international levels, to identify reasons for successes and failures in this process and to propose future action. It also formulated a four-year work programme with the following themes: reproductive rights and reproductive health, including population information, education and communication (1996); international migration, with special emphasis on the linkages between migration and development, and gender issues and the family (1997); health and mortality, with special emphasis on the linkages between health and development, and gender and age (1998); and population growth, structure and distribution, with special emphasis on sustained economic growth and sustainable development, including education (1999). In addition, in 1999, the Commission would consider a five-year review and appraisal of the overall implementation of the Programme (UN, 1995c: Para. 19).

These proposals were generally endorsed by ECOSOC through Resolution 1995/55 of 28 July 1995. But the negotiations on enlarging the membership of the Commission took longer. While the G77 wanted the membership to be expanded to equal that of the Commission on Sustainable Development (established to monitor the implementation of Agenda 21), the US and several other countries were in favour of a much smaller increase. Also, the formula for balanced regional representation on the Commission needed to be worked out. Finally, on 12 December 1995 ECOSOC agreed in its decision 1995/320 to increase the membership of the Commission from 27 to 47, with 12 members from Africa, 11 members from Asia, five members from Eastern Europe, nine members from Latin America and the Caribbean and ten members from Western Europe and other states. This formula was endorsed by the GA on 20 December 1995 in Resolution 50/124. Soon thereafter, ECOSOC elected the new members, and the expanded Commission on Population and Development met, for the first time, in March 1996.

The GA, in Resolution 50/124, also defines the nature of representation on the Commission:

> *the representatives of Governments that are to serve on the Commission should have a relevant background in population and development, in order to ensure that it fulfills its functions as reflected in its updated and enhanced mandate, taking into account the integrated multidisciplinary and comprehensive approach of the Programme of Action and the membership of the other functional commissions of the Council.*

In practice, the membership of the Commission has evolved over the last several years to include not only population experts but also programme managers. Several large countries appoint delegations of four or five members, including government officials drawn from ministries of health or population and diplomats from UN missions and foreign ministries. The composition of many individual delegations thus reflects both technical expertise and political and diplomatic experience.

GOVERNANCE OF UNFPA

The governing body of UNFPA, which is another subsidiary body of ECOSOC, was not part of the three-tiered structure envisaged in GA Resolution 49/128. However, as UNFPA was expected to play a major role in the follow-up to ICPD, particularly at the country level, its governing body was invited by the GA in the same resolution

> *to oversee, on a regular basis, the response of the Fund to the needs of countries regarding activities to strengthen national population and development programmes, including the specific requests from developing countries for assistance in the preparation of national reports, within its area of competence, and to report to the Economic and Social Council on this matter.* (GA Resolution 49/128)

What kind of a governing body UNFPA should have in future was another matter discussed by delegates, first at the 48th Session and, following the ICPD, at the 49th Session of the GA. Since 1973, the governing body of UNDP has also served as the governing body of UNFPA, though the Administrator of UNDP and the Executive Director of UNFPA report to it separately. Among many members of the G77 there was a great deal of sentiment in favour of giving UNFPA greater recognition and visibility after ICPD, by giving it a governing body which would be separate from that of UNDP. On the other hand, most of the donor countries wanted the existing arrangements to continue, while ensuring that more time and attention would be devoted to UNFPA matters. Some of them also felt that as the reforms on the governance of UN funds and programmes, which envisaged revised arrangements for the joint oversight of UNDP and UNFPA, had been initiated quite recently, any major changes in this regard ought to be considered later in the light of experience. In the meantime, they felt, the newly constituted UNDP/UNFPA Executive Board (which had replaced the Governing Council of UNDP) should devote more time to the consideration of UNFPA matters at its regular sessions (UN, 1995c: Para. 25).

The negotiations between the two groups were rather inconclusive. The GA, therefore, chose not to act on this issue but requested ECOSOC, at its 1995 substantive Session, to consider '[t]he establishment of a separate executive board of the United Nations Population Fund' (GA Resolution 49/128).

In order to take care of some of the concerns voiced during the GA, the governing body of the UNDP and the UNFPA, renamed the UNDP/UNFPA Executive Board, agreed in early 1995 on a set of practical measures that would give UNFPA a direct role in organizing and administering the sessions devoted to its items. Several changes were made in the procedure to allocate agenda items and time slots at the regular sessions of the Executive Board to ensure that both UNDP and UNFPA would get adequate time and attention. UNFPA was encouraged to play a more direct role in organizing the Executive Board meetings. On a separate track, UNFPA Executive Director's proposal to give UNFPA's country directors a clear profile and adequate visibility by designating them as UNFPA representatives gained the approval of the Executive Board, ECOSOC and the Assembly. These developments seemed generally to satisfy many of the delegates who were interested in giving the UNFPA greater attention than in the past. ECOSOC did not take any specific action in response to the GA request on the question of a separate executive board for UNFPA, and the entire matter has been put aside for the foreseeable future.

INSTITUTIONAL ARRANGEMENTS

Another matter under discussion was how the responsibilities and functions in the follow-up to the ICPD should be assigned within the UN. In the ICPD process, UNFPA and the Population Division had worked together well, under the direction of the Conference Secretary General (who was also the Executive Director of UNFPA). In the post-ICPD phase, would it be possible to establish a similar arrangement? The idea was given a good deal of thought, but ultimately it did not move forward. Whereas UNFPA was accountable to its own Executive Board on programme matters, the Population Division's work programme was considered and approved by the Population Commission. Those who did not favour a joint secretariat for ICPD follow-up took the position that such an arrangement would create considerable confusion with regard to the formulation of work programmes and reporting procedures.

The report of the UN Secretariat on the implementation of GA Resolution 49/128 emphasized the role that the DESIPA of the Secretariat, in particular the Population Division, has played as the focal point for the provision of integrated secretariat support to the Commission.

> *In the past, this role has consisted of the provision of substantive support, the preparation of documentation and the coordination of relevant inputs. Effective substantive support for the work programme of the Commission has required the involvement of many organizations of the United Nations system, in particular UNFPA, and could only have been carried out on the basis of cooperative and coordinated relationships. At the same time, UNFPA has taken the lead in coordinating and implementing operational activities in the field. It is proposed this basic pattern of work should continue with respect to provision of support for the Commission and implementation of the Programme of Action.* (UN, 1995c: Para. 28)

Under the arrangements proposed by the Commission on Population and Development in 1995, the Population Division remains the Secretariat of the Commission, while it shares with UNFPA the responsibility for preparing the documentation on ICPD follow-up. The Population Division prepares the report on world population monitoring, whereas UNFPA is responsible for four other reports: the monitoring of population programmes; the report of the inter-agency task force for the implementation of the Programme of Action; the report on the activities of intergovernmental and non-governmental organizations; and the report on the flow of financial resources. A decision taken by the Commission in 1997 eliminated the separate report on the activities of intergovernmental and non-governmental organizations, with the understanding that relevant information on these activities would be included in other reports.

AGENCY FOLLOW-UP AND INTER-AGENCY COLLABORATION

UNFPA also serves as the lead agency within the UN on promoting and coordinating inter-agency cooperation on ICPD follow-up. An Inter-Agency Task Force, under the chairmanship of the Executive Director of UNFPA, was established towards the end of 1994. It set up four working groups to develop proposals for inter-agency collaboration at the country level: (1) a common data system at the national level in the field of health, notably in the areas of infant, child and maternal mortality, led by UNICEF; (2) basic education, with special attention given to gender disparities, led by UNESCO; (3) policy-related issues, including the drafting of a common advocacy statement on social development issues, led by UNFPA; and (4) women's empowerment, led by United Nations Development Fund for Women (UNIFEM). Two other working groups were established in early 1995, on: (1) reproductive health, led by WHO; and (2) international migration, led by ILO. Five of these working groups produced guidelines for UN Resident Coordinators, to enable them to operationalize the ICPD Programme of Action and promote and strengthen inter-agency collaboration at the country level. The sixth developed a common advocacy statement, which emphasizes the importance of population as an integral component of development strategies. The statement was endorsed by the UN Administrative Committee on Coordination (ACC), which groups together executive heads of the UN's specialized agencies and major operational funds and programmes under the chairmanship of the Secretary General, in late 1996.

In October 1995, the Inter-Agency Task Force was expanded and reconstituted as the ACC Task Force on Basic Social Services for All, with UNFPA still serving as the lead agency. The ACC established, at the same time, two other task forces to focus on major goals and objectives emerging from global UN conferences and to promote more effective and better coordinated delivery of UN assistance at the country level, with a view to helping the implementation of these goals and objectives. These are the ACC Task Force on Employment and Sustainable Livelihoods, chaired by ILO, and the ACC Task Force on an Enabling Environment for Economic and Social Development, chaired by the World Bank. All three task forces are expected to liaise, on a regular basis, with the Inter-Agency Committee on Women and Gender Equality.

The ACC Task Force on Basic Social Services for All was asked to focus on six major topics under the general theme of poverty eradication: (1) population, with an emphasis on reproductive health and FP services; (2) basic education; (3) primary health care; (4) drinking water and sanitation; (5) shelter; and (6) social services in post-crisis situations. At its first meeting, on 23 February 1996, the Task Force decided to continue three of the previous working groups (reproductive health, international migration and a common approach to national capacity building in tracking child and maternal mortality). It also decided to establish a working group on primary health care and another one on basic education (to review and update the guidelines formulated by the previous group set up by the Inter-Agency Task Force).

The output of the ACC Task Force on Basic Social Services for All includes updated and revised guidelines for the UN Resident Coordinators, on primary health care, reproductive health, basic education, women's empowerment, international migration and national capacity building in measuring infant and maternal mortality. These are prepared on the basis of comments on earlier guidelines received from the Resident Coordinators, while taking into account six 'cross-cutting dimensions': the selection/use of performance indicators; financing and resource mobilization; gender perspective; the targeting of specific groups, including those in post-crisis/emergency situations; policy; and the involvement of civil society. In addition, the dimensions of nutrition, the environment and shelter are taken into consideration, as appropriate (UN, 1996d: Para. 9). Other end-products are a wall chart on social indicators, a publication on lessons learned/best practices in social sector assistance, the selection/use of indicators, a pocket card on advocacy and a compendium of international commitments on poverty alleviation and social integration.

Various inter-agency groups, including the ACC Task Force on Basic Social Services for All, have emphasized the need for reliable indicators to measure progress towards the goals of the ICPD and other global conferences. This was further emphasized by the GA in a resolution adopted at its 51st Session in 1996 (GA Resolution 51/176). The wall chart mentioned above, which provides country data in six key areas (population, primary health care, nutrition, basic education, drinking water and sanitation, and shelter), brings together currently available data and estimates, though further work is needed to revise and update them.

One of the areas that requires further work is the methodology for monitoring reproductive health programmes. The working group on reproductive health, led by WHO, has produced a list of 15 indicators that

> *meet certain essential criteria: they are considered to be ethical, useful, scientifically robust, representative and accessible. This short list of 15 indicators provides an overview of the reproductive health situation in different settings. It is not envisaged that these indicators can provide all the information needed for national or global monitoring or for the evaluation of programme impact. For the latter WHO advises that countries focus on national capacities for data generation, analysis and interpretation. To support countries in these endeavours,*

WHO has developed a guideline targeted to district health planners and managers which describes a process for the identification and selection of reproductive health indicators that meet essential criteria. (UN, 1997a: Para. 7)

In 1996, UNFPA used a set of seven indicators in developing its new approach to resource allocation in the light of the ICPD goals. These indicators, which relate to access to reproductive health services, the reduction of mortality, and education, particularly of women and girls, are currently being used by UNFPA and its field offices. Six of the seven indicators have also been used in preparing the wall chart on social services. While many of these indicators are accepted throughout the UN system, others are not. A system-wide agreement on common indicators is essential to developing common follow-up at both country and inter-country levels to the ICPD and other major UN conferences.

FOLLOW-UP BY UNFPA AND OTHER UN ORGANIZATIONS

UNFPA, UNICEF and WHO are the three UN organizations most directly concerned with the implementation of the ICPD recommendations on reproductive health issues. Each one of them has undertaken a series of actions in the context of its own mandates. The initial issues related to who does what seem to have been sorted out, and the three organizations are working together on several issues, including adolescent health, HIV/AIDS and female genital mutilation.

Immediately after ICPD, UNFPA organized a series of meetings for its headquarters and field staff to inform them of the outcome of ICPD and to seek their views on reorienting and reorganizing its work programme in the light of the ICPD Programme of Action. A number of task forces were also appointed to revise technical and programme guidelines to bring them in line with the ICPD Programme. UNFPA officials realize that this will be a continuing process, as the guidelines will have to be revised and updated on the basis of operational experiences.

With the approval of its Executive Board in 1995, UNFPA has reoriented its programme priorities to focus on three main areas: reproductive health, including family planning and sexual health, population and development strategies, and advocacy. A UN report notes:

UNFPA support for reproductive health is based on a public-health, pragmatic and participatory approach. UNFPA will support all aspects of family planning at the primary, secondary and tertiary levels. Support for other components of reproductive heath will be concentrated at the primary health-care level. Recognizing the need for strengthening referral services for the evaluation and treatment of reproductive health problems that cannot be managed at the primary health-care level, UNFPA will promote the appropriate strengthening of reproductive health services at the secondary and tertiary levels. (UN, 1996d: Para. 30)

The report further points out that:

[i]n order to position itself better to play a lead role in the follow-up to ICPD, UNFPA has reviewed and adjusted all its operational guidelines to align them with the recommendations of the ICPD Programme of Action. In 1995, UNFPA also held a series of regional follow-up consultations that yielded valuable insights into the differing needs of various countries and regions. As a result, country programmes are being designed or reoriented to reflect the priorities and commitments emerging from ICPD. Thus increased emphasis is being placed on the following themes and issues: adopting a reproductive health approach; increasing the role and responsibility of men in reproductive health and family life; expanding reproductive health services and information for youth and adolescents; ensuring women's empowerment and the gender perspective; and expanding partnerships with non-governmental organizations. (UN, 1996d: Para. 30)

In line with its revised programme strategies, UNFPA has also updated its strategy for resource allocation. This strategy, which was approved by its Executive Board in 1996, seeks to concentrate on those countries that, judged by several economic and social indicators, need most help in implementing ICPD goals and objectives. These countries (most of which are in sub-Saharan Africa and Southern Asia) will receive support in all major programme areas, whereas those countries that have already achieved significant success in reaching some of the ICPD goals will receive support in those specific programme areas where it is still needed. A third group of countries will receive mainly technical assistance. Countries of Eastern and Central Europe will receive special attention on a temporary basis.

In October 1994 the Executive Board of UNICEF requested its Executive Director to prepare and submit a report on the role of UNICEF in the follow-up to the ICPD. This report, which was submitted to the Board in March 1995, indicated that UNICEF would focus on strengthening its own strategies, advocacy and programme interventions to promote the reproductive health of women and youth, specifically by improving their access to essential and emergency obstetric care, promoting family planning and preventing STDs, including HIV/AIDS. UNICEF would also expand its efforts to provide universal access to basic education, improve gender equity, and enhance the status of girls and women in society. UNICEF has further clarified its position on family planning and reproductive health issues by indicating that it would include appropriate information on these topics in its information and advocacy campaigns, but that it would not fund contraceptive commodities or services, leaving this task to other organizations such as UNFPA. This clarification does not seem to have satisfied the Holy See, which announced in 1996 the withdrawal of its symbolic annual contribution of US$2000 to UNICEF, questioning its involvement in family planning and reproductive health issues.

WHO defined its role in the post-ICPD environment in a report entitled 'Reproductive Health: WHO's Role in a Global Strategy', which was submitted to the World Health Assembly in May 1995. According to this report, which was approved by the World Health Assembly, WHO's strategy will focus on four interrelated areas: (1) international and national advocacy for the concept of reproductive health and for the policies and programmes promoted by WHO; (2) research aimed at adapting and applying existing knowledge and developing new approaches and interventions as well as the coordination of global efforts in these areas; (3) normative functions, including policy development, strategic approaches, norms, standards and guidelines; and (4) technical support to member states and others in formulating, implementing and evaluating comprehensive national reproductive health policies and programmes (UN, 1995c: Para. 52).

Recent reports indicate that WHO, in addition to updating and revising various guidelines, is giving particular attention to the area of adolescent health. A joint WHO/UNFPA/UNICEF statement on action for adolescent health has been issued (WHO/UNFPA/UNICEF, 1997), as has a joint WHO/UNICEF publication on the status of adolescent health in developing countries (UN, 1997a: Para. 15). WHO is also working closely with other interested UN organizations on focusing world attention on the practice of female genital mutilation. Most observers agree that WHO's role, given its technical expertise and experience, will be crucial in providing guidelines, standards and benchmarks for integrated reproductive health programmes.

The UNAIDS, which is co-sponsored by six UN agencies and organizations (UNDP, UNICEF, UNFPA, WHO, UNESCO and the World Bank), came into existence soon after the ICPD. Its work plan on HIV/AIDS prevention focuses on the relevant objectives of the international community outlined in the ICPD Programme of Action. The technical expertise and advice this new Programme will be able to provide to national HIV/AIDS prevention programmes will play a crucial role in making their interventions effective.

Many other UN agencies and organizations (UNDP), the UN High Commissioner for Refugees (UNHCR), UNESCO, FAO, ILO, the World Bank and others) are involved in the ICPD follow-up and report on their activities through the ACC Task Force on Basic Social Services for All. I should also mention here some of the activities being undertaken by the UN regional commissions. The ESCAP continues to monitor the implementation of the regional programme of action adopted in Bali (1992) and its relevance to the ICPD programme of Action. It has also undertaken research on gender issues including gender equity, violence against women and maternal mortality. As many Asian countries are now increasingly concerned about the problems of ageing, ESCAP has also prepared and issued several research volumes on the subject, and provided technical assistance to several governments on development and the implementation of policies aimed at involving the elderly in economic and social development. The ECA is involved in monitoring the implementation of the Dakar/Ngor Declaration as from the ICPD Programme of Action. The ECE, with support from UNFPA, is assisting the countries with economies in transition in such areas as data collection and analysis and the compilation and dissemination of policy-relevant information.[7]

REORIENTATION OF POLICIES AND EMERGING ISSUES

The GA, in Resolution 49/128, affirmed that 'in the implementation of the Programme of Action, Governments should commit themselves at the highest political level to achieving its goals and objectives, which reflect a new, integrated approach to population and development, and take a lead in coordinating the implementation, monitoring and evaluation of follow-up actions'. This was reiterated by the GA in Resolution 51/176 of 16 December 1996.

The primary emphasis is thus on the implementation of the ICPD Programme of Action at the country level. In preparing its progress reports on national implementation, UNFPA has mainly relied on the information provided by its field offices. In addition, information on changes in policies and programme priorities that are taking place is available in the country programme documents prepared for submission to the UNDP/UNFPA Executive Board. All of these documents demonstrate a clear pattern of policy changes in many countries. Several illustrative cases are cited below.

Benin is one of the African countries where some of the most remarkable policy changes have taken place since Cairo. In 1996, the Government of Benin adopted a very comprehensive population policy, and with the technical assistance of Tunisia is establishing a framework for the provision of reproductive health services through local health centres. Another African country where major initiatives have been undertaken in consonance with Cairo is South Africa. The new constitution of South Africa prohibits discrimination based on gender, sex, pregnancy, marital status or sexual orientation and guarantees the right of individuals to make reproductive decisions and to have access to reproductive health services. The framework of its population-related policies is being formulated on the basis of a 'green' paper circulated in 1995 and wide-ranging consultations with NGOs and community groups.

In Latin America, Peru and Bolivia are two of the countries that have changed or clarified their positions since Cairo. Peru, which during the ICPD process sometimes took rather ambiguous positions on reproductive health issues, has instituted a new policy approach that supports the provision of a wide range of family planning/reproductive health services, within its health-care system. Bolivia has issued new rules and regulations giving women freer and easier access to maternal health and family planning services.

India is another of those countries that announced a major policy change after the ICPD. It decided to move away from the system of quotas and targets to be filled by family planning service providers that had been in place for decades. In 1995–1996, at the initiative of JC Pant, who was then the Secretary of Family Welfare in the Government of India, several districts were selected for an experiment in this regard. Having looked at the results of this experiment and after consulting with state officials, the central government announced that from April 1996 onwards the system would be abolished all over India and would be replaced by a new set of indicators on access to and availability of services to monitor programme performance. It is perhaps too early to say if the new policy has been fully understood and accepted by all the service providers. But the information on the experimental programmes introduced in some of the districts in 1995 seems quite encouraging. In the state of Rajasthan, two rural and densely populated districts – Tonk and Dausa – were selected in 1995 to launch a new programme, under a restructured institutional set-up which brought together under one manager all the health workers and midwives in a district. The programme did not prescribe quotas and targets. Instead, it sought to meet the need of couples for contraceptive services as well as pre- and post-natal care, based on the results of door-to-door surveys conducted by local health workers and auxiliary nurse midwives. Reports show that between 1995 and 1997 the CPR has gone up from 31 and 35 per cent to 47.4 and 48.9 per cent – a spectacular increase by any standards.

I was told during my visits to India in 1997 that a fully fledged effort was being made in various states to restructure the programmes and to reorient and retrain the service providers and their supervisors. The senior officials of the Ministry of Health and Family Welfare I spoke to seemed confident that the new policy would take root. These officials also took heart from the results of the latest surveys, which show that the annual population growth rate in India has continued to decline and is now around 1.8 per cent. There is also increasing realization in India that a standard formula would not fit all the states or, for that matter, all the districts within a state, and that sufficient authority would have to be given to local programme managers to adapt their programmes to the needs and wishes of the local population.

More recently, the Philippines has announced plans for a similar policy change (*The Straits Times*, 6 June 1997). The government believes that dropping the quotas and providing a full range of services, including family planning, will make them more easily accessible and available, particularly to women. Many other countries in Asia, as in Africa and Latin America, have similarly begun to move away from narrowly defined demographic goals and targets. Instead, they plan to focus on responding to individual needs for family planning and reproductive health information and services.

At the international level, the broad thrust of the reorientation of population policies and programmes advocated by Cairo has received further endorsements at subsequent UN conferences (Copenhagen, Beijing, Istanbul and Rome), but only after the vast majority of government delegates and NGO observers have thwarted the attempts made in each case by a very small group of delegations to revise or water down some of the key concepts and definitions accepted at Cairo. For those organizations (including NGOs and women's groups) and individuals involved in shaping the message of Cairo, it is necessary to continue working towards a broadly based understanding and acceptance of this message and to maintain and strengthen the networks and coalitions forged during the ICPD process that so effectively influenced the outcome of Cairo.

Maternal mortality has received increased attention since Cairo as an extremely important indicator of the status of women and their access to adequate health care. But the paucity and inadequacy of data continue to hamper the development of reliable and up-to-date estimates. The previous estimates of 500,000 maternal deaths per year have now been increased to 590,000 maternal deaths per year. In case of Africa, maternal mortality is now estimated at 880 deaths per 100,000 live births, compared with the previous estimate of 630 deaths per 100,000 live births. UN agencies and organizations such as WHO, UNICEF and the UNFPA plan to provide both technical advice and programme support to individual countries to reduce the incidence of high maternal mortality.

On the subject of international migration, there have been several follow-up activities to Cairo. GA Resolution 49/127 of 19 December 1994 requested the UN Secretary General to prepare a report on the possibility of convening a global conference on international migration. The report, which was prepared by the Population Division in 1995 and submitted to the substantive session of ECOSOC in 1995, did not find a consensus in favour of convening a global conference. The discussion continued at the 50th session of the GA, but without any results. The Commission on

Population and Development devoted a major part of its 1997 Session to the topic of international migration and approved plans for an international symposium on international migration in 1998.[8] So far, however, no agreement seems to be emerging on holding an international conference on migration in the near future. Apart from 'conference fatigue' in UN circles, there is the feeling shared among many countries that such a conference would not serve any useful purpose unless it were preceded by a set of carefully negotiated regional and sub-regional formulas and agreements on the vexing disputes and issues relating to international migration.

Following the adoption by the Commission on Population and Development of detailed plans for an international technical symposium on international migration, the Working Group on International Migration, which was set up by the ACC Task Force on Basic Social Services for All with ILO as the lead agency, has decided to organize the event in the Hague (the Netherlands) in 1998. The symposium is expected to examine various aspects of international migration and refugee movements and to suggest appropriate policy responses. Following the symposium, the proposal to hold an international conference on migration may be aired again in 1998.

In the post-ICPD era, one of the most interesting developments has been the emergence of the International Organization for Migration (IOM) as a dynamic player in all the discussions on international migration issues.[9] Though an intergovernmental organization with 61 members, IOM is not part of the UN system. However, since 1992 it has enjoyed special status at the UN GA. On 25 June 1996, it signed a cooperation agreement with the UN and subsequently with a number of other UN organizations. It also sits on the Working Group on International Migration. IOM has close operational links with the office of UNHCR, and increasingly with UNDP. With UNFPA support, it has carried out a major study on the dynamics of emigration in selected developing countries and regions. In future discussion and negotiations on international migration issues, IOM is most likely to play a significant and influential role.

THE INTEGRATION OF FAMILY PLANNING AND REPRODUCTIVE HEALTH SERVICES

In the post-ICPD era, the integration of family planning into a wide range of reproductive health services has been accepted as an operational objective by many developing countries. For example, the Government of Mexico decided, soon after Cairo, to put family planning and other reproductive health services under one common directorate, with the aim of providing integrated services. To this end, it has also established a National Committee of Reproductive Health which is chaired by the Minister of Health and includes representatives from several ministries as well as NGOs. This committee will promote and coordinate the necessary reforms in the health sector during 1995–2000. Gregorio Perez-Palacios, Director General of Reproductive Health in Mexico, says the reform process is moving forward quite well, with additional components being added to FP and MCH services.

Bolivia has established a new Maternity and Child Insurance Programme, which gives women free access to reproductive health care including pre-natal care, delivery and post-natal care, family planning, and PAP smear tests. The management of the complications of unsafe abortion is also included in its health services.

Ghana has formulated a national reproductive policy based on ICPD definitions, and aims at improving the delivery of services particularly in the marginal communities. Kenya has developed a new health framework with four major components: family planning, STD/HIV/ AIDS control, the early detection of reproductive organ cancers, and counselling on sexuality (see UNFPA, 1997b: 58–59).

The integration of family planning and other reproductive health services is also now a primary objective in many Asian countries. Vira Niyomwan, Deputy Director General of the Department of Health in Thailand, told me that providing integrated services including family planning, maternal and child care, the prevention of STDs, and the prevention of HIV/AIDS was the stated goal of the Ministry of Health, even before the ICPD. The ICPD Programme of Action has, however, underlined the importance of a 'holistic approach', and reproductive health care as defined by the Ministry of Health now includes family planning, sexual education, STDs, reproductive tract infection, post-fertility care for women, infertility treatment and abortion. Thai officials accept that many officials lack an understanding of the holistic or integrated approach. Even less well understood is the notion of reproductive rights. 'To women activists and staff of family planning NGOs . . . the most frequent form of reproductive rights violation occurs when clients are given incomplete information about contraceptive methods' (Chamsanit, 1996: 16). A lack of understanding of the integrated approach, the inadequacy of the information or choices offered to women and a lack of emphasis on the quality of care offered to clients are three of the most important issues that would have to be tackled by both government and NGO officials in Thailand, as in a very large number of other developing countries.

In Indonesia, there is a growing realization that while family planning programmes have achieved a remarkable degree of success, the treatment and prevention of STDs, and the fight against the pandemic of HIV/AIDS require much greater attention than in the recent past. Also, the reduction of maternal mortality, where Indonesia lags behind all other members of the Association of South-East Asian Nations (ASEAN), is being assigned a high priority. Abdullah Cholil, a senior Indonesian official who participated in all the sessions of the ICPD Preparatory Committee and the Cairo Conference, says that the maternal mortality rate (MMR) in Indonesia is 'intolerably high' (Cholil, 1996: 2). According to the *1996 Human Development Report* issued by UNDP, the MMR in Indonesia in 1993 was 650 per 100,000 live births. To drastically reduce maternal mortality, Dr Cholil proposes a six-point programme which brings us, again, to the integrated approach advocated by Cairo: advancement of the role and status of women; empowerment of pregnant women by giving them more knowledge and information; family planning for every couple in need; basic maternal care for all pregnant women; a community-based data collection and referral system; and accessible emergency obstetrical care for pregnant women at risk.

Malaysia, which already provides a wide range of reproductive health services for those who need them, including modern contraception, feels quite comfortable with the ICPD definition of reproductive health. Dr Raj Karim, who has served as Director General of the National Population and Family Development Board of Malaysia since 1992 and who was among the more active participants in the ICPD process, believes that Malaysia has acquired a great deal of experience in providing reproductive health services and says it is quite willing to offer training opportunities for programme managers from Central Asian countries. Her latest concern is how to deal with the problems faced by adolescents, something that will not come as a surprise to those who have some knowledge of the changing patterns of adolescent behaviour in many Asian countries.

Bangladesh, which has a highly effective family planning programme, accepts the need to establish an institutional framework and a timetable for integrating this programme with other reproductive health services. A sectoral review by the UNFPA field office in Bangladesh points out that

> [t]he family planning program has been driven by a single focus – gaining acceptors to meet demographic targets. This is not something which the program need be ashamed of at this juncture since the same motivations drove most of the world's successful family planning programs. However, to move from a target-driven, demographic approach to a client-centred reproductive health approach calls for sweeping changes. Not only do clinics need to be able to offer a wider range of services, the service providers need to change their attitudes in order to serve to a wider range of reproductive health needs, not simply immediate family planning services. (UNFPA Dhaka, 1996: 14)

I have mentioned earlier the case of India, which has officially decided to give up the quota and target system in favour of a client-centred approach. Its officials readily admit the conceptual and institutional shortcomings in implementing the new approach. They also argue that it will take some time to bring family planning and other reproductive health services together.

The cases I have cited here go to show that the ICPD definition of reproductive health is being embraced by an increasing number of countries in all parts of the world. However, we can already see that implementing it will require major reorientation and training of staff, changes in institutional and management structures, additional facilities and, of course, additional funding, based on local needs and circumstances.

At the international level, the ICPD definition of reproductive health has become the norm for WHO, UNFPA and a whole host of other intergovernmental and non-governmental organizations. It is being used to reformulate and update their own programme priorities and strategies. The definition has also been sustained at all the subsequent UN conferences, although, as I have pointed out earlier, an attempt was made each time by a small group of countries to water it down. The definition remained intact in the Platform for Action adopted at the Fourth World Conference on Women (Beijing, 1995) as well as in the recommendations of the Social Summit (Copenhagen, 1995), Habitat II (Istanbul, 1996) and the World Food Conference (Rome, 1996).

It is interesting to note that while the Holy See does not fully endorse the ICPD language on reproductive health and reproductive rights, it has ended up supporting the inclusion of this language in the recommendations of all subsequent UN conferences, in preference to other formulations offered. While its opposition to abortion remains unwavering, it also seems to have eased its stance on modern or 'artificial' contraception. A news dispatch in *The Times* (London) of 13 March 1997 says that the Pontifical Council for the Family has issued a new handbook for priests recommending that 'Catholics who admit using the Pill, the sheath or other forms of contraception should be given absolution, even if they carry out the "sin" repeatedly, as long as each time . . . they confess they are penitent and make a commitment "not to fall again into sin"'. The Catholic Church thus seems to acknowledge the reality that the vast majority of Catholics around the world are already using modern contraceptive methods.

In the post-Cairo period, some supporters of family planning have worried aloud that family planning might be neglected or lost sight of when advocating the broad reproductive health approach. At the other end of the spectrum, several women's groups have expressed apprehension that the approach adopted at Cairo would not really be put into practice in many countries because of political or religious opposition, a lack of political commitment or a lack of resources.

A declaration issued by the Eighth International Women's Health Meeting in Rio in March 1997 takes the view that 'in many countries what is occurring is a narrow interpretation of the Cairo and Beijing resolutions, the implementation of vertical models, and the renaming of pre-existing and newly-launched family planning programs as reproductive health' (*The Earth Times*, 1–15 April 1997). The countries which are attempting to change the vertical models would probably argue, with some justification, that it is impossible to change family planning programmes into reproductive health programmes overnight and that, given the limitations of infrastructure and resources, they have no option but to adopt an incremental approach to integrating family planning with other reproductive health services. This would also appear to be the general approach favoured by UNFPA in the case of those countries which have well established family planning programmes. I would agree, at the same time, that it will be important for NGOs, women's groups and other actors in civil society to keep the spotlight on how this process of integration and expansion is working or not working. This would help ensure that rhetoric is followed by real action.

Adolescent sexuality and health is another area of increasing concern to policy makers and programme managers in many countries around the world. Teenage pregnancies and the rising rates of STDs, including HIV/AIDS, particularly in Africa and Latin America, have made them acutely aware of the need to give adolescents accurate and adequate information on sexuality and its implications and consequences, and they are willing to consider plans to give them both information and counselling. However, the provision of services and contraceptive commodities to young people runs against social and religious mores and taboos in many societies. Both advocacy and advice from international and non-governmental organizations will be needed to register steady progress towards overcoming these obstacles.

THE EMPOWERMENT OF WOMEN

Though the recommendations of UN global conferences such as Cairo and Beijing are not legally enforceable, they set up standards, goals and benchmarks against which individual countries and the international community judge their accomplishments as well as failures. This is especially true of the recommendations concerning reproductive health, reproductive rights and the empowerment of women. As public attention continues to be focused on these recommendations and increasing support is voiced for their implementation, the policy makers are encouraged or persuaded of the urgency of the issues and of the need to act.

This happened during the Cairo process, as various issues regarding women's empowerment were being debated at the national level, and continued after the Cairo and Beijing conferences in the context of the call to implement their recommendations. For example, in 1995 South Africa and Vietnam adopted laws prohibiting discrimination in employment on the grounds of pregnancy and marital status. Also in 1995, Brazil approved legislation prohibiting the requirement that a woman furnish as a condition of employment a certificate indicating that she had been sterilized or that she was not pregnant; Peru amended its national population law to remove the provisions that excluded sterilization as a method of family planning (Boland, 1997).

The need to protect women against sexual and domestic violence is being recognized by an increasing number of individual countries. UNFPA (1997b) reports that Bolivia, Costa Rica, Ecuador and Panama have recently adopted laws against domestic violence and similar measures are under consideration in many other countries. The incidence of rape, abuse and domestic violence is being reported more widely by the media in both developing and developed countries, and there is evidence, as recorded by the media and the NGO community, to show that there is much greater public support than in the past for strong legal and judicial measures to deal with acts of sexual and domestic violence. While in many countries laws already exist to deal with such acts of violence and what is needed is more determined and vigorous action on the part of the authorities, in many other countries currently applicable laws will need to be amended. Both the media and civil society organizations, including population NGOs, women's groups and parliamentary organizations, have an extremely important role to play in this context.

These are encouraging examples of national action. But given deep-rooted traditional attitudes and patterns of male behaviour, the implementation of the Cairo and Beijing recommendations on women's issues and rights must be regarded as a long-term endeavour on the part of enlightened policy makers and leaders of civil society organizations.

THE INCREASING ROLE OF THE NGO SECTOR

NGOs and other civil society organizations (parliamentarians, academic groups and youth and women's groups) continue to play an active role in disseminating information about the ICPD Programme of Action. IWHC (1995) provides an analysis of the consensus forged at Cairo, and a summary of the main points in each chapter of the ICPD Programme of Action. Organizations such as IPPF, The Centre for Development and Population Activities (CEDPA) and Family Health International have produced and distributed among their constituents special publications on the ICPD.

Since Cairo, IPPF, which with 144 national member associations is the largest international NGO in the field of voluntary family health care, has organized numerous seminars and workshops at international and regional levels to focus the attention of its constituents and affiliates on the implementation of the ICPD Programme of Action. Ms Brueggemann, who succeeded Dr Hafdan Mahler as Secretary General of IPPF in 1995, and others in the IPPF leadership, point out that Cairo's goals and objectives are mostly the same as those outlined in the Vision 2000 plan, which was adopted by the IPPF member assembly in 1992. Cairo thus provides an extremely valuable framework, backed up by a wide-ranging international consensus, for IPPF's own work programme.

Many other international NGOs such as the Population Council, PAI, the Population Institute, the Center for Population and Development Activities, Family Health International and the Commonwealth Medical Association have sponsored or supported international or regional meetings where specific aspects of the implementation of the ICPD Programme of Action were analysed in depth.

Many NGOs have also been consulted by governments on follow-up national action plans and programmes, and an increasing number are involved in population programmes at the local level. UNFPA field offices have been encouraged to set up consultative groups or committees involving NGOs. At its headquarters, UNFPA has expanded and updated its guidelines for cooperation with NGOs, and an NGO Advisory Committee constituted by UNFPA's Executive Director has met annually since 1995. While still at UNFPA I was involved in the first meeting in 1995 and was struck at the time by the enthusiasm shown by a variety of NGOs in carrying forward the message of Cairo.

Advocacy and championing by NGOs of specific causes, as we have seen in earlier chapters, have convinced diplomats and officials to take significant action, and I believe this trend will continue. Under the agenda formulated by Cairo and Beijing, there are a number of issues – the reduction of maternal mortality, adolescent health, the education of young girls and the prevention of domestic abuse and violence – which are of particular concern to NGOs and will undoubtedly receive their continuing attention.

The issue of female genital mutilation is another of these issues, which has recently begun to receive increasing international attention, primarily through the efforts of a group of NGOs. Both Cairo and Beijing condemned the practice of female genital mutilation and called for its early eradication. It is, however, deep-rooted in the social and cultural traditions of many African and Arab countries. An uncompromising and sustained information and educational campaign on the part of the concerned NGOs will be needed to bring about an end to this practice. All the evidence suggests that NGOs are fully committed to this task.

Internationally, organizations such as WEDO are involved in NGO efforts to monitor the action taken by individual countries and international organizations to implement Cairo and to keep them focused on this task by constantly reminding them of the commitments they made there. A monitoring report covering more than 100 countries, sponsored by the Natural Resources Defense Council (NRDC) and WEDO, was issued in 1995 (Earth Summit Watch, 1995), and I understand there are plans to issue such a report on a regular basis in the future.

The involvement of NGOs in programme implementation at the national and local levels is being encouraged in a number of countries. In visits to several countries in Asia in 1996–1997 I was encouraged to find that the participation of NGOs in operational programmes was indeed growing. However, in some countries NGO officials expressed the suspicion or fear that governments, in providing financial support for NGO activities, might also seek to control them. On the other side, many government officials spoke of their concerns regarding the long-term sustainability of NGO operations, financial accountability and the lack of transparency in the governance of NGOs. While governments will have to allay NGO concerns, NGOs on their part will be expected to meet the standard financial and reporting requirements and to provide more information on their internal structures and planning and operational procedures.

THE MOBILIZATION OF RESOURCES

Soon after the ICPD, the OECD Development Assistance Committee (DAC) organized a meeting in Paris (29–30 November 1994) to give donors an opportunity to reflect on the implications of the ICPD Programme of Action. Dr Sadik and I were present at this meeting, which was chaired by DAC Chairman James Michel (US). In addition to representatives of the World Bank and the EC, representatives of all the donor countries (including many who had attended the Cairo Conference) participated in this meeting.

The participants in the Paris meeting endorsed the 'paradigm shift' at Cairo and agreed that they would work with UNFPA and other relevant bodies in defining the steps needed to implement the Cairo Consensus. When discussing the financing needs contained in the ICPD Programme of Action, '[t]he general view was that the further work envisioned in paragraph 13.15 is urgently needed to improve the estimates, especially for reproductive health, and, again to agree on definitions so that reporting from multiple sources will be comparable and transparent' (OECD, 1995: 6).

The donor countries also indicated at this meeting the approaches they were likely to pursue in allocating resources. They thought that overall aid levels were unlikely to grow in the future, and that achieving the indicative levels of contributions on the part of individual donors to reach ICPD goals would require shifts in their priorities. This was what one of the participants called in the corridors a 'reality check'. Many of them also expressed the view that if funding levels for population were to increase, bilateral programmes were more likely to expand than were multilateral programmes. Some of the other proposals mentioned in the meeting were about building up and strengthening staff capability relevant to the new approaches, the consideration of earmarked funding dedicated to the Cairo agenda, and encouraging priority attention to population issues by developing country authorities.

Six months later, a donor workshop, co-sponsored by the UK Overseas Development Administration (UKODA) and USAID, sought to discuss further the donor response to funding needs, particularly for reproductive health. The workshop (New York, 12–14 June 1995) underscored the success of the ICPD

in that the concept of reproductive health was adopted not only by technical experts but by politicians. Many policy officials are strongly in favor of the new concepts and goals articulated at the ICPD, but are asking how they will be implemented. Reproductive health goals therefore need to be articulated in more operational terms so that they can be fully funded. (UKODA/USAID, 1995: 29)

Since 1995, many bilateral donors, including USAID and ODA, have indeed reoriented many of their policies and approaches in the light of ICPD. At the international level, WHO and UNFPA have organized several workshops and seminars to clarify definitional and operational issues regarding reproductive health at international and regional levels, and various guidelines and guidance notes have been revised and updated. The process also continues at the national level, as these guidelines and notes are adapted to specific conditions and the infra-structure, commodity and servicing requirements of individual countries are clearly identified. All these efforts at various levels should help to clarify operational needs and requirements. But if individual donor agencies are to give adequate attention to those countries with the most urgent and pressing needs, they would need to strengthen, in line with the thinking articulated at the Paris and New York meetings, their technical capacity in the area of population and to allocate much greater support to population programmes than they have provided so far.

Since 1995, the Executive Director of UNFPA has organized an annual consultation with multilateral and bilateral donors, coinciding with the annual sessions of the Commission on Population and Development. These meetings have provided a useful opportunity to exchange inform-ation and engage in a general review of progress toward raising the funds needed to reach the ICPD goals. But these meetings have not always been attended by all the major donors, and the information provided there provides an incomplete picture of what is being done to mobilize resources. At the 1997 meeting, many of the donors asked UNFPA to prepare an update on global funding for population programmes. A provisional version of the report prepared in response was distributed at the UNDP/UNFPA Executive Board Meeting in May 1997 and the final version at the Board Meeting in September 1997 (UN, 1997d).

The report indicates that the funding for population did go up in 1994 and 1995, but it seems likely that the total amount did not increase in 1996; it may be lower than in 1995. A lower rate of exchange *vis-à-vis* the US dollar was partly responsible for this decrease. But there are other, more important reasons we should take note of.

Though the US administration, under President Clinton, remains firmly committed to the Cairo agenda, the majority of the US Congress (particularly in the House of Representatives) seems less sympathetic to providing more money for population assistance. The money provided by the US to population assistance has gone down every year since 1995, and there is considerable uncertainty as to how much population assistance the US would provide in future. Japan, the biggest donor to UNFPA, is reducing its overall ODA commitments by 10 per cent, though it is not clear what impact this would have on the population sector. Almost all of the European donors have seen the value of their contributions fall because of the soaring value of the US dollar, and some of them are also reducing their overall commitments to ODA, including population assistance. But there are also encouraging developments. The Netherlands, following a resolution adopted by its parliament, is committed to raising the amount devoted to population assistance to 4 per cent of its ODA by the year 2000, and the UK, under the new Labour government, is expected to strengthen the UK commitment to Cairo.

There are also two bright spots on the international scene provided by the World Bank and the EU. The World Bank has increased its support for reproductive health and population-related activities from around US$300 million in 1994 to US$448 million in 1995 and around $600 million in 1996. It remains committed to providing even greater support if the countries want it. The EU has reiterated the commitment it made in 1994 to provide approximately US$300 million for population by the year 2000. Most recently, it has provided through UNFPA a grant of US$35 million to NGOs in Asia and committed US$200 million to the Government of India for reproductive health programmes (Europe Information Service, 1997).

The 1997 UNFPA report also points out that following the ICPD the developing countries have substantially increased their investments in the population sector. The total amount of domestic resources allocated in 1995 is estimated at US$7.5 billion, including US$6.1 billion in government funds and US$1.1 billion from domestic private resources.

If we add this amount to approximately US$2.0 billion provided by international sources, the total funding for population programmes in 1995 would come to US$9.5 billion. The total of US$7.5 billion allocated by developing countries is not that far from the US$11.3 billion projected as their contribution toward the ICPD goals in the year 2000. In fact, now they are contributing around 78 per cent of resources, whereas Cairo agreed that their share of resources by the year 2000 should be around 67 per cent.

To put the contribution of developing countries into a proper perspective, it is important to note that the amount of US$7.5 billion includes very substantial allocations by a few large countries such as China, India and Indonesia, whose programmes are financed to a great extent through domestic budgets. In many other developing countries, including the least developed countries and most of those in sub-Saharan Africa, domestic resources can only support part of the population programme costs, and an increasing amount of external support will continue to be needed, especially if these countries are to register significant progress toward ICPD goals.

On the other side, donor assistance, after recording an impressive rate of growth during 1993–1995, has ceased to grow and it may even be declining. The amount of about US$2 billion for population assistance in 1995 shows an impressive 40 per cent increase over 1994, which in turn was 40 per cent more than in 1993. But in 1996 there was probably no increase over 1995, and the prognosis for 1997 is no better. At current rates, donor assistance cannot be expected to rise to US$5.7 billion (the donor share of US$17.0 billion) by 2000.[10]

The UNFPA report paints a grim picture of the consequences of a shortfall in resources:

> *the magnitude of the negative effects of failing to fully implement the ICPD Program of Action . . . should be sobering to all who are committed to the goals of ICPD. If the implementation of the Program of Action were to fall short of the agreed targets and goals, many reproductive-health outcomes would suffer incrementally. Millions of individuals or couples who would have used family-planning services would not be able to do so because fewer services will be available or accessible. Many millions more unintended pregnancies would thus result over this period and millions of these pregnancies would end in abortions. Hundreds of thousands more women would die than otherwise, either in childbirth or while undergoing unsafe abortions. Several times that number of mothers would suffer life-threatening morbidities. Millions of unwanted children, born from unintended pregnancies, would die in their infancy or early childhood. While the exact estimates may change when more data become available, the order of magnitude of this grave – yet avoidable – consequence will not change.* (UN, 1997d: 63)

There is clearly an urgent need to refocus international attention on the funding needs in the population field and on ways and means of meeting these needs. The US, as the largest donor in the field, is expected by other donors and by developing countries to find a way to reinforce and strengthen its financial commitment to the Cairo goals. A similar responsibility lies on other donors, including traditional major donors and other countries whose contribution to population is limited (Table 7.1 provides an estimate of the percentage increases required in the

Table 7.1 Donor Assistance for Population in 1995 and Possible Patterns for the Year 2000

Country	Population assistance in 1995 (US$ millions)	ICPD target reached using gross domestic product (1995) (US$ millions)	Annual rate of growth to meet ICPD resource target (per cent)
Australia	27	57	16
Austria	3	38	68
Belgium	6	44	51
Canada	37	93	20
Denmark	50	28	—
Finland	22	21	—
France[a]	13	252	80
Germany	145	395	22
Ireland	3	10	28
Italy	4	178	109
Japan	94	837	55
Luxembourg	1	3	26
Netherlands	87	65	—
New Zealand	1	9	51
Norway	47	24	—
Spain[a]	1	93	176
Sweden[a]	45	37	—
Switzerland	17	50	24
UK	98	180	13
US	667	1157	12
Total[b]	1368	3570[c]	21

Source: UN (1997d).

[a] For France and Spain, 1993 data were used. For Sweden, 1994 data were used.

[b] Due to rounding, columns may not sum exactly to totals.

[c] Reaching the necessary US$5.67 billion would also require US$2.10 billion from development banks, multilateral organizations and private institutions.

contributions of individual donor countries to reach the ICPD resource target by the year 2000).

Funding by the private sector (including corporations, foundations and NGOs) has gone up in the last several years and may indeed increase further if private donors could be persuaded to support more worthwhile projects. 'Debt-swaps' may present another potentially large source of funding for population programmes. In its report, UNFPA indicates that it would like to encourage agreements between lenders and debtors at governmental and private levels under which creditors would forgive a portion of debt in exchange for an agreement on the part of the debtor countries to use equivalent local resources for reproductive health and related population programmes. So far this approach has been tried in a few selected cases to obtain local funds for environmental projects. There is no reason why it could not also work for population projects.

While NGO and private channels could and should provide greater support to population programmes, those governments which provide ODA and several others in a position to provide such assistance in the future need to be reminded that for many developing countries, particularly in sub-Saharan Africa, ODA will remain the major source of external financial support towards the implementation of international commitments in the foreseeable future.

In the final analysis, a very logical and persuasive case can be made, on three grounds, for greater support to population activities in the future. First, investments in the population sector have, within a relatively short period of 25–30 years, shown impressive, in some cases even extraordinary, results, which cannot be said of investments in many other sectors of development. Second, the programme areas where investments are needed have been clearly identified. And third, the amounts needed are not mind-boggling. In fact, they are relatively small and, with a little bit of extra effort, can be found within the current projections for ODA budgets of donor countries.

IMPLEMENTING CAIRO

Implementing the new global consensus on the reorientation of population policies, the integration of population, environment and development strategies and the operationalization of the broadly based concepts of reproductive health and reproductive rights will require in each country the evolution of a national consensus on the policy, legal and institutional implications of these concepts and on the action needed to convert them into reality. Not only the governments but also all the actors in civil society have to commit themselves fully and unequivocally to this process.

In implementing the ICPD Programme of Action which embodies this new global consensus, it will be important for countries to learn from success stories, but it will be equally important for them to identify, early on, the problems and constraints that impede progress. Reorienting population policies in order to focus on a human rights approach and on the need to provide comprehensive and adequate information and services to 'individuals and couples' will require radical changes at policy, institutional and managerial levels. In those countries where family planning services have been organized vertically and run parallel to other health services, efforts at integration would require policy decisions, the retraining of staff and major changes in operational and supervisory structures. In countries like India and Bangladesh, where such efforts are under way, bureaucratic obstacles and turf problems need to be overcome. In the same part of the world, Thailand provides a good example of how the integration of services can be planned and promoted. A lack of infrastructure and trained personnel and a serious shortfall of resources remain serious problems in most African countries and will slow down their efforts to realize the commitments they accepted at Cairo, unless the international community demonstrates a clear resolve to help them overcome these constraints.

Full involvement of the NGO sector, including women's groups, in policy dialogues and consultation at all levels, and increasing their participation in advocacy, information and service delivery projects, is not only desirable but necessary. It should be actively sought and promoted to help ensure that the projects respond to the specific needs of individuals and the community on a continuing and flexible basis.

Members of the international community (including, in particular, the UN organizations concerned with health and population issues) have an extremely important and crucial role to play in undertaking coordinated advocacy campaigns highlighting the messages from Cairo, providing technical advice and expertise for national action aimed at implementing the ICPD Programme, and mobilizing international resources to complement domestic resources in support of such action. Finally, regular monitoring of the implementation of the ICPD Programme at both national and international levels, including that envisaged for the 'ICPD+5' process in 1999,[11] is needed to ensure that governments, NGOs and the international community undertake all the necessary efforts to implement the promises they made at Cairo.

NOTES AND REFERENCES

1 BUCHAREST, MEXICO AND CAIRO

1 Because the EU was listed as a full participant at Cairo, the number of participating countries has sometimes been given as 180. The *Report of the International Conference on Population and Development* gets around this problem by identifying the participants as 'States and regional economic integration organizations' (UN, 1995a: 117).

2 This phrase was used by Caspar Weinberger, head of the US delegation, in his statement to the Conference.

3 The US recorded the following statement, while joining the consensus: 'The United States strongly protested the inclusion of this issue, believing it politically divisive and extraneous to the work of the Conference. The United States also challenged the competence of the Conference to interpret one of the most critical international instruments governing the rules of war, the Geneva Convention' (UN, 1984: 26).

4 In organizing the Amsterdam Forum, I was ably assisted by Stirling Scruggs and Joyce Bratich-Cherif. On the Dutch side, Karel de Beer, head of the UN Aid Section of the Ministry of Foreign Affairs, and Pauline Kruseman, Director of Corporate Affairs at the Royal Tropical Institute, were immensely helpful.

5 In addition to Mr Payton, the ICPD Secretariat based at UNFPA included Ranjit Atapattu, Senior Adviser, Stafford Mousky, Senior Adviser, and Ms Bratich-Cherif, Arthur Erken, Renata Lok, Linda Libront, Petri Tiukkanen and Christa Giles as Advisers. In the case of the UN Population Division, Birgitta Bucht, Deputy Director, UN Population Division, Armindo Miranda, Technical Adviser, and Virginia Aquino, Associate Population Affairs Officer, were extensively involved in the substantive preparatory activities. Many other staff members of the UN Population Division and the UNFPA Technical and Evaluation Division handled specific responsibilities with regard to expert group meetings, round tables and Preparatory Committee sessions. I would like to mention, in particular, David Horlacher, Ellen Brennan, Hania Zlotnik, Mary Beth Weinberger and Aminur Khan from the Population Division and M Nizamuddin, Nicholas Dodd, OJ Sikes, Catherine Pierce, Arnfin Jorgensen-Dahl and Michael Vlassoff from UNFPA.

6 Nabil El-Arabi, the Egyptian Ambassador to the UN, and his colleagues were consistently helpful to us in helping to sort out ICPD-related matters. In Cairo, Maher Mahran, the head of the National Population Council, who was appointed to the post of Minister of Population some months prior to the Conference, and Amre Moussa, Foreign Minister, played an active role in resolving various political and practical problems.

7 A synthesis of the expert group meetings, brief summaries and recommendations from each of the expert group meetings can be found in the *Population Bulletin of the United Nations* (UN, 1993a). The reports from expert group meetings, which are discussed further in the following chapters, were submitted to the PrepCom II meeting, and carry separate document numbers.

8 A synthesis of the five regional conferences, brief summaries and recommendations from each of them can be found in the *Population Bulletin of the United Nations* (UN, 1994a). The reports from regional conferences, which are discussed further in the following chapters, were submitted to the PrepCom II meeting, and carry separate document numbers.

9 All of these reports were distributed by national delegations at the Cairo Conference. In many cases, they also received wide distribution within the countries concerned.

10 During 1992–1993, these media seminars and other related activities were organized by Hirofumi Ando, UNFPA Director of Information and External Relations, in cooperation with Alex Marshall, Senior Information Officer, and Hugh O'Haire, Information Officer. In late 1993, Mr Scruggs took over these responsibilities when Mr Ando was appointed Deputy Executive Director, UNFPA. At the Cairo Conference, a joint UN–UNFPA team including Ayman El-Amir of the UN and Mr Scruggs was responsible for organizing media liaison and media briefings.

2 FROM FAMILY PLANNING TO REPRODUCTIVE HEALTH

1 The International Conference on Better Health for Women and Children through Family Planning was sponsored by five UN organizations and two NGOs: the UN Children's Fund (UNICEF), the UN Development Programme (UNDP), UNFPA, the World Bank, WHO, IPPF and Population Council.

2 This text was distributed by WHO representatives at PrepCom III and is quoted in WHO (1994, Para. 89).

3 Mr Sinding did a further analysis before the Cairo Conference in which he looked at government demographic targets in some 17 developing countries and at what fertility would be if only the unmet need for contraception in those societies – as represented by unwanted childbearing – were met. The result of his analysis, which was received with great interest by several ICPD delegations, showed that in 13 of the 17 countries, simply meeting the family planning needs of couples wishing to avoid unwanted fertility would actually result in even lower population growth than the rates that the countries had themselves established as their demographic targets (see Sinding, 1996).

191

4   A colourful account of what transpired in the meeting is to be found in Bernstein and Politi (1996). In the course of gathering material for the book, Mr Bernstein had met Dr Sadik and asked her to give him a gist of the conversation between Pope John Paul and herself. Mr Politi, the coauthor, covers the Vatican for an Italian newspaper and may have gathered additional information in Rome.

5   The titles given to the 16 chapters of the Draft Final Document as presented to PrepCom III remained mostly intact in the Draft Programme of Action presented to the Conference and the ICPD Programme of Action. The title of chapter VII, 'Reproductive Rights, Reproductive Health and Family Planning', was changed to 'Reproductive Rights, [Sexual and Reproductive Health] and Family Planning' in the Draft Programme of Action, and finally to 'Reproductive Rights and Reproductive Health' in the Programme of Action. The title of chapter XI, 'Population Information, Education and Communication', was changed to read 'Population, Development and Education' in the Programme of Action. For a listing of the chapters in the Programme of Action, see note 12 below.

6   The year 1994 was declared by the UN as also the International Year of the Family.

7   A comprehensive survey of governmental policies on abortion in 174 countries is to be found in UN (1992b).

8   For an analysis of Islamic teachings on reproductive health issues, see Omran (1992). On Buddhist views, see Gnanawimala (1993). The Hindu view is presented in Rao (1978).

9   A cable sent by the US Department of State to all its diplomatic and consular posts on 16 March 1994, which became available to many participants at PrepCom III, may have been a contributing factor. In the language of the cable, '[t]he United States believes that access to safe, legal and voluntary abortion is a fundamental right of all women' (US Department of State, 16 March 1994).

10 Remarks by Al Gore at the National Press Club, Washington, DC, on the UN Population Conference (Federal News Service, 25 August 1994).

11 Remarks by Timothy Wirth at the State Department regular briefing at Washington, DC (Reuters, 31 August 1994).

12 The ICPD Programme of Action consists of the following chapters: (I) 'Preamble'; (II) 'Principles'; (III) 'Interrelationships between Population, Sustained Economic Growth and Sustainable Development'; (IV) 'Gender Equality, Equity and Empowerment of Women'; (V) 'The Family, its Roles, Rights, Composition and Structure'; (VI) 'Population Growth and Structure'; (VII) 'Reproductive Rights and Reproductive Health'; (VIII) 'Health, Morbidity and Mortality'; (IX) 'Population Distribution, Urbanization and Internal Migration'; (X) 'International Migration'; (XI) 'Population, Development and Education'; (XII) 'Technology, Research and Development'; (XIII) 'National Action'; (XIV) 'International Cooperation'; (XV) 'Partnership with the Non Governmental Sector'; and (XVI) 'Follow-Up to the Conference'.

13 The idea of 'decriminalizing' abortion was brought up again by EU members and several other countries at the Fourth World Conference on Women (Beijing, 4–15 September 1995), and gained enough support to be included in the Beijing Platform of Action under Para. 106(k), which after endorsing

Para. 8.25 of the ICPD Programme of Action calls on governments to 'consider reviewing laws containing punitive measures against women who have undergone illegal abortions' (UN, 1996a).

3   POPULATION AND DEVELOPMENT

1   The International Convention on the Protection of the Rights of All Migrant Workers and Their Families was approved by the GA on 20 December 1990. It contains 93 articles providing an international definition of a migrant worker, categories of migrant workers and members of their families and spelling out their rights, proposing minimum standards of protection for them that will be universally acknowledged and accepted (GA Resolution 45/158, 18 December 1990).

2   The GA reviewed at its 50th Session in 1995 the proposal to convene an international conference on migration, but there was no great enthusiasm for such a conference. For further discussion of this topic, see Chapter 7.

4   THE EMPOWERMENT OF WOMEN

1   The International Women's Health Conference for Cairo 1994 was held in Rio de Janeiro from 24 to 28 January 1994, with the participation of 215 women from 79 countries. The ICPD Secretariat had provided an advance copy of the Draft Final Document (UN, 1994d) to the organizers to enable them to discuss what was being proposed in the Document.

2   These are China, India, Indonesia, Pakistan, Bangladesh, Egypt, Nigeria, Mexico and Brazil. All of them are involved in an initiative on Education for All, launched by UNESCO in 1993.

5   PARTNERSHIP WITH THE NON-GOVERNMENTAL SECTOR

1   Among 1254 accredited NGOs for the ICPD, only 153 were in Consultative Status with ECOSOC. The breakdown of the accredited NGOs by type of organization is as follows: Women's groups, defined as groups which are led by women or which target women in their programming, 210; population/FP/health groups, 295; environment groups, 87; youth groups, 51; development groups, including those organizations which deliver multi-sectoral programmes that may also include interventions in the health/population field, 323; research groups/universities, 60, 60; and others, including, among others, professional associations, trade unions, religious groups and parliamentarian organizations, 128 (UN, 1994h).

6   MOBILIZING RESOURCES FOR POPULATION PROGRAMMES

1   The three studies were eventually issued as the Family Health International study (Janowitz *et al.*, 1990), the Research Triangle Institute study (Kocher and Buckner, 1991) and the USAID study (Gillespie *et al.*, 1989).

2   The Amsterdam estimates were prepared by Rao (1990). In addition to the three draft studies mentioned above, he used the analyses prepared by Bulatao (1985).

3   The figure of US$5.6 billion was based on estimated costs of US$15 per user for Africa and US$10 per user for Asia and Latin America. The US$11 billion figure was based on estimated costs of US$30 per user for Africa and US$20 per user for Asia and Latin America.

4   The first study by Parker Mauldin (Mauldin, 1991) was published in February 1991. The second study was prepared by Mauldin in collaboration with Vincent C. Miller of the Population Council and published in time for the Cairo Conference (UNFPA, 1994a). For the second study, Mary Beth Weinberger of the UN Population Division prepared the projections of married women aged 15–49, and Randy Bulatao of the World Bank contributed a section entitled 'Unmet Need as Basis for Projection of Contraceptive Prevalence'.

5   The Secretariat advanced the methodology by adapting exploratory analyses carried out by Bulatao and Bos (1994) on the dynamics of unmet need and prevalence increase to the task of producing regional projections. The refinement and implementation of the methodology for the resource estimates and its dissemination and review were undertaken by Stan Bernstein of UNFPA, in collaboration and consultation with several experts. The process was intensive and extensive, including both the formal and informal meetings noted in this chapter and frequent information consultations.

6   The evolution of these estimates was shaped by the valuable inputs and recommendations provided by many experts and advocates including Jose Luis Bodadillo (and his colleagues on the Mother–Baby package for WHO and the World Bank), Charlotte Leighton, Joseph Speidel, Deborah Maine, Judith Bruce, Joan Dunlop and Rachel Kyte.

7   This background note was revised and issued informally on 13 July 1994 as UNFPA (1994b).

8   These meetings were held to review and disseminate the estimates. The USAID meeting included representatives from the Office of Population and the Office of Health and invited experts from cooperating agencies working on USAID projects. The OMB meeting included John Stover, Jim Knowles, Mr Bulatao and Scott Radloff of the Office of Population and served as part of the OMB's review of the proposed USAID budgetary request. The meeting at the Center for Population and Development Studies at Harvard University on 29 June 1994 was attended by academic experts (Christopher Murray, Peter Berman, Allan Hill, John Bongaarts, David Bell, Sissela Bok, George Brown, Adrienne Germain, Robert Cassen, Lincoln Chen, George Zeidenstein and Tamina Rahman), NGO representatives (Susan Davis, Joseph Speidel, Carmen Barrosso and Ms Dunlop), international organization staff and Secretariat members (Eva Jespersen, Ashok Nigam, Mr Bulatao, Peter Cowley, Stafford Mousky and Stan Bernstein), US Government officials (Nils Dulaire, Faith Mitchell and Barbara Crane) and political advisers (Joseph Wheeler, Mr Biegman and Tone de Jong).

9   The Social Development Summit (1996) agreed 'on a mutual commitment between interested developed and developing country partners to allocate,

on average, 20 per cent of ODA and 20 per cent of the national budget, respectively, to basic social programmes' (UN, 1996c: Para. 88(c)).

7 IMPLEMENTING CAIRO

1 Interview with Senator Wirth, Washington, DC, 6 January 1997.
2 Interview with Ambassador Biegman, New York, 20 February 1997.
3 Interview with Mr Suyono, Jakarta, Indonesia, 16 January 1997.
4 Interview with Ms Abzug, New York, 10 September 1997.
5 Interview with Ms Dunlop and Ms Germain, New York, 24 September 1997.
6 Interviews with Ms Brueggemann and Mr Laskin, London, 6 October 1997. Exchanges of views and impressions of the ICPD with Mr Fornos and other NGO representatives took place mainly in New York and Washington, DC, over 1996–1997.
7 For further information on the activities of the regional commissions in the follow-up to the ICPD, see UN (1997a).
8 Four of the reports submitted to the 30th Session of the Commission on Population and Development (1997) deal with international migration: UN (1996e, f; 1997b, c).
9 Established in 1951, the IOM, with its Secretariat in Geneva, has 60 governments as its members, while another 50 participate in its meetings as observers.
10 The estimates for international population assistance included in Para. 14.11 and all other relevant estimates are in 1993 US dollars. Though the rate of inflation in the US in the past several years has been running quite low, these estimates, if recalculated in 1998 dollars, will be higher.
11 The plans for review and appraisal of the implementation of the ICPD Programme of Action in 1999 (outlined in GA document A/52/208/Add.1 of 12 September 1997) include regional and technical meetings in 1998, an international forum on operational experiences to be organized by UNFPA in early 1999 and a Special Session of the GA to consider the outcome of the review process. The GA resolution calls for a three-day Special Session from 30 June to 2 July 1999, to be preceded by an open-ended session of the Commission on Population and Development serving as the Preparatory Committee for the Special Session. The Resolution says that the overall review will be undertaken 'on the basis of and with full respect for the Programme of Action' and 'that there will be no renegotiation of the existing agreements contained therein'.

BIBLIOGRAPHY

Angel, William D. (1995) *The International Law of Youth Rights: Source Documents and Commentary* Martinus, Dordrecht

Bernstein, Carl and Marco Politi. (1996) *His Holiness: John Paul II and the Hidden History of Our Time*. Doubleday, New York

Boland, Reed (1997) *Promoting Reproductive Rights: A Global Mandate* Center for Reproductive Law and Policy, New York

Bongaarts, John (1991) 'The KAP-gap and the unmet need for contraception', *Population and Development Review* 17: 293–313

Bulatao, Rodolfo A (1985) 'Expenditures on population programs in developing regions: current levels and future requirements' Working Paper no. 679, Population and Development Series, World Bank, Washington, DC

Bulatao, Rodolfo A and Eduard Bos (1994) 'Projecting contraceptive prevalence from unmet need, and vice versa' presented at the PAA Annual Meeting, May 1994

Center for Population and Family Health (1994) *Declaration of Ethical Principles, Round Table on Ethics, Population and Reproductive Health* Columbia University, New York

Chamsanit, Varaporn (1996) *Change in Population Policies and Programs Post Cairo: The Case of Thailand* Center for Health Policy Studies, Mahidol University, Nakornprathom

Cholil, Abdullah (1996) 'Mother (women) friendly movement' unpublished paper

Cleland, John (1996) 'ICPD and the feminization of population and development issues' *Health Transition Review* 6: 107–110

Earth Negotiations Bulletin (25 April, 1994) 'Report of PrepCom III: the Programme of Action' vol 6, no.30.

Earth Negotiations Bulletin (19 May, 1993) 'PrepCom highlights: Tuesday, 18 May 1993' vol 6, no. 8

Earth Negotiations Bulletin (2 June, 1993) 'Summary of the second substantive Session of the ICPD Preparatory Committee' vol 6, no. 11

Earth Negotiations Bulletin (7 September, 1994) 'ICPD highlights: Tuesday, 6 September 1994' vol 6, no. 33

Earth Negotiations Bulletin (10 September, 1994) 'ICPD highlights: Friday, 9 September 1994' vol 6, no. 36

Earth Negotiations Bulletin (14 September, 1994) 'Summary of the ICPD: 5–13 September 1994' vol 6, no. 39

Earth Summit Watch (1995) 'One year after Cairo: assessing national action to implement the International Conference on Population and Development'

Europe Information Service (3 September 1997) 'European report'

Family Life Education Sub-Committee CONGO (1994) 'Cairo Youth Declaration on Population and Development' International NGO Youth Consultation for the ICPD, 31 August–4 September 1994, Cairo, Egypt

Fathalla, Mahound F. (1989) 'New contraceptive methods and reproductive health' in: SJ Segal, AO Tsui and SM Rogers (eds) *Demographic and Programmatic Consequence of Contraceptive Innovations*. Plenum, New York

Fathalla, Mahound F. (1991) 'Reproductive health: a global overview' *Annals of New York Academy of Science* 626 (June): 1–10

Federal News Service (25 August, 1994) Remarks by Vice President Al Gore on UN Population Control Conference, at National Press Club, Washington, DC

Finkle, Jason and Barbara Crane (1985) 'Ideology and politics at Mexico City: the United States at the 1984 International Conference on Population' *Population and Development Review* 11(1): 1–28

Gille, Halvor (1982) 'International population assistance, in: JA Ross (ed) *International Encyclopedia of Population*, 374–382, The Free Press, New York

Gillespie, Duff G, Harry E Cross, John H Crowley and Scott R Radloff (1989) 'Financing the delivery of contraceptives: the challenge of the next twenty years' in: S Segal, A Tsui and S Rogers (eds) *Demographic and Programmatic Consequences of Contraceptive Innovations* Plenum, New York

Gnanawimala, B (1993) 'Free to choose: the Buddhist view' *Asiaweek* 27 October, 54

Harkavy, Oscar (1995) *Curbing Population Growth: An Insider's Perspective on the Population Movement* Plenum, New York

Inter Press Service (5 April, 1994) 'Population: women's groups and NGOs criticize Vatican' reported by Thalif Deen

IPPF (1993) *Vision 2000: Strategic Plan* London

IWHC (1995) *The Cairo Consensus: The Right Agenda for the Right Time* New York

IWHC and CEPIA (1994) *Reproductive Health and Justice: International Women's Health Conference For Cairo '94, January 24–28, 1994 Rio de Janeiro* New York

Janowitz, Barbara, John H Bratt and Daniel B Fried (1990) *Investing in the Future: A Report of the Cost of Family Planning in the Year 2000* Family Health International, Research Triangle Park, NC

Keyfitz, Nathan (1995) 'What happened in Cairo: a view from the internet' *Canadian Journal of Sociology* 20(1): 81–90

Knodel, John and Gavin W Jones (1996) 'Post-Cairo population policy: does promoting girls' schooling miss the mark?' *Population and Development Review* 22(4): 683–702

Kocher, James E and Bates C Buckner (1991) 'Estimates of global resources required to meet population goals by the year 2010' Staff Working Paper, Center for International Development, Research Triangle Park, NC

Kuroda, Toshio (1996) *From Bucharest to Cairo: 20 Years of United Nations Population Conferences*, Resource Series 2 Asian Population and Development Association, Tokyo

Mauldin, W Parker (1991) 'Contraceptive requirements and demand for contraceptive commodities in developing countries in the 1990s' Technical Report, UNFPA

McIntosh, C Alison and Finkle, Jason (1995) 'The Cairo Conference on Population and Development: a new paradigm?' *Population and Development Review* 21(2): 223–260

Mertens, Walter (1995) *The 1994 International Conference on Population and Development: Context and Characteristics* International Union for the Scientific Study of Population, Liege, Belgium

OECD (1995) 'Meeting on population and development, 29–30 November 1994' (OCDE/GD(95)37) Paris

Omran, Abdel (1992) *Family Planning in the Legacy of Islam* Routledge, New York

Operations Research Group (1988–89) *Family Planning Practices in India*, Third All-Indian Survey

Park Ridge Center (1994) *World Religions and the 1994 United Nations International Conference on Population and Development* Chicago, IL

Pollard, Robert, Ruth West and Will Sutherland (eds) (1992) *Alternative Treaties: Synergistic Processes for Sustainable Communities and Global Responsibility* International NGO Forum, 1–14 June, Ideas for Tomorrow Today and International Synergy Institute, Rio de Janeiro

Presser, Harriet B (1997) 'Demography, feminism, and the science–policy nexus' *Population and Development Review* 23(2): 295–331

Rao, Seshagiri K (1978) 'Population ethics: a Hindu perspective' *Encyclopedia of Bioethics* Free Press, New York

Rao, Sethuramiah LN (1990) 'Resource requirements for population programmes in the year 2000: an update' unpublished paper, UNFPA

Reuters (6 April 1994) News dispatch

Reuters (31 August 1994) 'Vatican attacks US and UN over population' (Philip Pullella)

Sadik, Nafis (1994) *Making a Difference: Twenty-five Years of UNFPA Experience* Banson, London

Sai, Fred T (1984) 'A tremendous success' *Populi* 11(4): 21–25

Salas, Rafael (1977) *People: An International Choice*, 2nd edition, Pergamon, Oxford

Salas, Rafael (1984) 'Guidelines for a decade' *Populi* 11(4): 36–41

Sinding, Steven W (1993) 'Getting to replacement: bridging the gap between individual rights and demographic goals' in: P Senanayake and R Kleinman (eds) *Family Planning – Meeting Challenges: Promoting Choices* Parthenon, New York

Sinding, Steven W (1996) 'Reproductive health and population: what has happened since Cairo?' unpublished paper

Singh, Jyoti S (1974) 'Conference commentary' *Populi* 1(5): 10–11

Singh, Prabeen (1994) 'Women, health and population in India' unpublished paper

Tabah, Leon (1984) 'A turning point' *Populi* 11(4): 13–20

The Earth Times (1–15 April 1997) 'Cairo consensus on rights is being "Distorted", critics charge' (Jack Freeman)

The Earth Times (21 April 1994) Editorial by Robert S. Hirschfield

—— (14 September 1994) 'Into history' Jack Freeman

The New York Times (24 April 1994) 'Abortion is divisive issue at population talks' (Susan Chira)

The Straits Times (Singapore) (6 June 1997) 'Manila to stop setting birth-control targets' (Nirmal Ghosh)

The Times (London) (13 March 1997) 'Vatican has modified its stance on birth control' (John Phillips)

UKODA/USAID (1995) 'Implementing reproductive health programmes: report of a donor workshop, New York, June 12–14, 1995'

UN (1966) 'World population: challenge to development, summary of the highlights of the World Population Conference, Belgrade, Yugoslavia, 20 August to 10 September 1965' (sales no. 66.XIII.4)

UN (1968) 'Final act of International Conference on Human Rights Tehran, 22 April–13 May 1968' (sales no. 68.XIV.2)

UN (1975) 'Report of the United Nations World Population Conference, 1974, Bucharest, 19–30 August 1974' (sales no. E 75.XIII.3)

UN (1984) 'Report of the International Conference on Population, 1984, Mexico City, 6–14 August 1984' (sales no. E.84.XIII.8)

UN (1985a) 'World population trend, population and development interrelations and population policies: monitoring report, 1983' (ST/ESA/SER.A/93)

UN (1985b) 'The Mexico City Conference: the debate on the review and appraisal of the world population Plan of Action' Population Division,

Department of International Economic and Social Affairs

UN (1986) 'Report of the World Conference to review and appraise the achievements of the United Nations Decade for Women: equality, development and peace, Nairobi, 15–26 July 1985' (sales no. 85.IV.10)

UN (1989) 'Report of the Executive Director on the policy implications of the findings and conclusions of the UNFPA's exercise on review and assessment of population programme experience' (DP/1989/37, 14 April)

UN (1990) 'Report on the implications for population programmes of the Amsterdam Declaration and on efforts to develop further the analysis of resource requirements for international population assistance' (DP/1990/44, 17 April)

UN (1991a) 'Report of the Population Commission acting as the Preparatory Committee for the 1994 International Meeting on Population' (E/1991/47, 14 May)

UN (1991b) 'Population questions: preparations for a 1994 International Meeting on Population' (E/1991/5, 19 February)

UN (1992a) 'Recommendations of the Expert Group Meeting on Population and Women' (E/CONF.84/PC/6, 16 December)

UN (1992b) 'Abortion policies: a global review, vol I: Afghanistan – France; vol II: Gabon–Norway (UN, 1993); vol. III: Oman–Zimbabwe' (UN, 1995)

UN (1992c) 'Recommendations of the Expert Group Meeting on Population, Environment and Development' (E/CONF.84/PC.4, 28 August)

UN (1992d) 'Recommendations of the Expert Group Meeting on Population Policies and Programmes' (E/CONF.84/PC15, 28 August)

UN (1993a) 'Population bulletin of the United Nations, nos. 34/35, special issue on the expert group meetings convened as part of the substantive preparations for the ICPD' Department of International Economic and Social Affairs

UN (1993b) 'Recommendations for the Expert Group Meeting on Family Planning, Health and Family Well-Being' (E/CONF.84/PC/7, 17 March)

UN (1993c) 'Proposed Conceptual Framework of the Draft Recommendations of the Conference' (E/CONF.84/PC/11, 26 April)

UN (1993d) 'Report of the Fourth Asian and Pacific Population Conference' (E/CONF.84/PC/14, 29 April)

UN (1993e) 'Report of the Third African Population Conference' (E/CONF.84/PC/13, 27 April)

UN (1993f) 'Report of the European Population Conference, Geneva, 23–26 March 1993' (E/CONF.84/PC/15, 28 April)

UN (1993g) 'Second Amman Declaration on Population and Development in the Arab world adopted at the Arab Population Conference' (E/CONF.84/PC/16, 10 May)

UN (1993h) 'Latin American and Caribbean Consensus on Population and Development, adopted at the Latin American and Caribbean Regional Conference on Population and Development' (E/CONF.84/PC/17, 10 May)

UN (1993i) 'Goals for 2015' informal conference room paper

UN (1993j) 'Report of the Preparatory Committee for the International Conference on Population and Development on its second Session' (E/1993/69, 3 June)

UN (1993k) 'Progress report on the preparations for the conference: annoted outline of the final document of the conference' (A/48/430/ADD.1, 14 October)

UN (1993l) 'Earth Summit: Agenda 21: the United Nations Programme of Action for Sustainable Development' (sales no. E.93.1.11)

UN (1993m) 'Recommendations of the Expert Group Meeting on Population Distribution and Migration' (E/CONF.84/PC/9, 30 March)

UN (1994a) 'Population bulletin of the United Nations: special issue on the five regional population conferences and meetings convened as part of the substantive preparations for the International Conference on Population and Development' no. 37/38, New York

UN (1994b) 'Synthesis of the sub-regional meetings and conferences convened as part of the substantive preparations for the conference' (A/CONF.171/PC/7/Add.1, 4 March)

UN (1994c) 'Progress report on the preparations for the International Conference on Population and Development' (A/CONF.171/PC/2, 4 February)

UN (1994d) 'Draft Final Document of the Conference: Draft Programme of Action of the Conference' (A/CONF.171/PC/5, 18 February)

UN (1994e) 'Draft Programme of Action of the International Conference on Population and Development' (A/CONF.171/L.1, 13 May)

UN (1994f) 'Synthesis of the regional meetings or conferences convened as part of the substantive preparations for the conference' (A/CONF.171/PC/7, 31 January)

UN (1994g) 'Fourth review and appraisal of the World Population Plan of Action' (A/CONF.171/4, 27 July)

UN (1994h) 'Directory of non-government organizations accredited to the ICPD 94' ICPD Secretariat, New York

UN (1995a) 'Report of the International Conference on Population and Development: Cairo, 5–13 September 1994' (sales no. E.95.XIII.18)

UN (1995b) 'Vienna Declaration and Programme of Action: 14–25 June 1993' (sales no. 95.I.21)

UN (1995c) 'Implementation of General Assembly Resolution 49/128 on the report of the International Conference on Population and Development' (E/50/190 or E/1995/73, 20 June)

UN (1996a) 'The Fourth World Conference on Women: Beijing, September 1995' (sales no. 96.IV.13)

UN (1996b) 'World population prospects: the 1996 revision' Annex I, Department for Economic and Social Information and Policy Analysis, New York

UN (1996c) 'World Summit for Social Development: Copenhagen, 6–12 March 1995' (sales no. 96.IV.8)

UN (1996d) 'Implementation of the Programme of Action of the International Conference on Population and Development' (A/51/350, 25 September)

UN (1996e) 'International migration and development' (E/CN.9/1997/2, 24 December)

UN (1996f) 'Monitoring of population programmes' (E/CN.9/1997/3, 31 December)

UN (1997a) 'Implementation of the Programme of Action of the International Conference on Population and Development' (A/52/208, 24 June)

UN (1997b) 'Report of the ACC Task Force on Basic Social Services for All' (E/CN.9/1997/4, 7 January)

UN (1997c) 'Activities of intergovernmental and non-governmental organizations in the area of international migration' (E/CN.9/1997/5, 10 January)

UN (1997d) 'Meeting the goals of the ICPD: consequences of resource shortfalls up to the year 2000' (DP/FPA/1997/12, 10 July)

UNDP (1991) Human Development Report 1991, Oxford University Press, New York

UNDP (1994) 'The 20/20 initiative achieving universal access to basic social services for sustainable human development' New York

UNFPA (1983) 'Preparation for International Conference on Population 1984' (UNFPA/IACC/XXII/5, January)

UNFPA (1984) 'Population Perspectives: Statements by World Leaders' New York

UNFPA (1988) 'Global Population Assistance Report, 1982–1985' New York

UNFPA (1989a) 'Report of the International Forum on Population in the Twenty-First Century: Amsterdam, the Netherlands, 6–9 November 1989' New York

UNFPA (1989b) 'Global population assistance report, 1982–1988' New York

UNFPA (1989c) 'Population in the twenty-first century: policies and programmes for the 1990s and beyond 2000' (A/E/5. 18 September)

UNFPA (1992a) 'Guidelines for UNFPA: support to family planning programmes' (UNFPA/CM/83/14 Rev. 3, 29 December)

UNFPA (1992b) 'Global population assistance report 1982–1990' New York

UNFPA (1993) 'Report of the Round Table on Women's Perspectives on Family Planning, Reproductive Health and Reproductive Rights' New York

UNFPA (1994a) 'Contraceptive use and commodity costs in developing countries, 1994–2005' Technical Report 18

UNFPA (1994b) 'Background note on the resource requirements for population programmes in the years 2000–2015' unpublished background paper

UNFPA (1995) 'National perspectives on population and development: synthesis of 168 national reports prepared for the International Conference on Population and Development, 1994' New York

UNFPA (1996) 'Global population assistance report 1994' New York

UNFPA (1997a) 'Global population assistance report 1995' New York

UNFPA (1997b) 'The state of world population 1997' New York

UNFPA Dhaka (1996) 'Reproductive health in Bangladesh: a sectoral review' Dhaka

UNICEF (1993) *State of the World's Children 1993* Oxford University Press, New York

US Department of State (16 March 1994) 'Request for Demarche: final PrepCom for the International Conference on Population and Development (the Cairo Conference)' cable to all diplomatic and consular posts

van de Kaa, Dirk (1996) 'The Cairo Conference: a demographer's view' in: Hans van den Brekel and Fred Deven (eds) *Population and Family in the Low Countries 1995*, 21–39, Kluwer, Dordrecht

WEDO (1992) 'World Women's Congress for a Healthy Planet' New York

WEDO (1993a) 'Suggested revisions to the Conceptual Framework for the Draft Recommendation of the ICPD, offered by women's groups from all regions'

WEDO (1993b) 'Suggested points for inclusion' (distributed at PrepCom II)

WEDO (1994) 'Recommendations on bracketed text in the Draft Programme of Action of the ICPD'

Westoff, Charles and L Ochoa (1991) 'Unmet need and the demand for family planning' *Demographic and Health Surveys Comparative Studies* no. 5, Columbia, MD

WHO (1994) 'Health population and development' WHO Position Paper, Geneva

WHO/UNFPA/UNICEF (1997) 'Action for adolescent health: towards a common agenda' Geneva

APPENDIX 1: CHRONOLOGY OF MAJOR EVENTS RELATING TO INTERNATIONAL CONFERENCE ON POPULATION AND DEVELOPMENT

1987 ECOSOC requests Secretary General of the UN to prepare a document outlining options for a global population conference in 1994 (23 June–9 July).

1989 ECOSOC (5–28 July), following a recommendation of Population Commission, decides to convene an International Meeting on Population in 1994.

1990 Secretary General appoints Executive Director of UNFPA as Secretary General of the Conference. Population Division and UNFPA constitute a Joint Secretariat for the Conference.

1991 PrepCom I (3–8 March) recommends changing the name of the Conference to International Conference on Population and Development (ICPD), specifies priority topics and recommends to ECOSOC the convening of six expert group meetings and five regional conferences. ECOSOC endorses the recommendations.

1992 Expert Group Meeting on Population, Environment and Development, New York (20–24 January).

Expert Group Meeting on Population Policies and Programmes, Cairo (Egypt) (12–16 April).

Expert Group Meeting on Population and Women, Gaborone (Botswana) (22–26 June).

ECOSOC (29 June–31 July; 18 August) welcomes the offer of Egypt to host the Conference and decides on the dates of ICPD, 5–13 September 1994.

Regional Conference: Asian and the Pacific Population Conference, Denpasar (Indonesia) (19–27 August).

Expert Group Meeting on Family Planning, Health and Family Well-being, Bangalore (India) (26–29 October).

Expert Group Meeting on Population Growth and Demographic Structure, Paris (France) (16–20 November).

Regional Conference: 3rd African Population Conference, Ngor, Dakar (Senegal) (11–12 December).

GA 47th Session decides to have two additional meetings of the Preparatory Committee.

1993   Expert Group Meeting on Population Distribution and Migration, Santa Cruz (Bolivia) (18–22 January).

ECOSOC (26 January; 2–5 February; 29–30 April) defines dates for PrepCom II and III and adopts criteria for accreditation of NGOs.

Regional Conference: European Population Conference, Geneva (Switzerland) (23–26 March).

Regional Conference: Arab Population Conference, Amman (Jordan) (4–8 April).

Regional Conference: Latin American and Caribbean Regional Conference on Population and Development, Mexico City (Mexico) (29 April–4 May).

PrepCom II (10–21 May) receives recommendations from expert group meetings and regional conferences and a Conceptual Framework of the Draft Recommendation.

ECOSOC (28 June–30 July) recommends that the Preparatory Committee becomes a subsidiary body of the GA.

Maghreb Conference on Population and Development, Tunis (Tunisia) (7–10 July).

Round Table Meeting: Family Planning, Reproductive Health and Reproductive Rights, Ottawa (Canada) (26–27 August).

South Pacific Ministerial Meeting on Population and Sustainable Development, Port Vila (Vanuatu) (9–10 September).

Round Table Meeting: Demographic Impact of AIDS, Berlin (Germany) (28 September–1 October).

Round Table Meeting: Population and Development Plans and Strategies, Bangkok (Thailand) (17–19 November).

SAARC Ministerial Conference on Women and Family Health, Kathmandu (Nepal) (21–23 November).

Round Table Meeting: Population, Environment and Sustainable Development, Geneva (Switzerland) (24–26 November).

GA (48th Session) accepts ICPD Preparatory Committee as its subsidiary body. Discusses an Annotated Outline of the Draft Recommendations.

Andean Meeting on Population and Development, Lima (Peru) (1–3 December).

Round Table Meeting: Population and Communication, Vienna (Austria) (2–3 December).

Caribbean Meeting of Experts for a Regional Plan of Action on Population and Sustainable Development, Port-of-Spain (Trinidad) (2–3 December).

1994   Meeting of Eminent Persons in Population and Development, Tokyo (Japan) (26–27 January).

Round Table Meeting: Population and Food, Washington, DC (14–16 February).

Round Table Meeting: Ethics, Population and Reproductive Health, New York (8–10 March).

PrepCom III (4–22 April) reviews and revises Draft Programme of Action of the Conference, prepared by the secretariat, and transmits the revised version to the Main Conference.

Consultative Meeting of Countries with Economies in Transition on the ICPD, Budapest (Hungary) (19–20 July).

International NGO Youth Consultation on Population and Development, Cairo (Egypt) (31 August–4 September).

International Conference of Parliamentarians on Population and Development, Cairo (Egypt) (3–4 September).

NGO Forum '94, Cairo (Egypt) (4–13 September).

International Conference on Population and Development (ICPD), Cairo (Egypt) (5–13 September).

GA (49th Session) endorses the ICPD Programme of Action.

INDEX